IMAGES
of Rail

Greater Wyoming Valley Trolleys

On the cover: **ACCIDENT AT MOUNT GREENWOOD CROSSING, 1939.** Wilkes-Barre Railway Corporation trolley No. 356 bound for Dallas collided with an automobile in Kingston Township on the final day of trolley service to Dallas on April 30, 1939. Note the chain attached to the wrecked automobile. Emergency trolley No. 390 was on the scene to remove the wreck from underneath the trolley. Trolley No. 356 was ordered from the J. G. Brill Company on February 27, 1911. The Dallas line started at the public square in Wilkes-Barre. Following the accident, the trolley remained in service after the Dallas line was abandoned. The trolley was sold in 1942, and it became Sudbury-Copper Cliff Suburban Electric Railway trolley No. 37. (Edward S. Miller collection.)

IMAGES
of Rail

GREATER WYOMING VALLEY TROLLEYS

Harrison Wick

ARCADIA
PUBLISHING

ISBN 978-0-7385-6587-3

Published by Arcadia Publishing
Charleston, South Carolina

Printed in the United States of America

Library of Congress Control Number: 2009921626

For all general information contact Arcadia Publishing at:
Telephone 843-853-2070
Fax 843-853-0044
E-mail sales@arcadiapublishing.com
For customer service and orders:
Toll-Free 1-888-313-2665

Visit us on the Internet at www.arcadiapublishing.com

Dedicated to my parents, Charles and Virginia Wick.

Contents

ACKNOWLEDGMENTS

Greater Wyoming Valley Trolleys was made possible by dedicated rail enthusiasts, the work of photographers Edward S. Miller and Michael J. Lavelle Sr., and authors Harold E. Cox and Benson W. Rohrbeck. All the photographs in the book, unless otherwise specified, are from the collection of Edward S. Miller. I want to thank the following people for their assistance: Dr. Michael A. MacDowell and Dani Vaughn-Tucker from Misericordia University, Amanda Fontenova and the Luzerne County Historical Society, the Back Mountain Historical Association, Donald Britt and Joan Coolbaugh Britt, Stephen B. Killian, Harold D. Owens Jr., F. Charles Petrillo, Pauline Shaver Roth, Roger Samuels, Dorothy King Wadas and Frank Wadas, William Wentz, and Rev. James Wert. I want to acknowledge my friends at Misericordia University and my colleagues at the Patrick J. Stapleton Jr. Library at Indiana University of Pennsylvania. I thank my great-aunt Sally Bruce McClatchey, whose early guidance encouraged my archival career and interest in local history. The book was made possible by people like you who have shared your family history and donated collections to historical organizations.

INTRODUCTION

Greater Wyoming Valley Trolleys offers a new perspective on the Wyoming Valley with rare glimpses of the trolley system and community life from the 1890s to 1950. The book features photographs collected by Edward S. Miller with contributions from the National Railway Historical Society and the Misericordia University archives. The majority of photographs were taken in the 1930s and 1940s by photographers Edward S. Miller and Michael J. Lavelle Sr. The book shows the Wyoming Valley at a time when anthracite coal was king, and the photographs chronicle more than 60 years of the trolley system.

The Wyoming Valley has a rich history of transportation and industrial development. Judge Jesse Fell was the first to experiment with burning anthracite coal for domestic heating in Wilkes-Barre on February 11, 1808. His experiment sparked the demand for anthracite coal that fueled the Industrial Revolution. Northeastern Pennsylvania was home to many mining operations and company towns, and the people of the Wyoming Valley needed affordable local transportation. The trolley system provided a cheap, clean, and effective way of getting around. The history of trolleys in the Wyoming Valley began with horse-drawn streetcars in Wilkes-Barre. The first electrified trolley ran in Wilkes-Barre on March 19, 1888. Trolleys were an integral part of daily life, taking people to church, work, and recreation in the Wyoming Valley. One of the most popular destinations was Sans Souci Park in Hanover.

Greater Wyoming Valley Trolleys shows photographs taken from the Wyoming Valley trolley lines in the lower valley, Wilkes-Barre, upper valley, and west side. The trolleys went through the boroughs and townships of Ashley, Courtdale, Edwardsville, Forty Fort, Hanover, Kingston, Larksville, Luzerne, Miners Mills, Nanticoke, Parsons, Pittston, Plains, Plymouth, Sugar Notch, West Pittston, West Wyoming, Wilkes-Barre, and Wyoming. The trolleys underwent many improvements and changes in management over 60 years. During the Great Depression, newer trolleys were purchased from other transit companies to update the fleet. The book focuses on the trolleys operated by the Wilkes-Barre Railway and Wilkes-Barre Transit Corporation. Hanover and Nanticoke were the last Wyoming Valley trolley lines to close in 1950. The abandonment of the trolley system was the result of a steady decline in the number trolley passengers as more people drove automobiles. Trolleys were replaced by trackless trolleys and bus routes. The trolley system was an innovation, and it played a vital role in the history of rail transportation in northeastern Pennsylvania.

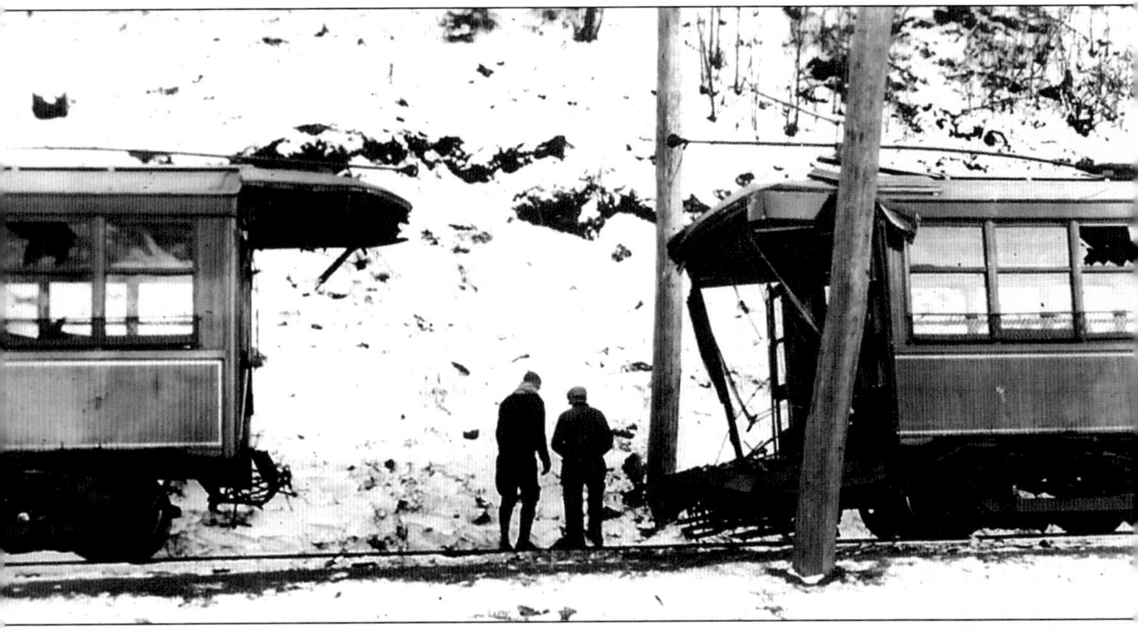

COLLISION IN KINGSTON TOWNSHIP, 1935. Wilkes-Barre Railway Corporation trolley No. 328 outbound and trolley No. 322 inbound accidently collided on the Dallas line near the Birch Grove station in Kingston Township on Thursday, January 24, 1935. The trolleys were ordered from the J. G. Brill Company in Philadelphia on February 27, 1911, and were delivered in August 1911. After the collision, trolleys No. 328 and No. 322 were repaired and both trolleys remained in service. Both trolleys were scrapped after the Dallas line was abandoned on April 30, 1939.

One

Lower Valley

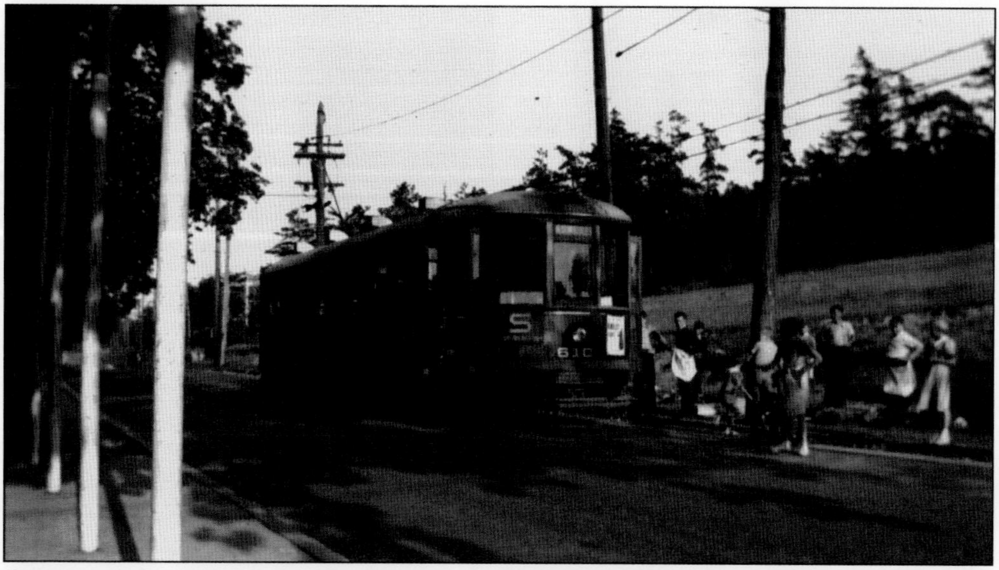

Chestnut Street at Front Street in Warrior Run, 1937. Wilkes-Barre Railway Corporation trolley No. 610 is pictured on Thursday, September 23, 1937, at the end of the Sugar Notch trolley line. Trolley service on the Sugar Notch line was temporarily discontinued when the South Street Bridge was closed on Wednesday, August 6, 1941. Service resumed on Monday, September 1, 1942.

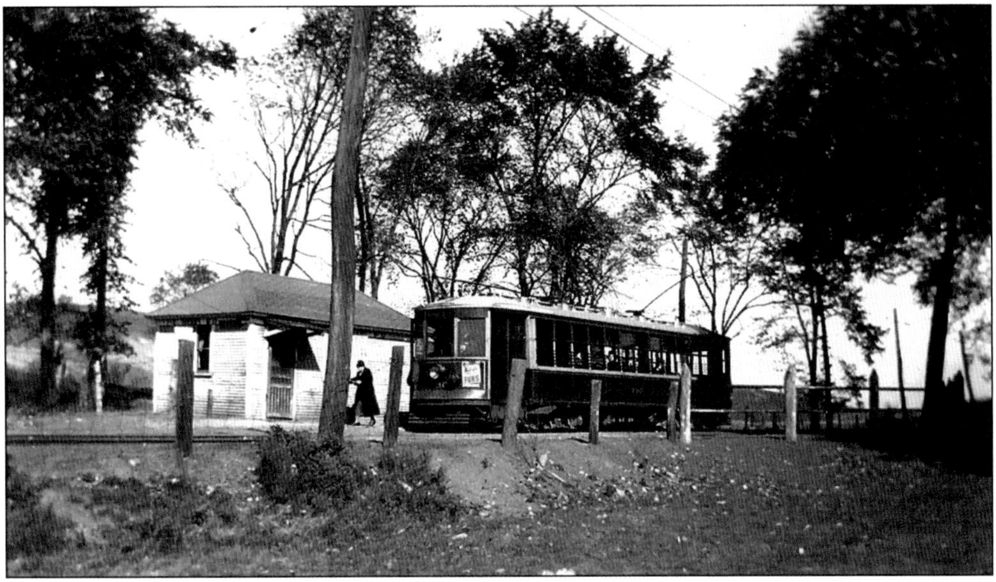

Summit Station in Hanover, 1937. Wilkes-Barre Railway Corporation trolley No. 790 is shown on Sunday, October 17, 1937. The trolley was ordered from the J. G. Brill Company on April 2, 1924, for the Eastern Pennsylvania Railway in Pottsville. It was delivered to the Wilkes-Barre Railway in September 1933. The last day of service on the Nanticoke line was Saturday, October 14, 1950.

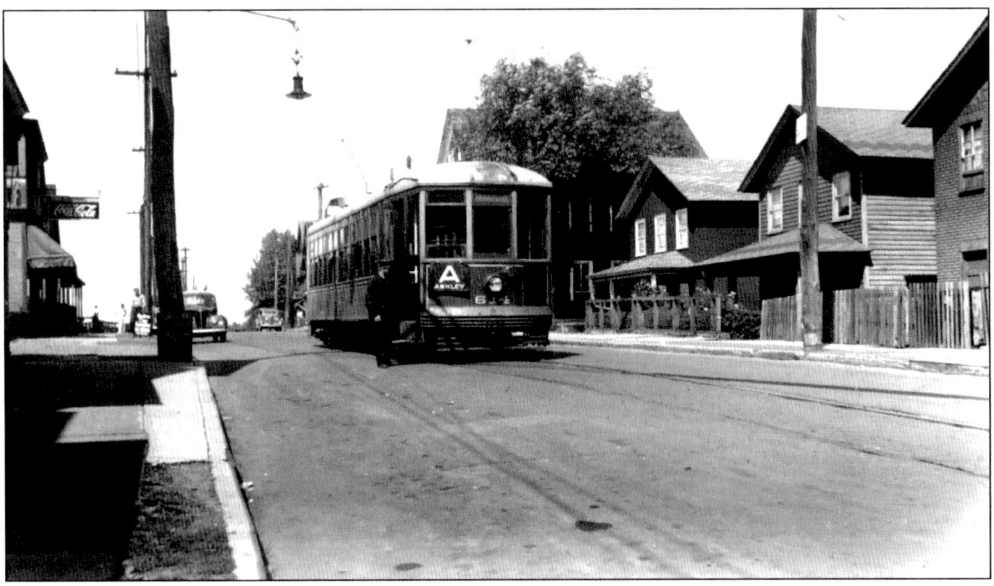

South Main Street at Fall Street in Ashley, 1938. Wilkes-Barre Railway Corporation trolley No. 614 was photographed on Tuesday, June 14, 1938, at the end of the Ashley line. The trolley was ordered from the J. G. Brill Company on April 23, 1918, and it was delivered to the Wilkes-Barre Railway in the early 1920s. The last day of service on the Ashley line was Friday, September 6, 1946. Trolley No. 614 was scrapped in 1948.

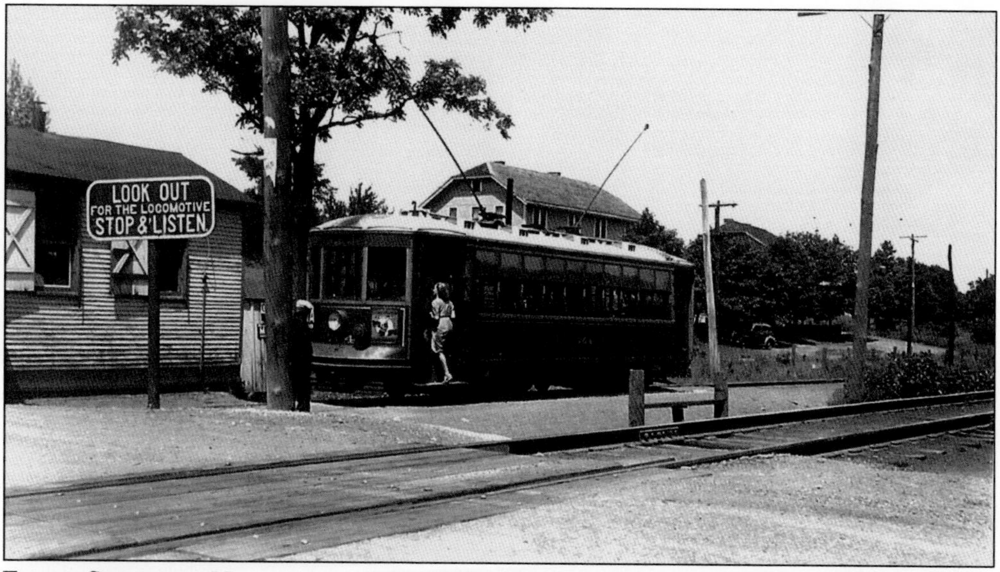

FRONT STREET IN NANTICOKE, 1938. Wilkes-Barre Railway Corporation trolley No. 764 is shown on Front Street at Truesdale Terrace Road on Tuesday, June 14, 1938, at the end of the Hanover line. The trolley was ordered from the J. G. Brill Company on April 2, 1924. It was built for the Eastern Pennsylvania Railway, and the trolley was delivered to the Wilkes-Barre Railway in September 1933.

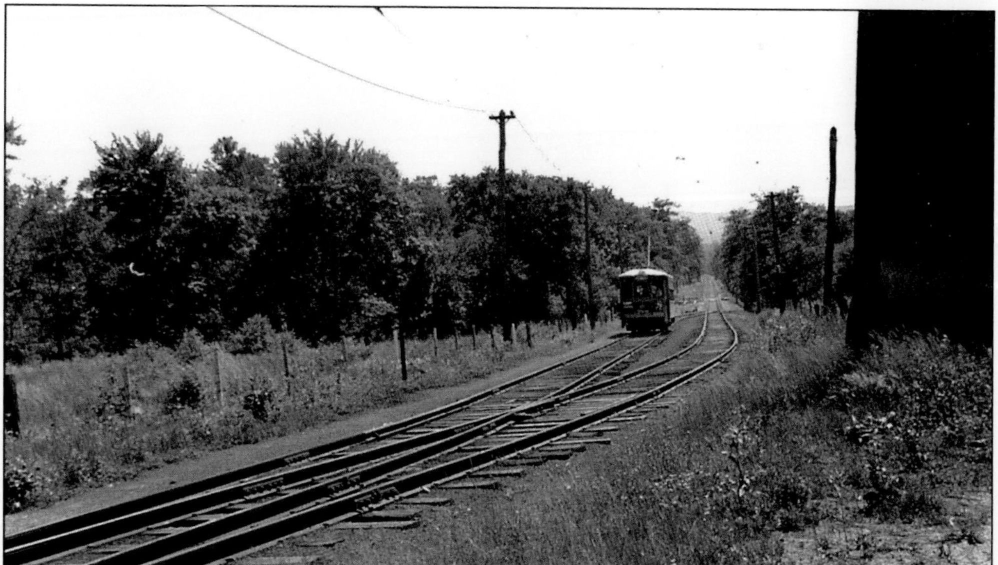

NEAR SANS SOUCI PARK IN HANOVER, 1938. Wilkes-Barre Railway Corporation trolley No. 764 was photographed on Tuesday, June 14, 1938. Built in 1924, the trolley was nearly 39 feet long. It was scrapped in August 1948. The last day of service on the Hanover line was Saturday, October 14, 1950. The final day on the Hanover line was the last day of trolley service in the Wyoming Valley.

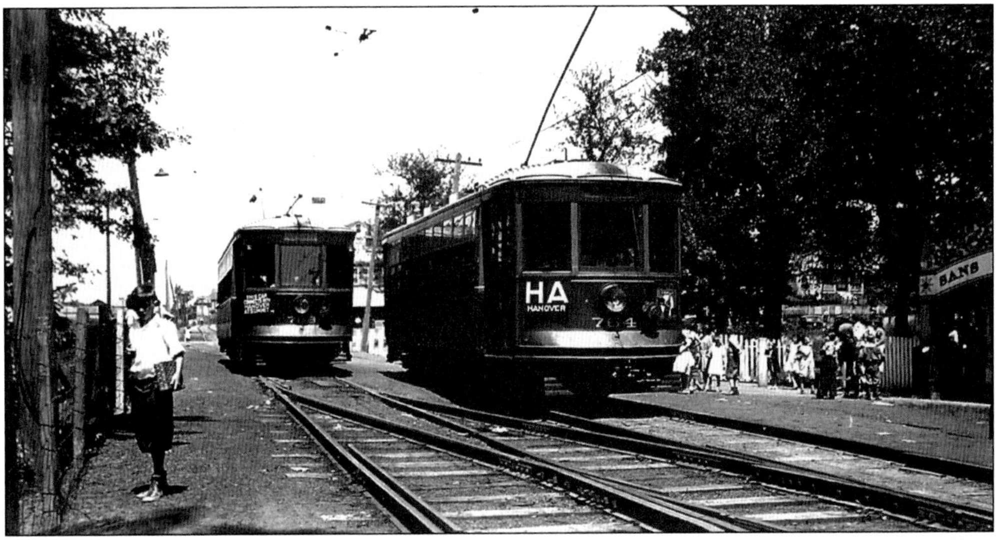

Sans Souci Park on the Hanover Line, 1938. Wilkes-Barre Railway Corporation trolleys No. 788 and No. 764 are seen at Ashley Road in Hanover on Tuesday, June 14, 1938. Both trolleys were ordered from the J. G. Brill Company for the Eastern Pennsylvania Railway and were delivered to the Wilkes-Barre Railway in September 1933. Trolley No. 788 was two windows longer than trolley No. 764.

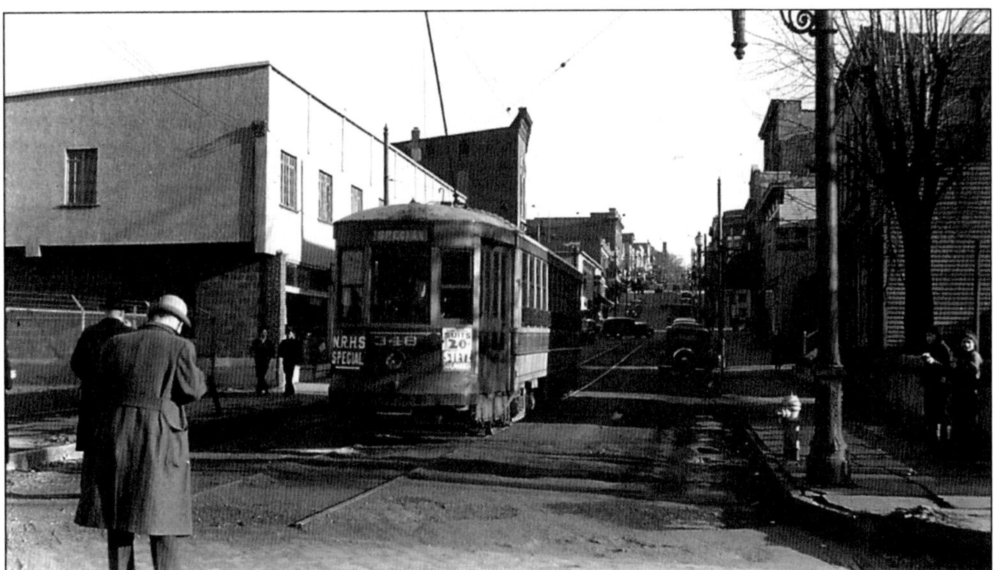

Railway Fan Trip on the Nanticoke Line, 1939. The Wilkes-Barre Railway Corporation trolley No. 348 special is seen on North Market Street at Hill Street in Nanticoke on Sunday, March 19, 1939, at the end of the Nanticoke line. Chartered by the National Railway Historical Society (NRHS), the trolley was ordered from the J. G. Brill Company on February 27, 1911. The Wilkes-Barre Railway Corporation took over the operations of the Wilkes-Barre Railway Company on July 1, 1924.

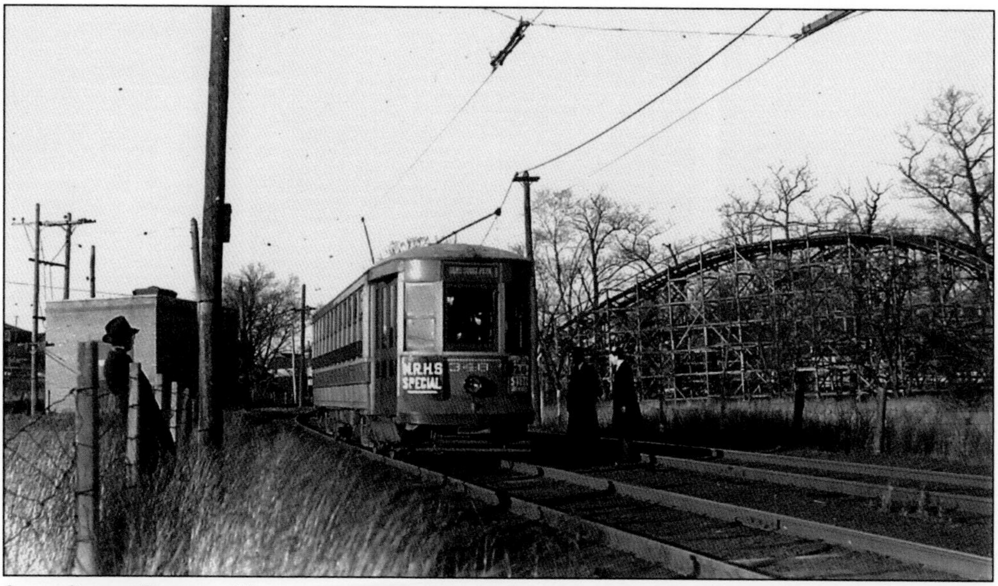

SANS SOUCI PARK IN HANOVER, 1939. The Wilkes-Barre Railway Corporation trolley No. 348 special chartered by the NRHS is seen on the Hanover line on Sunday, March 19, 1939. Howard E. Johnston is standing close to the front of the trolley on the left. The Bear Cat roller coaster at Sans Souci Park is in the background. Sans Souci Park was called Hanover Park when it was leased as a picnic grounds to the Delaware, Lackawanna and Western Railroad in July 1893.

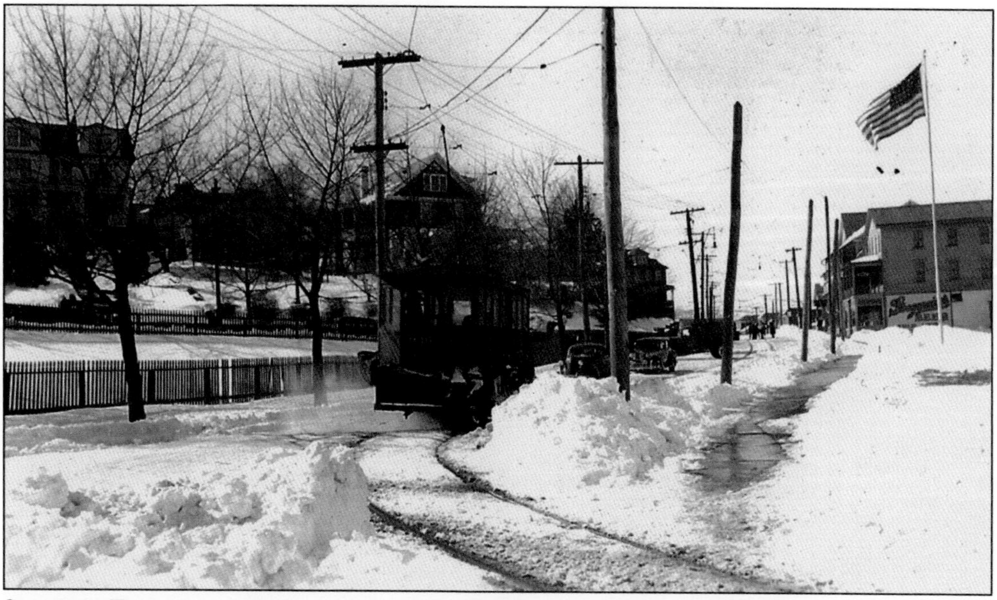

SWEEPER TROLLEY IN NANTICOKE, 1940. Wilkes-Barre Railway Corporation sweeper trolley No. 036 was photographed on the Nanticoke line on East Main Street at Mills Corners on Friday, February 16, 1940. The trolley is cleaning the tracks after a snowstorm on February 14. It was ordered from the J. G. Brill Company on October 10, 1895. The sweeper trolley was scrapped in 1946.

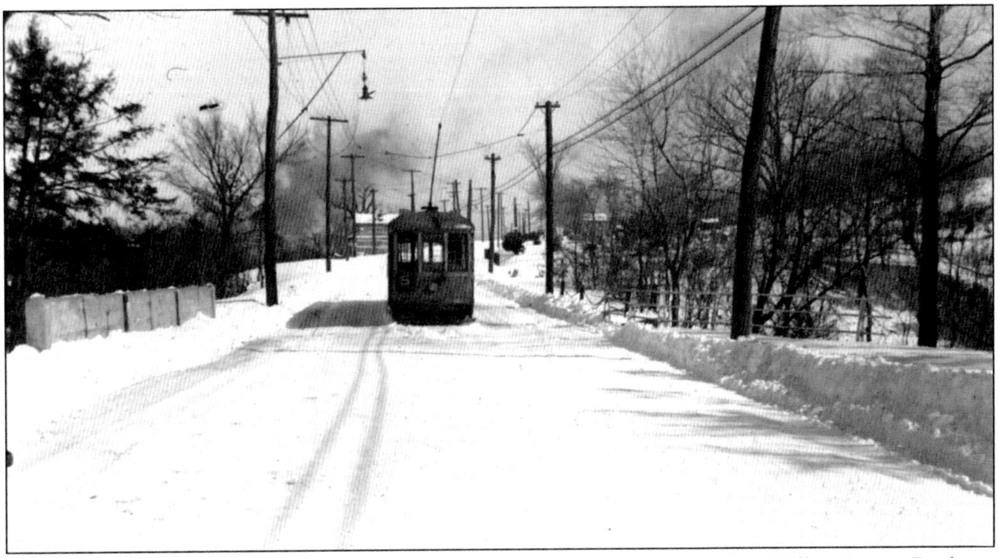

MAIN STREET NEAR GAUGHAN STREET IN SUGAR NOTCH, 1940. Wilkes-Barre Railway Corporation trolley No. 622 is pictured on Friday, February 16, 1940. The trolley was ordered from the J. G. Brill Company on April 23, 1918, and it was purchased secondhand by the Wilkes-Barre Railway in the 1920s. The trolley was on the Sugar Notch line, and the creek was the dividing line between Sugar Notch and Warrior Run. The trolley was marooned for three days by the storm on February 14.

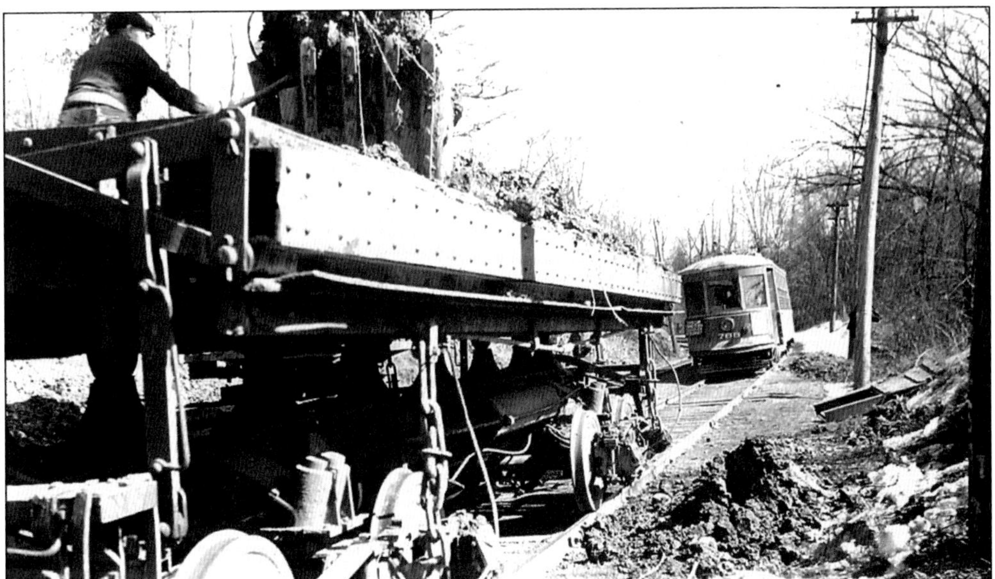

BETWEEN SANS SOUCI PARK AND NANTICOKE, 1940. Wilkes-Barre Railway Corporation work trolley No. 021 and trolley No. 788 were photographed on Monday, March 11, 1940, near the Loomis Colliery in Hanover on the Nanticoke line. The work trolley was a steel-sided dump trolley ordered from Western Wheeled Scraper on August 22, 1913. It was scrapped at the Wood Street trolley yard in Wilkes-Barre by Shapiro scrap dealers in March 1950.

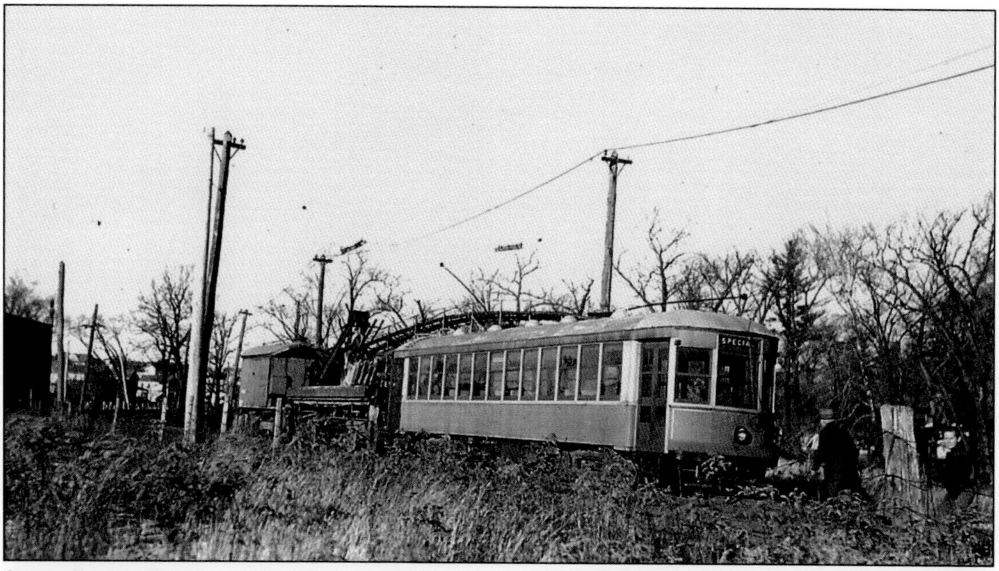

SANS SOUCI PARK IN HANOVER, 1940. Wilkes-Barre Railway Corporation trolley No. 380, work trolley No. 021, and shovel No. 050 are all on the Hanover line on Monday, March 11, 1940. Trolley No. 380 was ordered from the J. G. Brill Company on February 20, 1913, and it was delivered in August 1913. Shovel No. 050 was purchased in 1913, and it was often used as a repair crane without the shovel. Sans Souci Park opened in 1905.

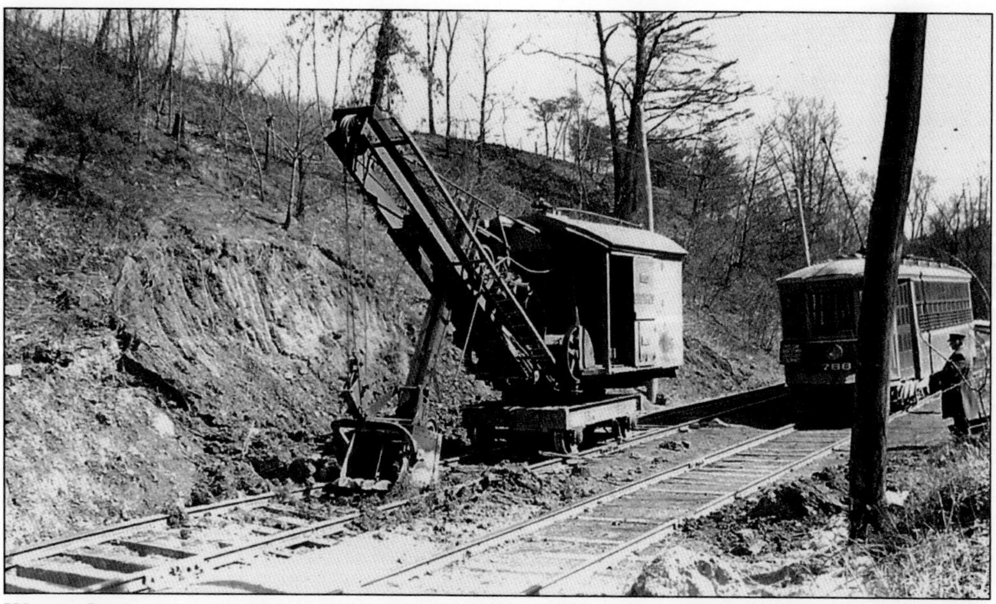

WORK SITE ON THE NANTICOKE LINE, 1940. Wilkes-Barre Railway Corporation trolley No. 788 and shovel No. 050 are captured near the Loomis Colliery in Hanover on Monday, March 11, 1940. Shovel No. 050 was used by being towed to a work site, and it was powered by a removable hook that was connected to the live trolley wire. In 1939, a permanent trolley pole was installed on the shovel so it could be operated under its own power. Shovel No. 050 was scrapped in July 1950.

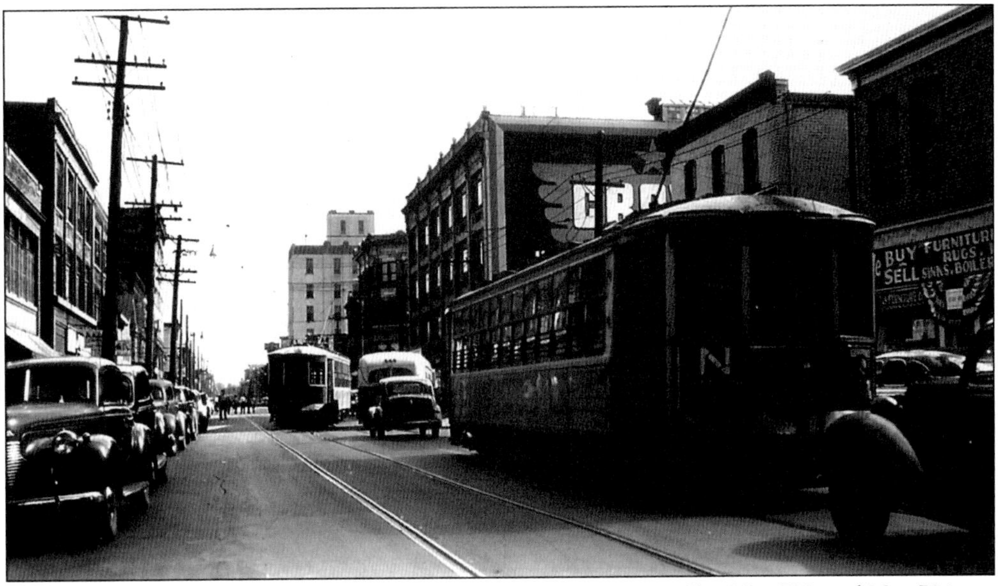

NANTICOKE LINE, 1940. Wilkes-Barre Railway Corporation trolley No. 782 and No. 784 are in action on Sunday, April 21, 1940. Both trolleys were ordered from the J. G. Brill Company in 1924 for the Eastern Pennsylvania Railway in Pottsville and were sold to the Wilkes-Barre Railway in September 1933. Trolley No. 782 was scrapped in November 1950.

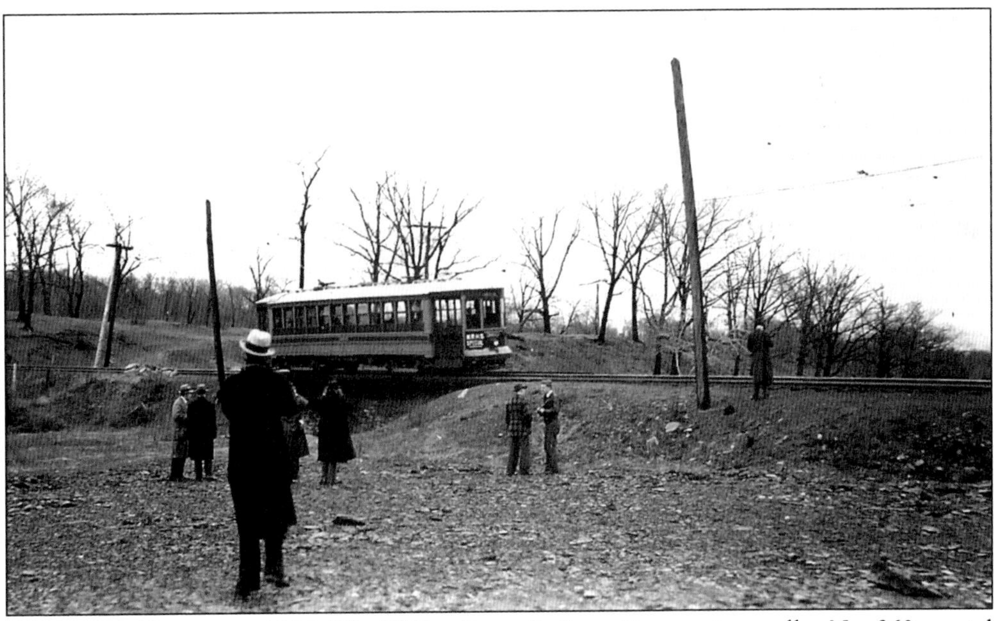

TRESTLE IN HANOVER, 1940. The Wilkes-Barre Railway Corporation trolley No. 360 special was chartered by the NRHS and is pictured during a rail fan trip. The trolley was stopped near Middle Road, Front Street, and Bauer Street in Hanover on Sunday, April 21, 1940. The final day of service on the Hanover line was Saturday, October 14, 1950.

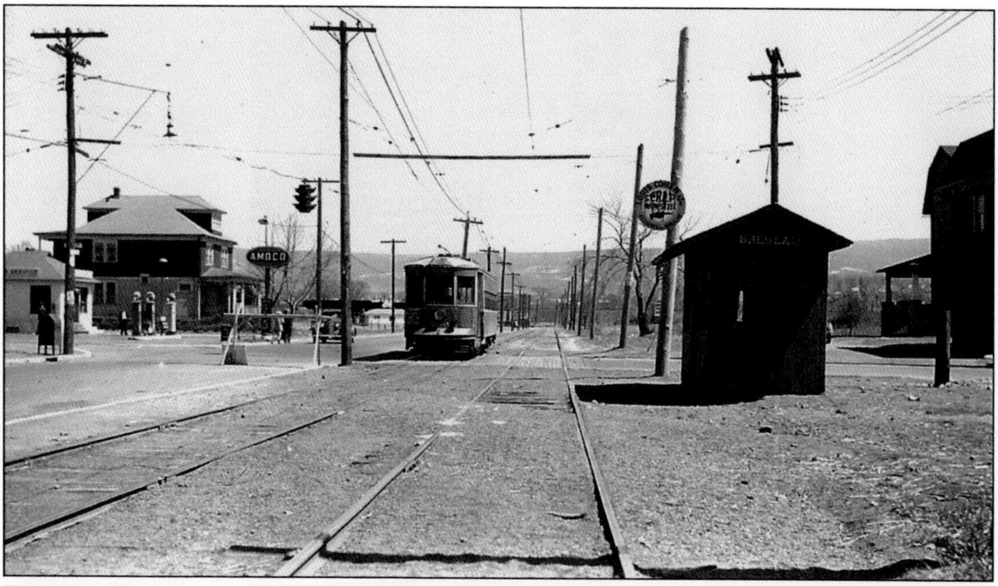

BRESLAU STATION IN HANOVER, 1940. Wilkes-Barre Railway Corporation trolley No. 786 was photographed on West End Road at Lynnwood Avenue on the Plymouth line on Sunday, May 5, 1940. Note the directional sign behind the Breslau station to the Louis Cohen and Son scrap yard on Fellows Street. The construction of the Plymouth line was delayed until the completion of the Carey Avenue bridge in 1895. The last day of service on the Plymouth line was Sunday, August 31, 1947.

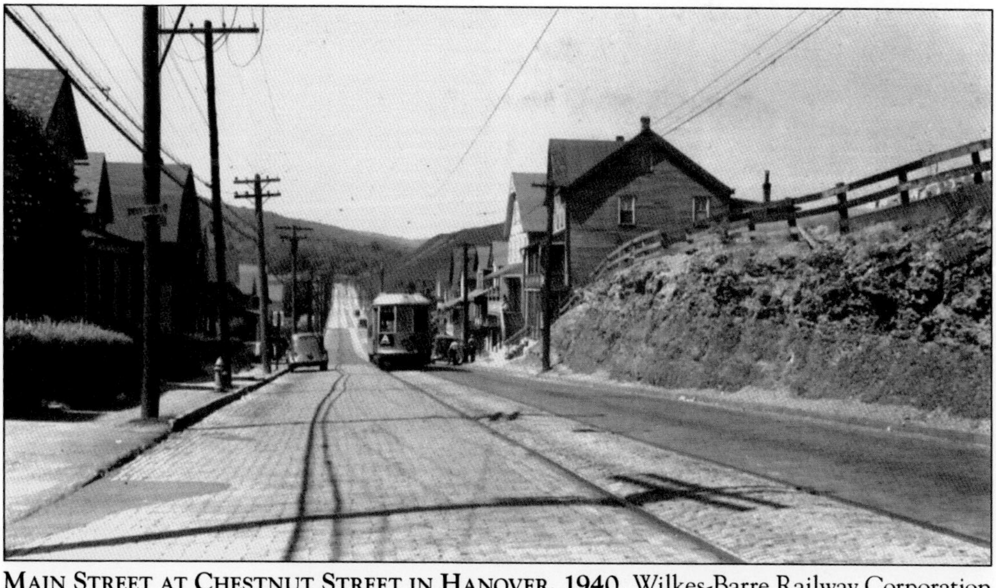

MAIN STREET AT CHESTNUT STREET IN HANOVER, 1940. Wilkes-Barre Railway Corporation trolley No. 614 was on the Ashley line on Saturday, August 3, 1940. The Ashley and Hanover trolley lines served mining operations near Sans Souci Park. Trolley No. 614 was reconditioned by the J. G. Brill Company for the Wilkes-Barre Railway Corporation. Service on the Hanover line was suspended after the August 1947 flood when the tracks were washed out, but trolley service was restored in September.

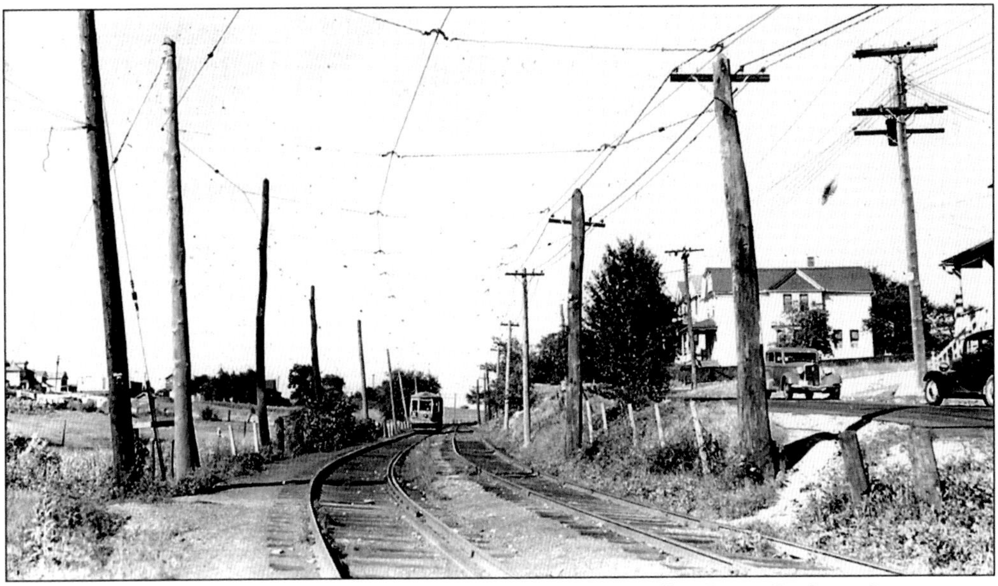

DIAMOND STREET AT ELM STREET IN HANOVER, 1940. Wilkes-Barre Railway Corporation trolley No. 774 was photographed along the Nanticoke line on Saturday, August 3, 1940. The 45-foot trolley was ordered from the J. G. Brill Company on May 8, 1923, for the Eastern Pennsylvania Railway in Pottsville. The Nanticoke line was the main trolley line south of Wilkes-Barre, and it was first used in 1893.

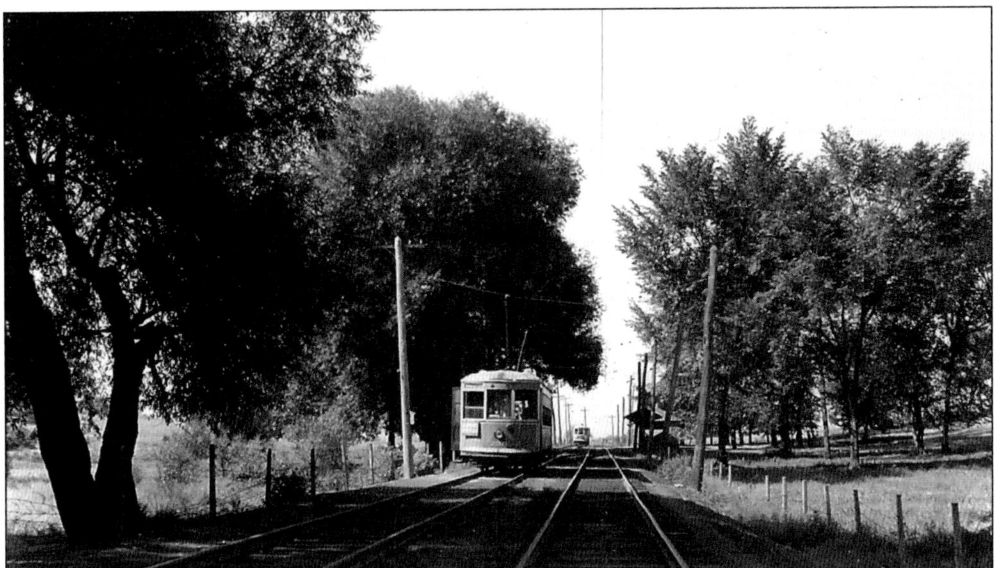

SUMMIT STATION IN HANOVER, 1940. Wilkes-Barre Railway Corporation trolley No. 756 was photographed on Saturday, September 21, 1940, at the north end of the Hanover line. The trolley was ordered from the J. G. Brill Company in Philadelphia on October 28, 1924, for the Coast Cities Railway of Asbury Park, New Jersey. Trolley No. 756 was purchased secondhand by the Wilkes-Barre Railway.

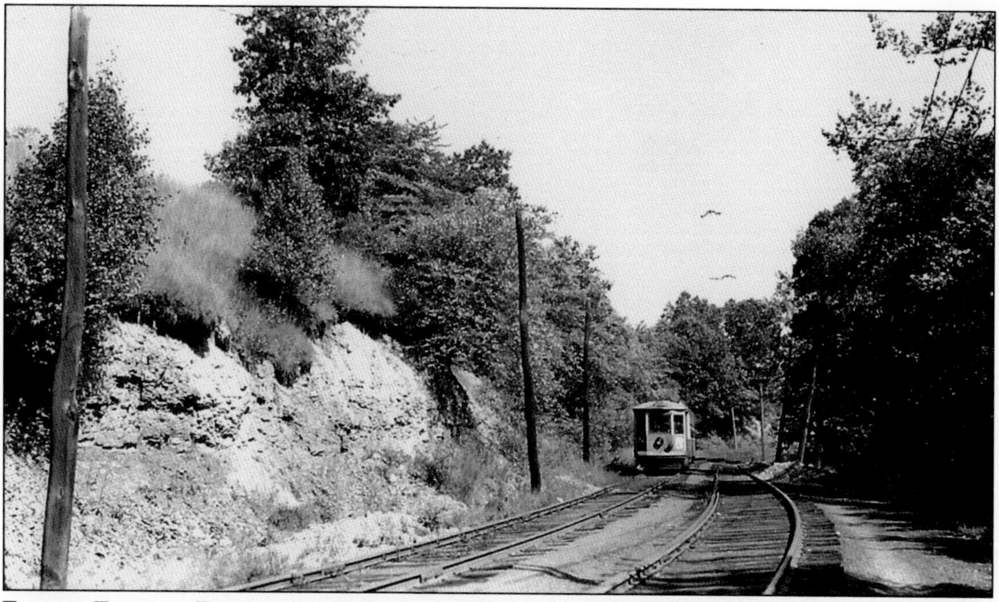

FORMER EASTERN PENNSYLVANIA RAILWAY TROLLEY, 1940. Wilkes-Barre Railway Corporation trolley No. 772 handles a curve on the Nanticoke line on Saturday, September 21, 1940. It was ordered from the J. G. Brill Company on May 8, 1923, for the Eastern Pennsylvania Railway. The trolley was delivered to the Wilkes-Barre Railway in September 1933. Trolleys No. 772 and No. 774 had the same interior with rattan seats.

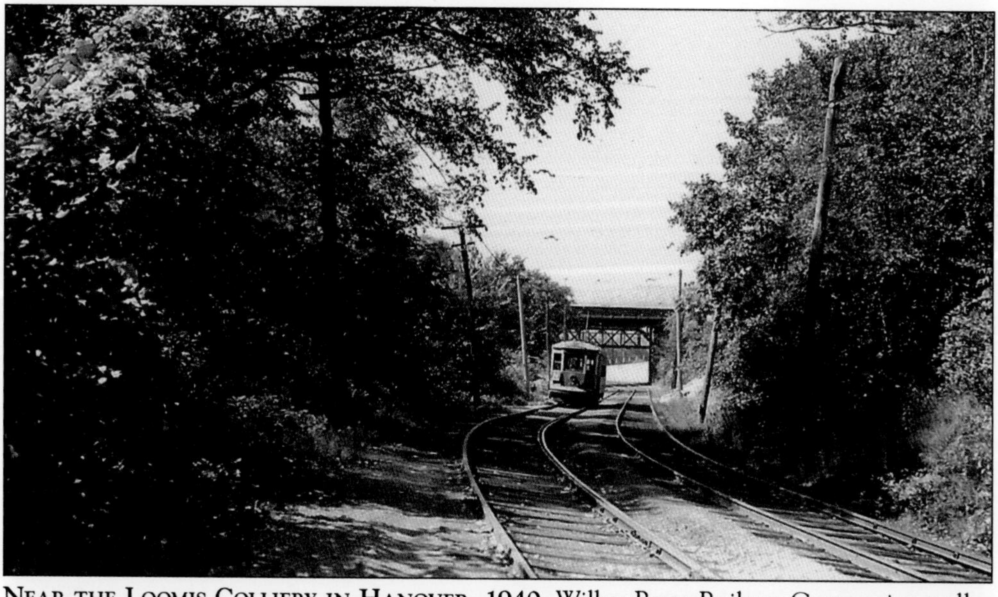

NEAR THE LOOMIS COLLIERY IN HANOVER, 1940. Wilkes-Barre Railway Corporation trolley No. 774 manages the curve near the Loomis Colliery on the Nanticoke line on Saturday, September 21, 1940. The trolley was ordered from the J. G. Brill Company for the Eastern Pennsylvania Railway. It was delivered to the Wilkes-Barre Railway in 1933. Trolleys No. 772 and No. 774 were equipped with steel vestibule framing, one vestibule at each end of the trolley.

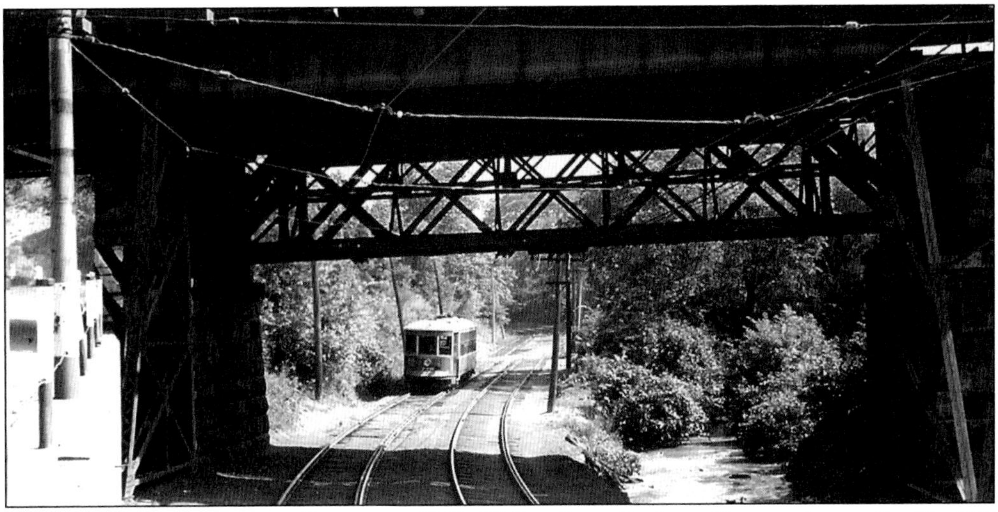

TRESTLE NEAR THE LOOMIS COLLIERY, 1940. Wilkes-Barre Railway Corporation trolley No. 778 is pictured at a curve near the Loomis Colliery in Hanover on the Nanticoke line on Saturday, September 21, 1940. The trolley was ordered from the J. G. Brill Company on April 2, 1924, for the Eastern Pennsylvania Railway, and it was delivered to the Wilkes-Barre Railway in 1933. Trolley No. 778 was scrapped in March 1948.

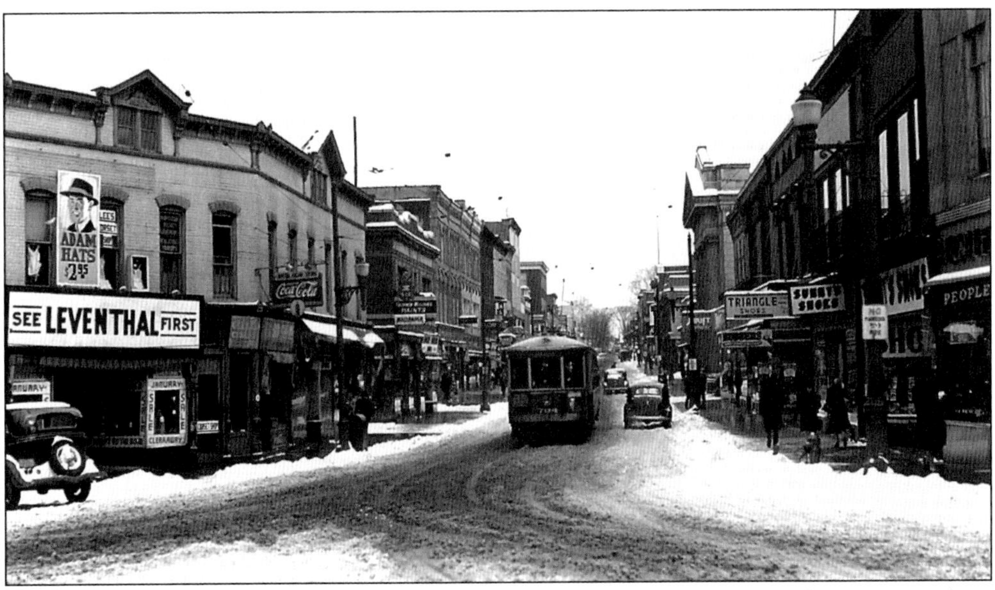

EAST MAIN STREET AT NORTH MARKET STREET IN NANTICOKE, 1941. Wilkes-Barre Railway Corporation trolley No. 784 is seen on the Nanticoke line on Saturday, January 25, 1941. The trolley was ordered from the J. G. Brill Company on April 2, 1924, for the Eastern Pennsylvania Railway. Trolley No. 784 was in an accident with work trolley No. 020 on May 24, 1949, and it was scrapped that November.

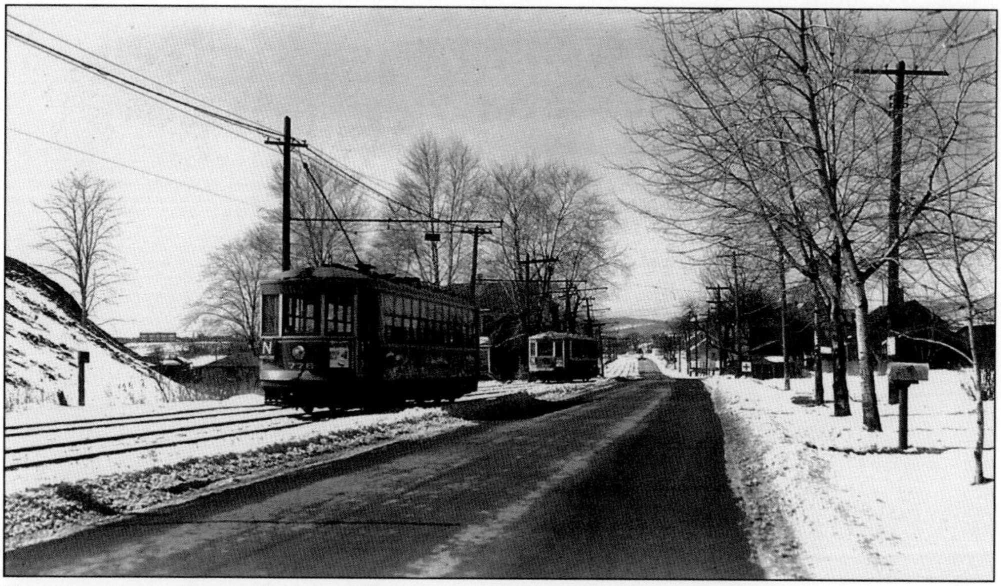

TROLLEYS NEAR RIVER ROAD IN HANOVER, 1941. Wilkes-Barre Railway Corporation trolleys No. 776 and No. 772 work near River Road close to Dundee Cross Road on the Nanticoke line on Sunday, March 2, 1941. Trolley No. 776 was originally ordered from the J. G. Brill Company on April 2, 1924, for the Eastern Pennsylvania Railway, and it was sold to the Wilkes-Barre Railway in 1933.

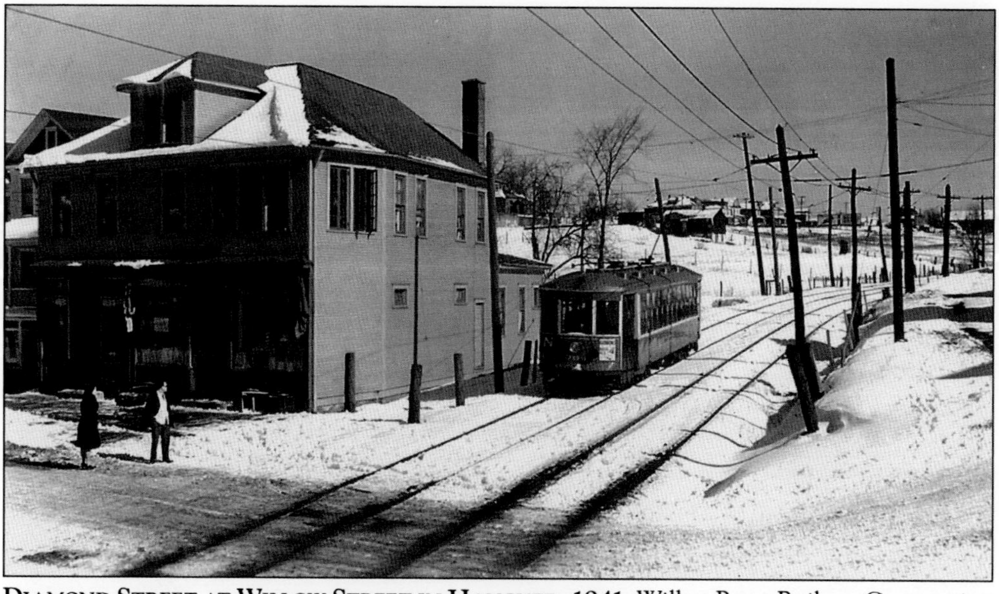

DIAMOND STREET AT WILLOW STREET IN HANOVER, 1941. Wilkes-Barre Railway Corporation trolley No. 784 was photographed on the Nanticoke line on Sunday, March 2, 1941. In December 1941, the creation of the bus line through Nanticoke and Hanover led to a decline of trolley passenger service. The last day of service on the Nanticoke trolley line was Saturday, October 14, 1950.

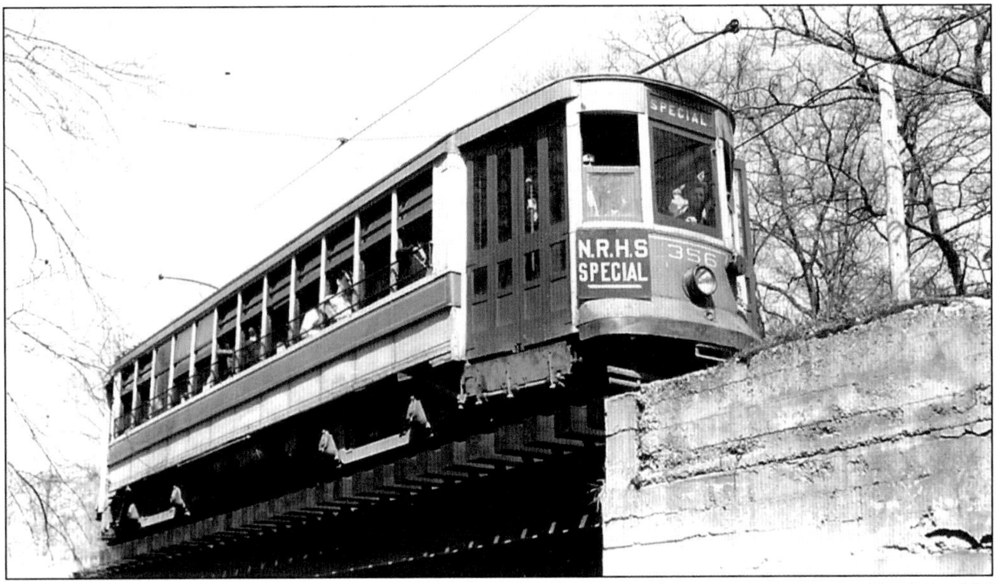

RAILWAY FAN TRIP IN HANOVER, 1941. The Wilkes-Barre Railway Corporation trolley No. 356 special, chartered by the NRHS, is shown on a trestle near Sans Souci Park on the Hanover line on Sunday, April 20, 1941. The trolley was ordered from the J. G. Brill Company on February 27, 1911, and it was delivered that August. It was equipped with a smoking compartment that was later removed. In April 1942, the trolley was sold to the Sudbury-Copper Cliff Suburban Electric Railway in Ontario, Canada.

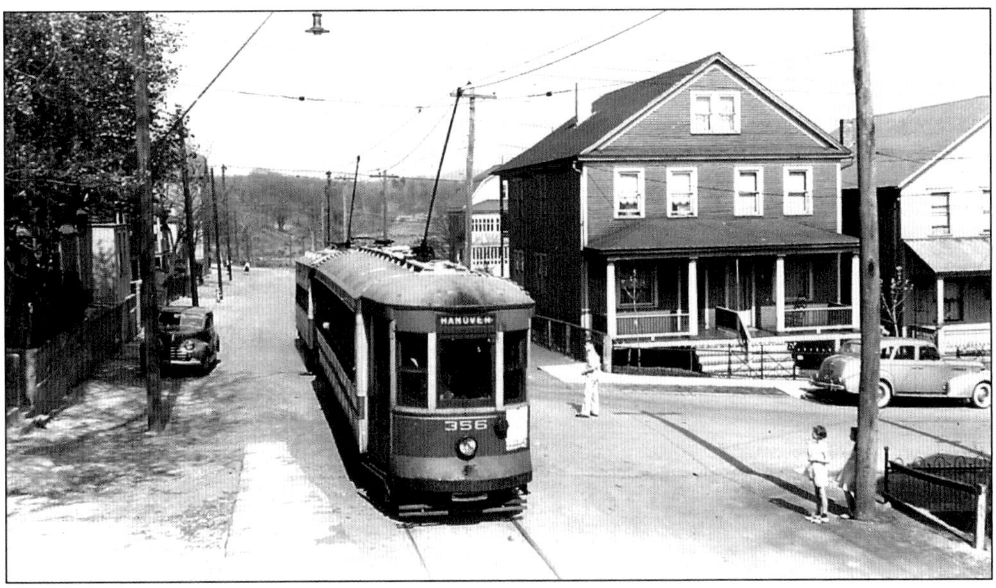

BAUER STREET AT ORCHARD STREET IN HANOVER, 1941. Wilkes-Barre Railway Corporation trolleys No. 356 special and No. 760 work on the Hanover line on Sunday, April 20, 1941. Trolley No. 760 was forced to back up to the Summit Station to allow trolley No. 356 special chartered by the NRHS to pass. Trolley No. 760 was ordered from the J. G. Brill Company on April 2, 1924, for the Eastern Pennsylvania Railway in Pottsville.

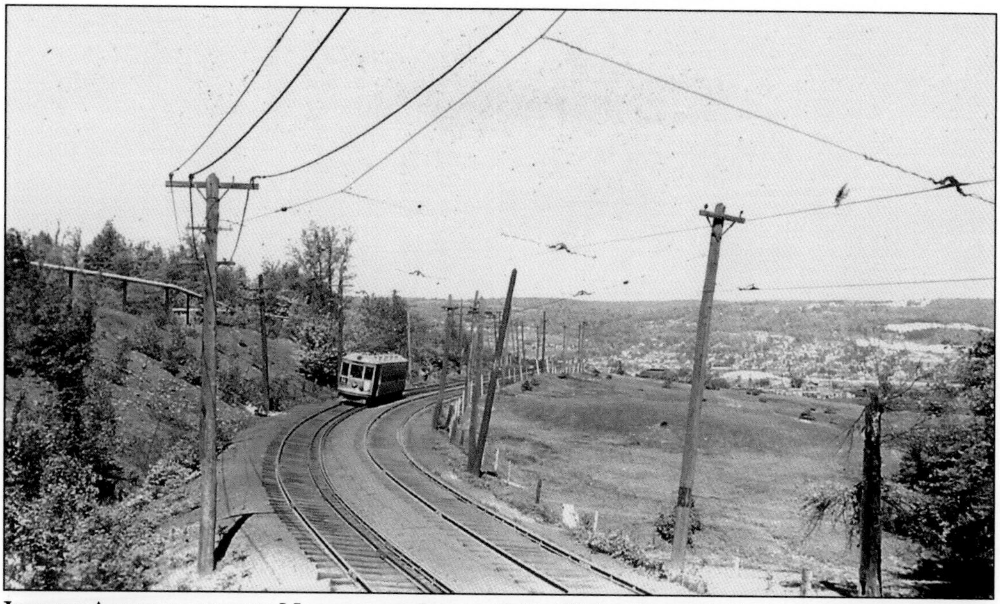

Inman Avenue on the Nanticoke Line, 1941. Wilkes-Barre Railway Corporation trolley No. 784 inbound handles a curve near Inman Avenue and Sivelley Street in Hanover on Sunday, May 18, 1941. The first test passenger trolley on the Nanticoke line ran from the public square in Wilkes-Barre to Inman's Hill on April 16, 1893. The first trolley reached Nanticoke on May 1, 1893, and on the first day of service one of the trolleys struck a cow.

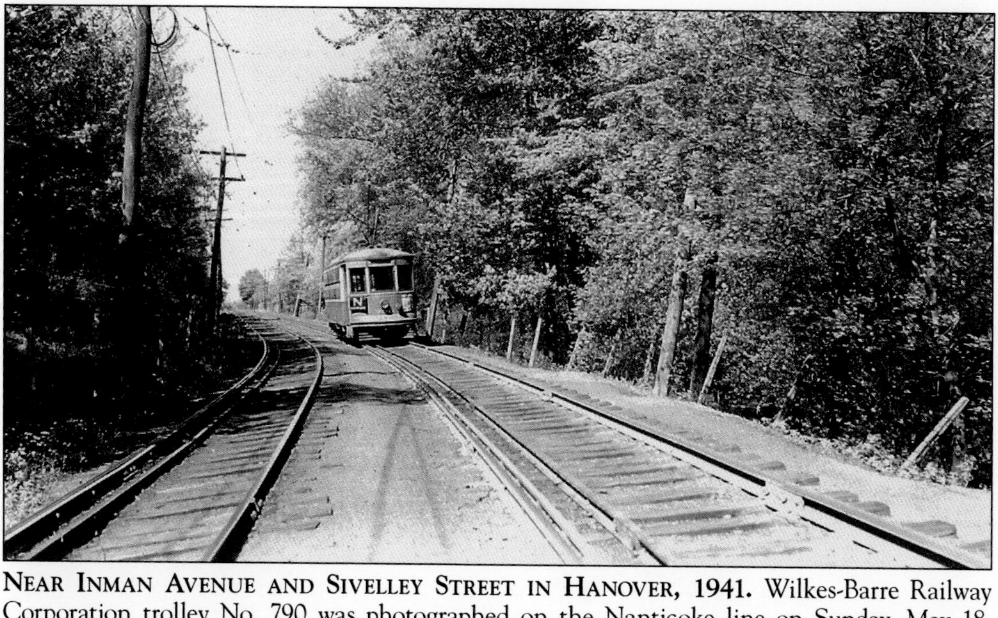

Near Inman Avenue and Sivelley Street in Hanover, 1941. Wilkes-Barre Railway Corporation trolley No. 790 was photographed on the Nanticoke line on Sunday, May 18, 1941. The trolley was ordered from the J. G. Brill Company on April 2, 1924, for the Eastern Pennsylvania Railway. In 1933, the trolley was delivered to the Wilkes-Barre Railway. It was scrapped in November 1950.

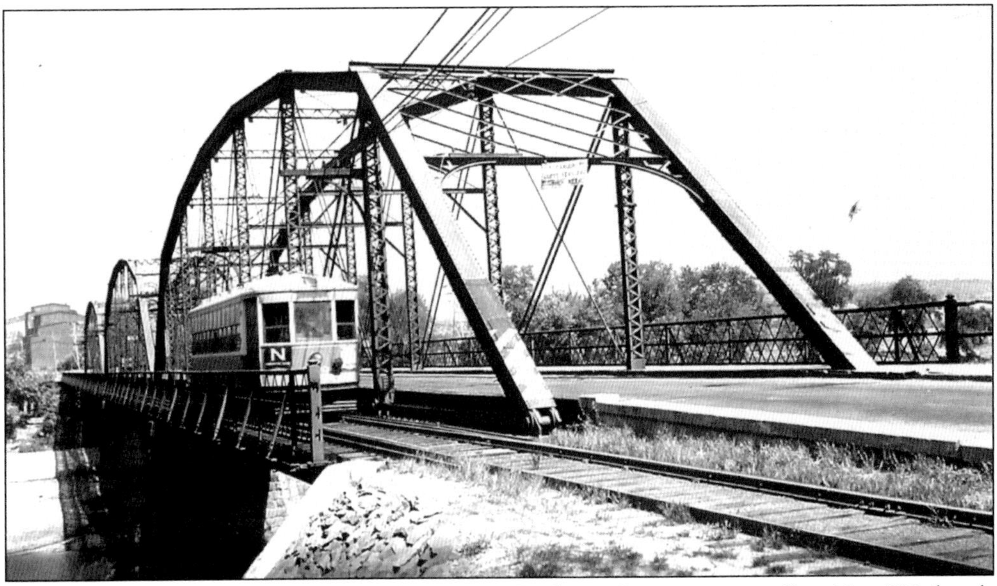

Carey Avenue Bridge, 1941. Wilkes-Barre Railway Corporation trolley No. 790 heads inbound to Wilkes-Barre at the Hanover end of the Carey Avenue bridge on the Plymouth line on Saturday, August 30, 1941. The sign on the bridge indicated routing of the Nanticoke and Plymouth trolley lines through Wilkes-Barre. Regular service on the Plymouth line over the Carey Avenue bridge started on July 15, 1895. The Plymouth line was one of only two trolley lines that provided late-night service from Wilkes-Barre.

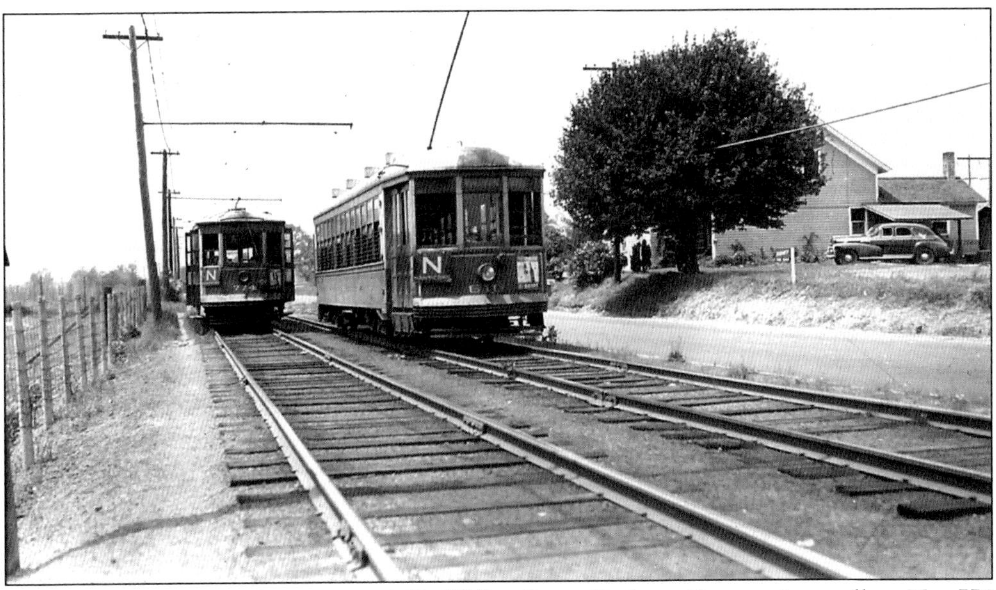

Old River Road in Hanover, 1942. Wilkes-Barre Railway Corporation trolleys No. 774 and No. 610 are south of Dundee Cross Road on the Nanticoke line on Sunday, June 7, 1942. Trolley No. 610 was ordered from the J. G. Brill Company on April 23, 1918. It was built for the Emergency Fleet Corporation at the Hog Island shipyard in Philadelphia. The trolley was delivered to the Wilkes-Barre Railway in the 1920s. Trolley No. 610 was scrapped in March 1948.

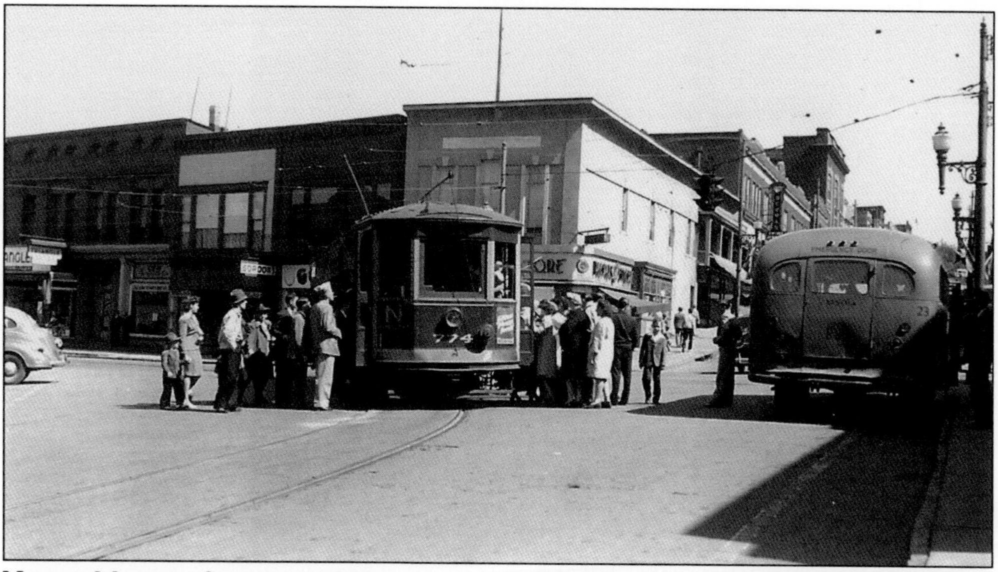

North Market Street at Main Street in Nanticoke, 1945. Wilkes-Barre Railway Corporation trolley No. 774 and bus No. 23 were captured on Wednesday, May 30, 1945, along with the holiday crowd heading to Sans Souci Park in Hanover. Trolley No. 774 had steel vestibule framing, but one of the vestibules was replaced with a wooden vestibule after an accident. The trolley was scrapped in October 1950.

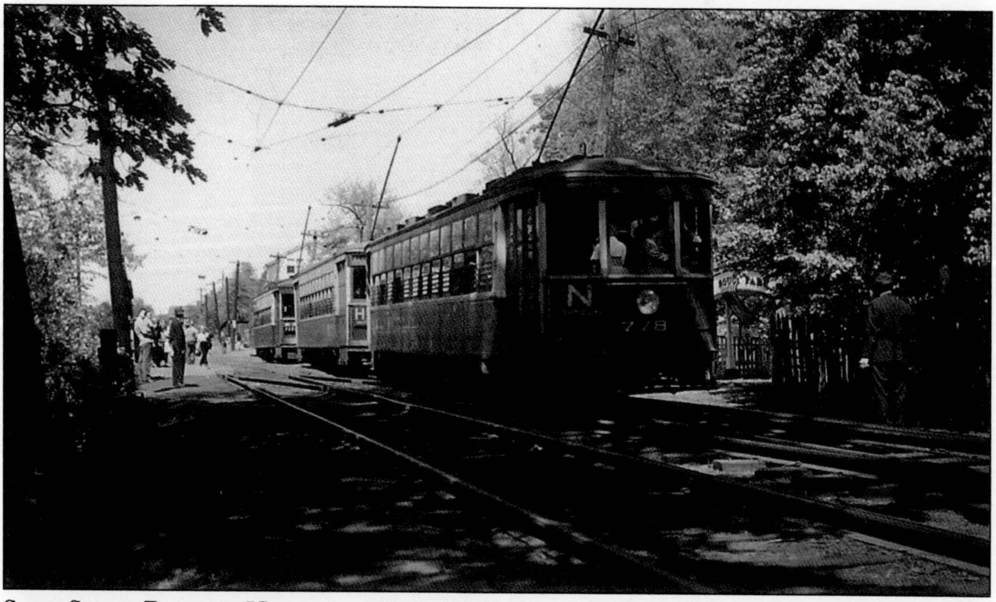

Sans Souci Park in Hanover, 1945. Wilkes-Barre Railway Corporation trolleys No. 778, No. 758, and No. 764 work on the Nanticoke line in Hanover on Wednesday, May 30, 1945. The trolleys were ordered from the J. G. Brill Company in 1924 and were purchased secondhand by the Wilkes-Barre Railway in 1932 and 1933. Trolley No. 758 was later sold to the Coast Cities Railway of Asbury Park, New Jersey.

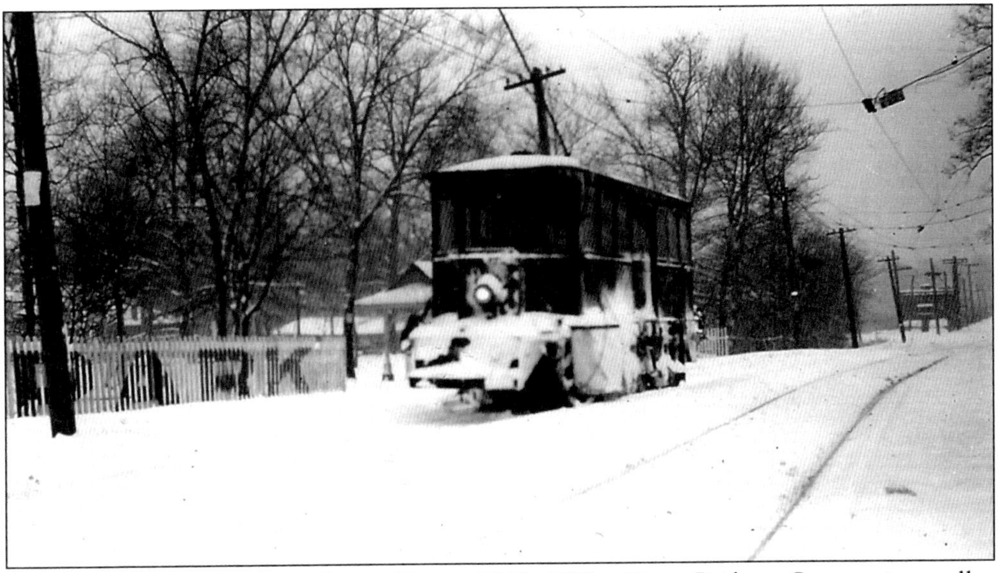

SWEEPER TROLLEY AT SANS SOUCI PARK, 1945. Wilkes-Barre Railway Corporation trolley No. 040 cleans the tracks on the Nanticoke line in Hanover on Wednesday, December 19, 1945. It was ordered from the J. G. Brill Company on August 7, 1899, for the Wilkes-Barre, Dallas and Harvey's Lake Railway. The sweeper trolley was scrapped in 1950. The Bear Cat roller coaster at Sans Souci Park was designed by Herbert Paul Schmeck, and it was built by the Philadelphia Toboggan Coasters, Inc., in 1928.

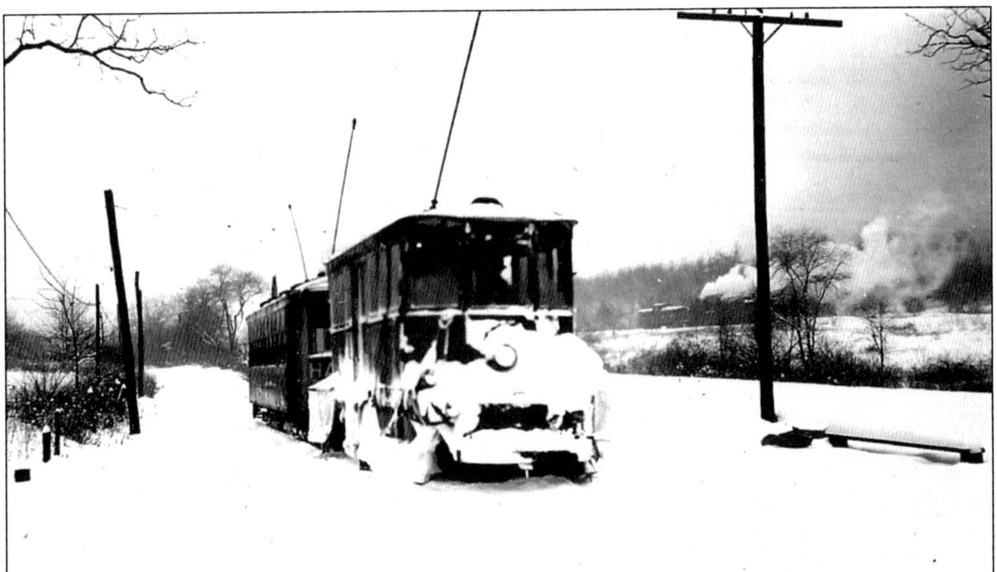

FRONT STREET AT TRUESDALE TERRACE ROAD IN NANTICOKE, 1945. Wilkes-Barre Railway Corporation sweeper trolley No. 040 and trolley No. 760 are busy on the Hanover line on Wednesday, December 19, 1945. The locomotive and caboose in the background were on the Lehigh Valley Railroad main line. The last day of trolley service on the Hanover line was Saturday, October 14, 1950.

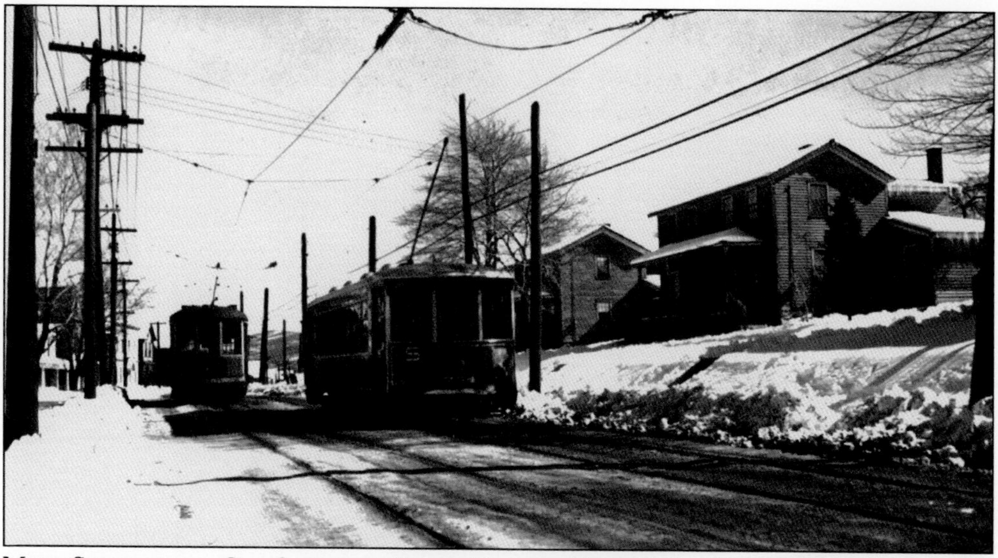

Main Street near Oak Street in Sugar Notch, 1946. Wilkes-Barre Railway Corporation trolleys No. 602 and No. 754 are pictured on the Sugar Notch line on Thursday, February 21, 1946. Trolley No. 602 was ordered from the J. G. Brill Company on April 23, 1918. The trolley was delivered to the Wilkes-Barre Railway in the 1920s, and it was scrapped in 1948.

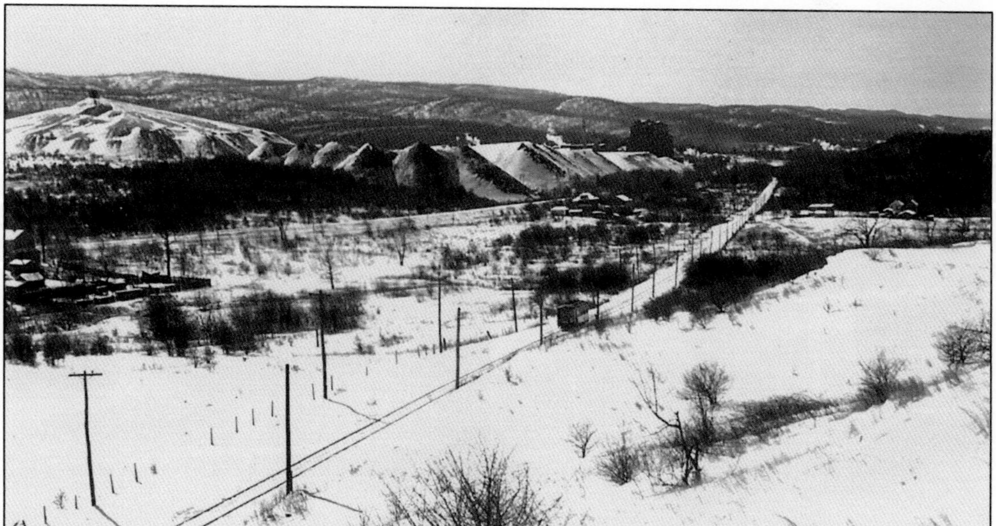

Bauer Street and Clark Cross Road in Hanover, 1946. Wilkes-Barre Railway Corporation trolley No. 760 is shown on the Hanover line on Thursday, February 21, 1946. The Truesdale Colliery was owned by the Glen Alden Coal Company, and it was the largest colliery in the Wyoming Valley. The colliery was destroyed by a fire on February 26, 1953.

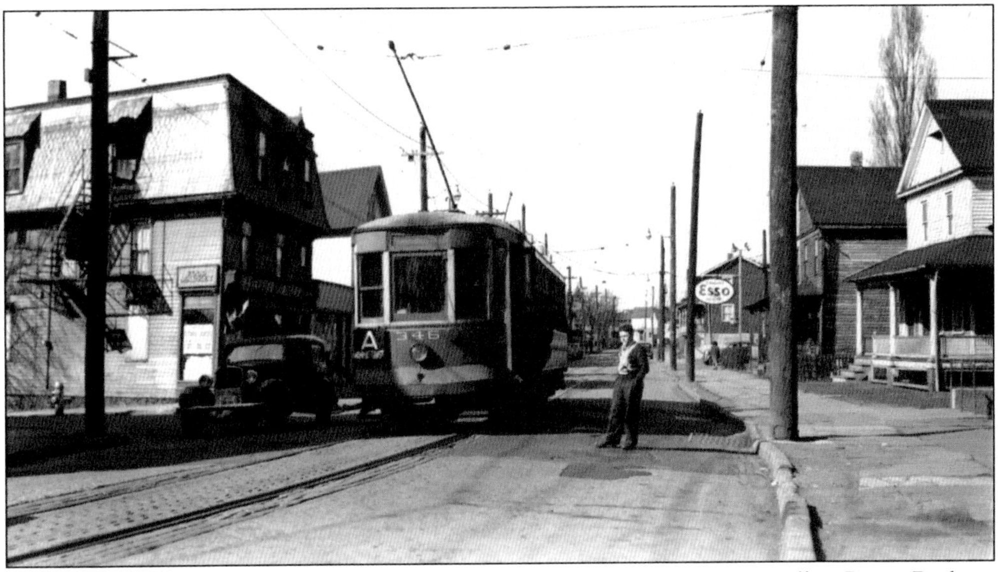

NORTH MAIN STREET AT MANHATTAN STREET IN ASHLEY, 1946. Wilkes-Barre Railway Corporation trolley No. 346 works during afternoon rush hour on Thursday, April 11, 1946. The trolley was ordered from the J. G. Brill Company on February 27, 1911, and it was delivered to the Wilkes-Barre Railway. Trolley No. 346 was scrapped in March 1948.

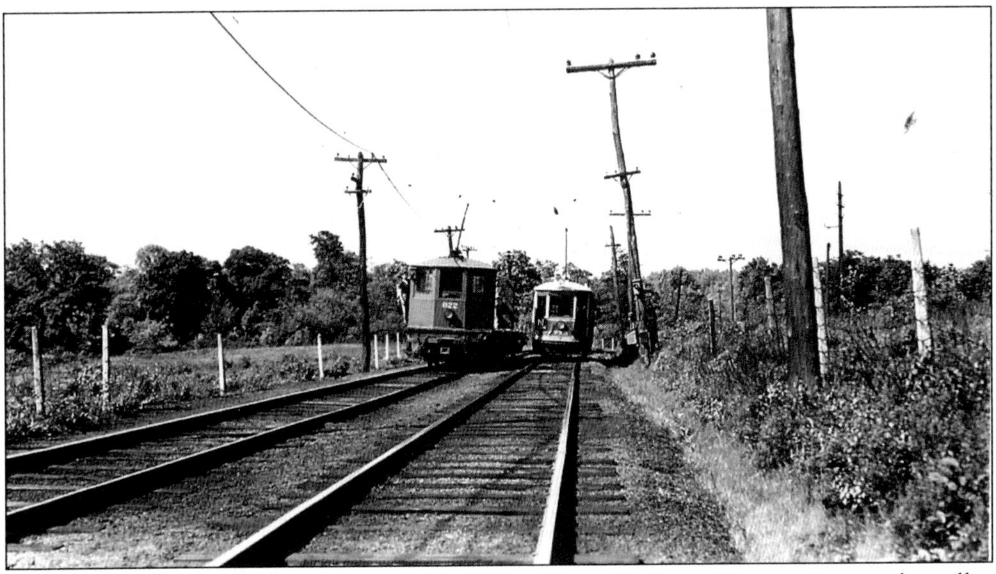

NANTICOKE LINE IN HANOVER, 1946. Wilkes-Barre Railway Corporation work trolley No. 022, flatbed trailer No. 08, and trolley No. 772 are outbound on a curve near Sans Souci Park on Friday, May 31, 1946. Workmen were repairing the roadbed at Dundee after it was washed out during a storm. Flatbed trailer No. 08 was ordered from the J. G. Brill Company in 1912, and it was equipped with air brakes operated by the towing trolley.

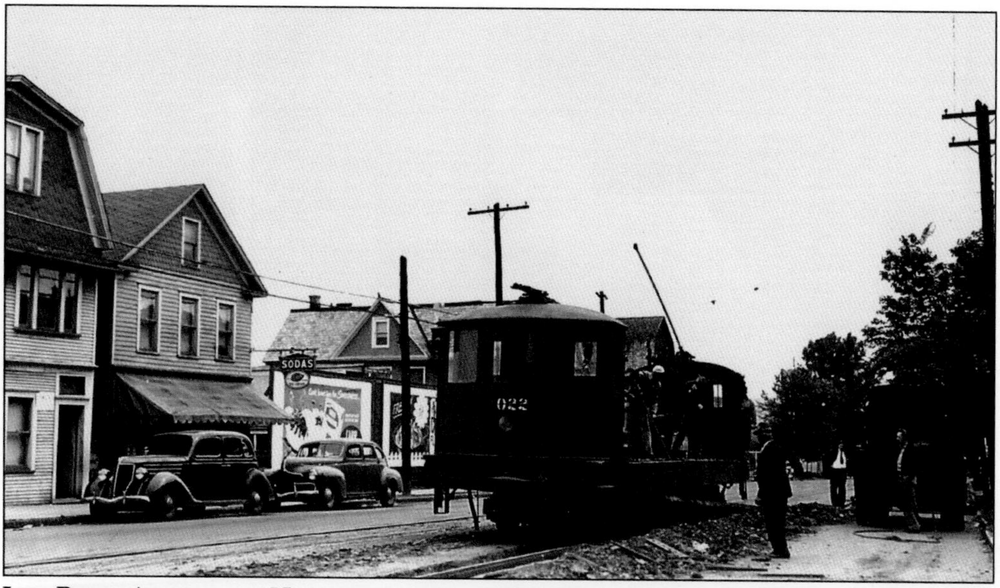

LEE PARK AVENUE IN HANOVER, 1946. Wilkes-Barre Railway Corporation work trolley No. 022 is near Oxford Street replacing rails on the Nanticoke line on Thursday, June 6, 1946. Foreman Herbert Dewitt is in the background wearing a coat and tie. Work trolley No. 022 was a 43-foot steel crane trolley was ordered from the J. G. Brill Company on May 6, 1912.

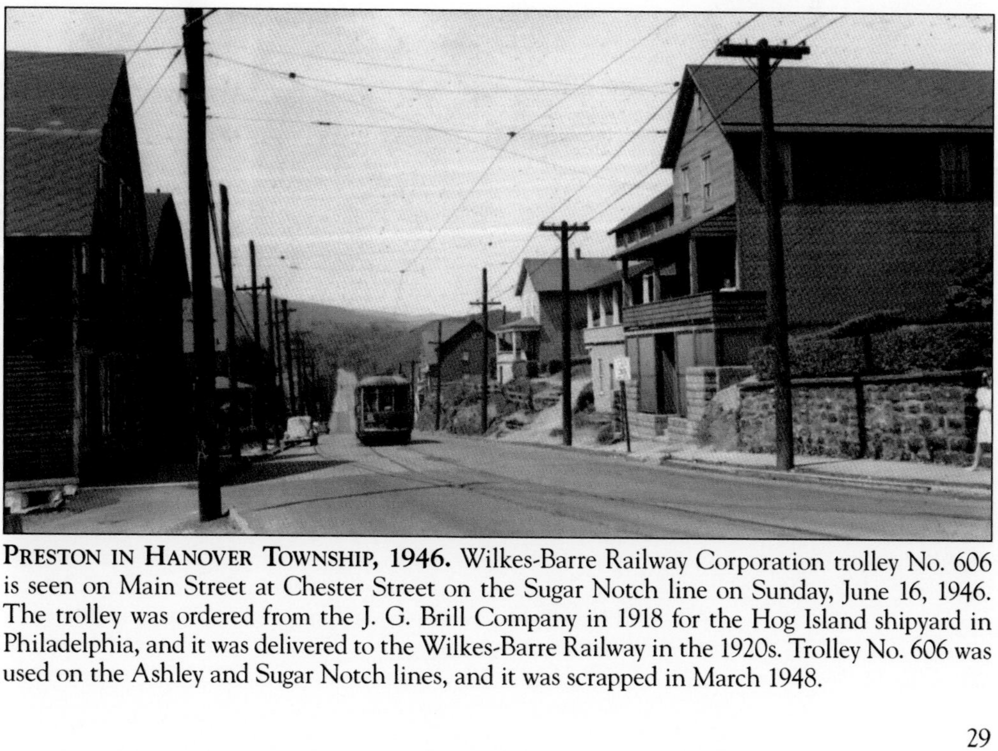

PRESTON IN HANOVER TOWNSHIP, 1946. Wilkes-Barre Railway Corporation trolley No. 606 is seen on Main Street at Chester Street on the Sugar Notch line on Sunday, June 16, 1946. The trolley was ordered from the J. G. Brill Company in 1918 for the Hog Island shipyard in Philadelphia, and it was delivered to the Wilkes-Barre Railway in the 1920s. Trolley No. 606 was used on the Ashley and Sugar Notch lines, and it was scrapped in March 1948.

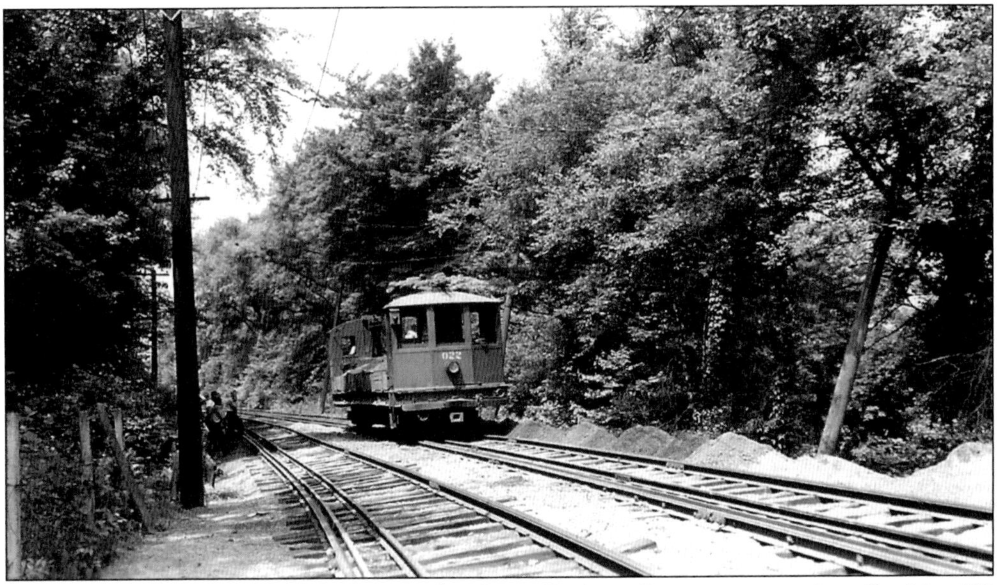

BUTTONWOOD IN HANOVER, 1946. Wilkes-Barre Railway Corporation work trolley No. 022 uses cinder fill to repair the damage due to mine settlement along the trolley line at the curve near Buttonwood on the Nanticoke line on Thursday, June 27, 1946. Work trolley No. 022 was ordered from the J. G. Brill Company, and it was finished at the Northampton Street trolley yard in Wilkes-Barre.

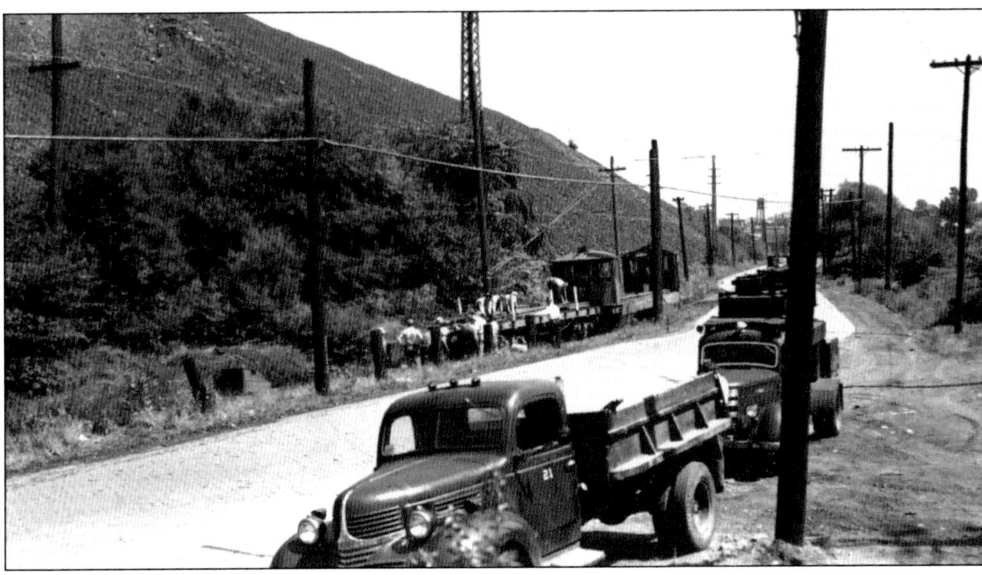

MAIN STREET IN PRESTON, HANOVER TOWNSHIP, 1946. Wilkes-Barre Railway Corporation work trolley No. 022 and flatbed trailer No. 08 remove rails from the abandoned Sugar Notch line on Thursday, August 8, 1946. Flatbed trailer No. 08 was scrapped in August 1950 at the Wood Street trolley yard in Wilkes-Barre. Work trolley No. 022 was the last trolley on the Wyoming Valley trolley system.

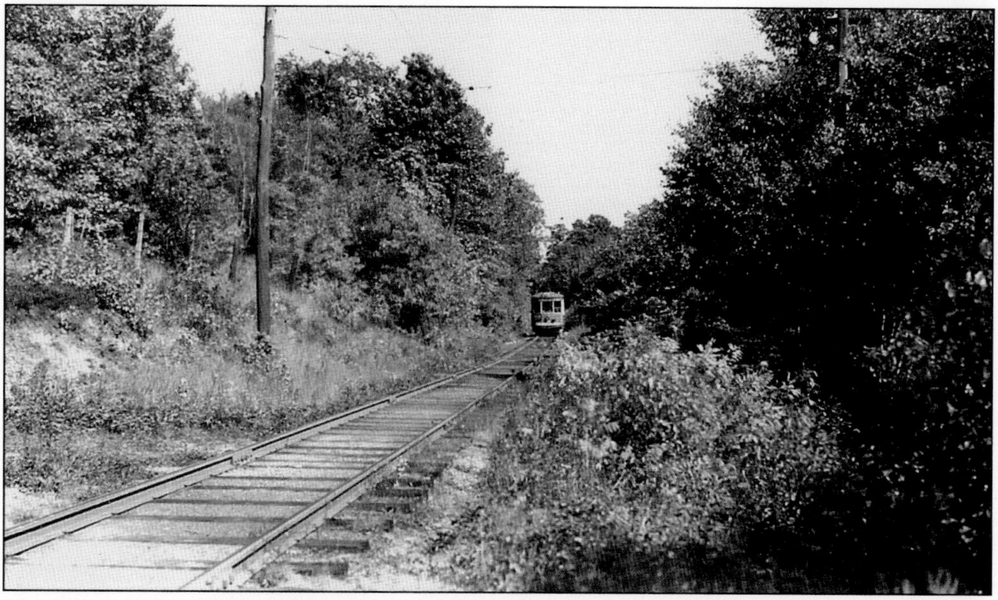

Hanover Line, 1946. Wilkes-Barre Railway Corporation trolley No. 760 is opposite the Truesdale Colliery in Hanover on Thursday, September 26, 1946. The trolley was ordered from the J. G. Brill Company on April 2, 1924, for the Eastern Pennsylvania Railway in Pottsville before it was delivered to the Wilkes-Barre Railway in 1933.

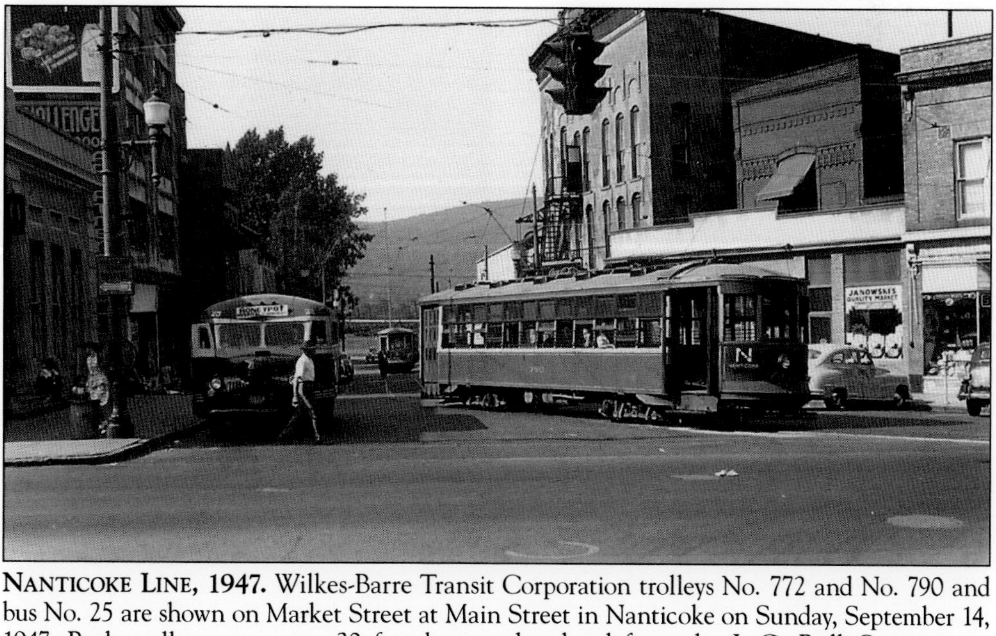

Nanticoke Line, 1947. Wilkes-Barre Transit Corporation trolleys No. 772 and No. 790 and bus No. 25 are shown on Market Street at Main Street in Nanticoke on Sunday, September 14, 1947. Both trolleys were over 30 feet long and ordered from the J. G. Brill Company in Philadelphia. They were delivered to the Wilkes-Barre Railway in September 1933.

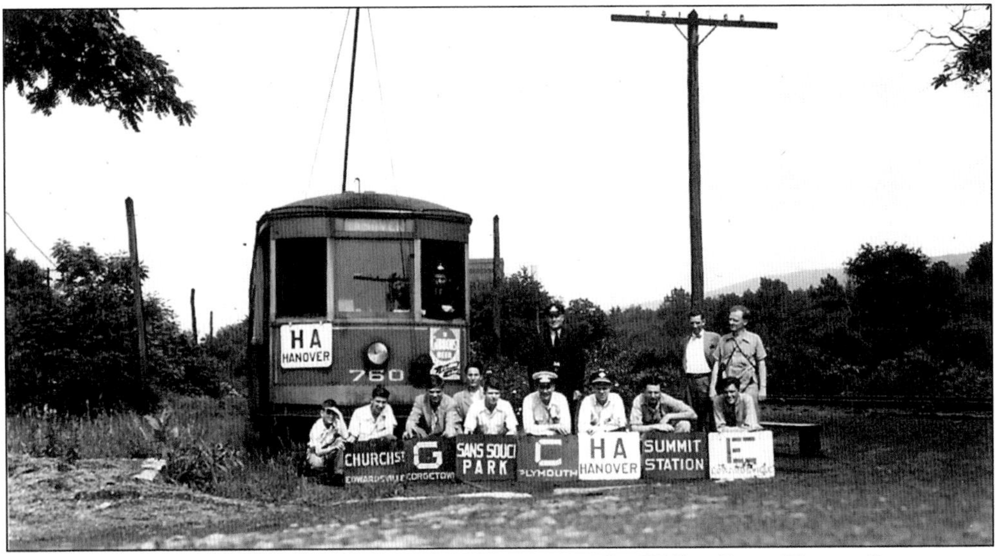

FRONT STREET AT TRUESDALE TERRACE ROAD, 1948. The Wilkes-Barre Transit Corporation trolley No. 760 special chartered by the NRHS is at the end of the Hanover line in Nanticoke on Sunday, June 27, 1948. Rail enthusiast passengers are displaying trolley line signs from Edwardsville, Georgetown, Hanover, Plymouth, Sans Souci Park, and Summit Station. Trolley No. 760 was the last regular passenger trolley on the Hanover line. The Wilkes-Barre Transit Corporation was incorporated on August 29, 1947, and assumed all local transportation routes.

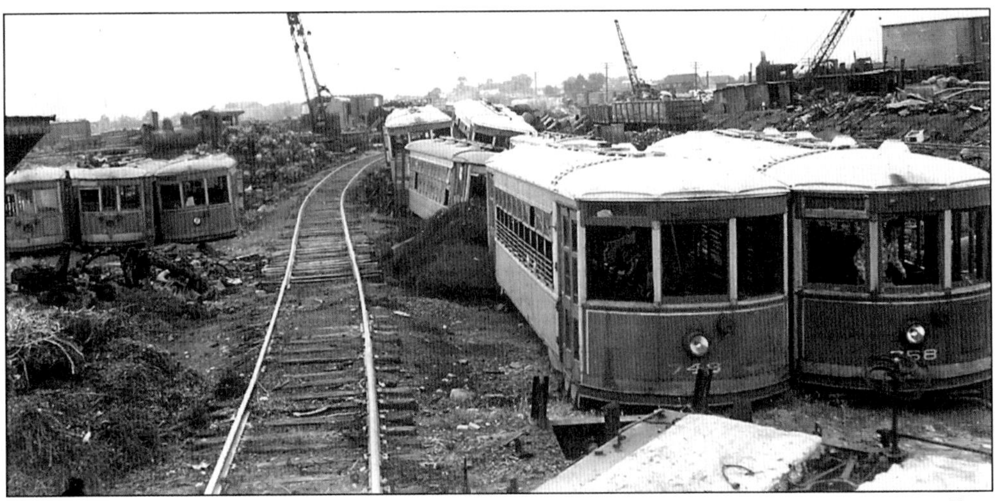

THE END OF THE LINE IN HANOVER, 1948. Former Wilkes-Barre Transit Corporation trolleys No. 720, No. 722, No. 724, No. 746, No. 748, No. 750, No. 752, No. 758, and No. 764 wait to be demolished at the Louis Cohen and Son scrap yard on Fellow Street in Hanover on Saturday, August 10, 1948. Trolleys No. 720, No. 722, and No. 724 were built in 1923 for the Sistersville and New Martinsville Traction Company in West Virginia and were delivered to the Wilkes-Barre Railway on December 27, 1925.

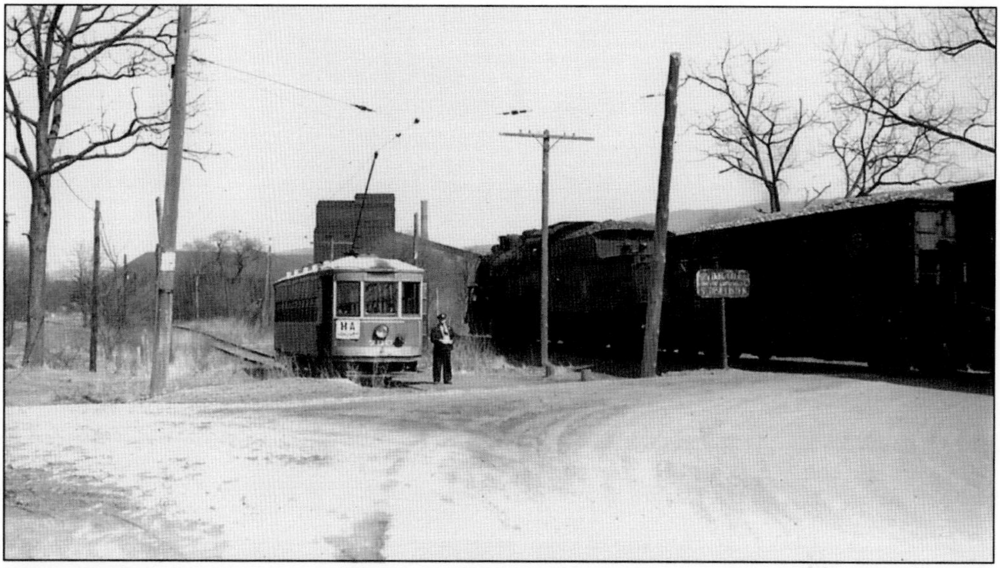

Front Street at Truesdale Terrace Road in Nanticoke, 1950. Wilkes-Barre Transit Corporation trolley No. 780 is at the end of the Hanover line on Wednesday, April 26, 1950, at the Central Railroad of New Jersey crossing. The operator was Felix Novokowski. The trolley was ordered from the J. G. Brill Company in 1924 for the Eastern Pennsylvania Railway. It was delivered to the Wilkes-Barre Railway in 1933.

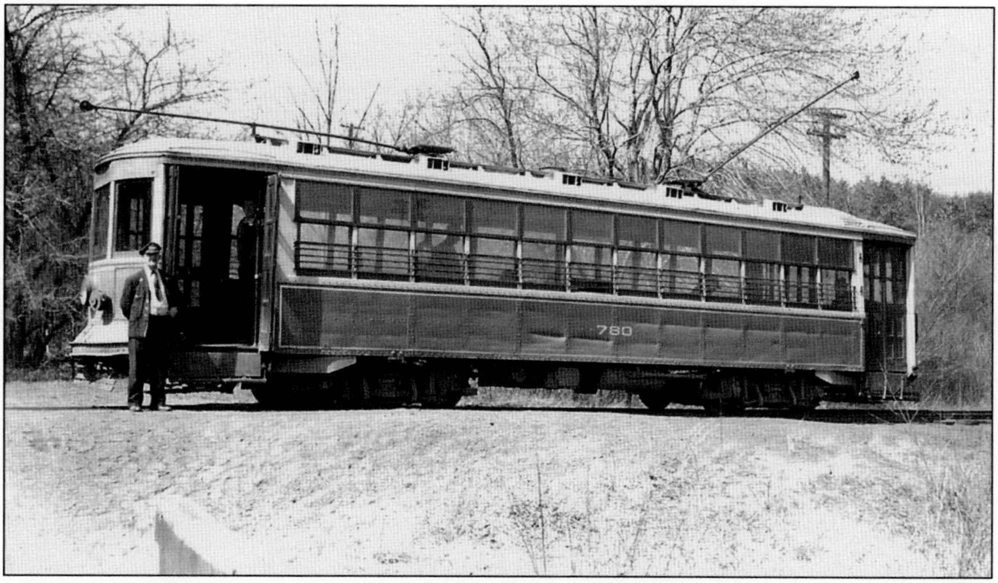

Opposite the Truesdale Colliery in Hanover, 1950. Wilkes-Barre Transit Corporation trolley No. 780 is pictured on Wednesday, April 26, 1950. The trolley was operated by Felix Novokowski and was scrapped after the final day of service on the Hanover line on Saturday, October 14, 1950, when all trolley service in the Wyoming Valley ended.

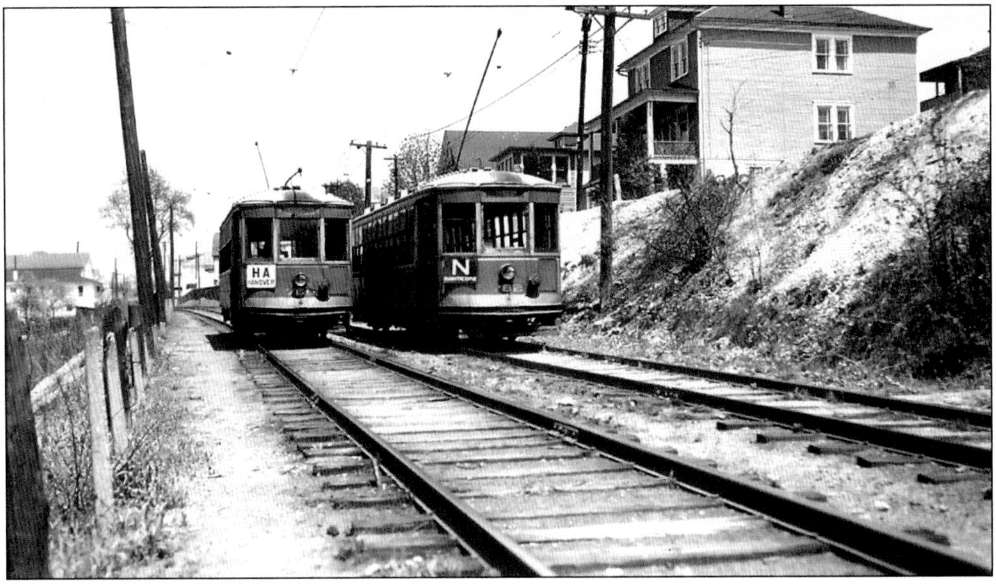

Hanover Line near Sans Souci Park, 1950. Wilkes-Barre Transit Corporation trolleys No. 760 bound for Hanover and No. 782 on the Nanticoke line in Hanover are shown on Tuesday, May 9, 1950. Both trolleys were ordered from the J. G. Brill Company on April 2, 1924, for the Eastern Pennsylvania Railway in Pottsville, and the trolleys were delivered to the Wilkes-Barre Railway in 1933. The former Pottsville trolleys were equipped with air-operated doors on the right side and manually operated doors on the left.

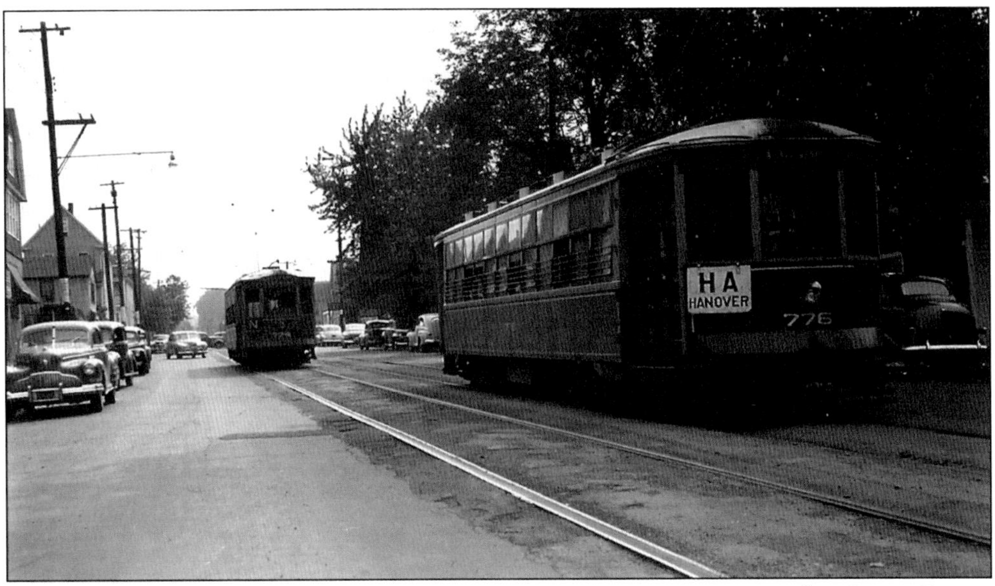

Lee Park Avenue near Oxford Street in Hanover, 1950. Wilkes-Barre Transit Corporation trolley No. 774 is on the Nanticoke line and No. 776 is on the Hanover line on Thursday, August 3, 1950. Both trolleys were ordered from the J. G. Brill Company for the Eastern Pennsylvania Railway in Pottsville and were delivered to the Wilkes-Barre Railway in September 1933. Trolley No. 774 was scrapped in October 1950.

Two

WILKES-BARRE

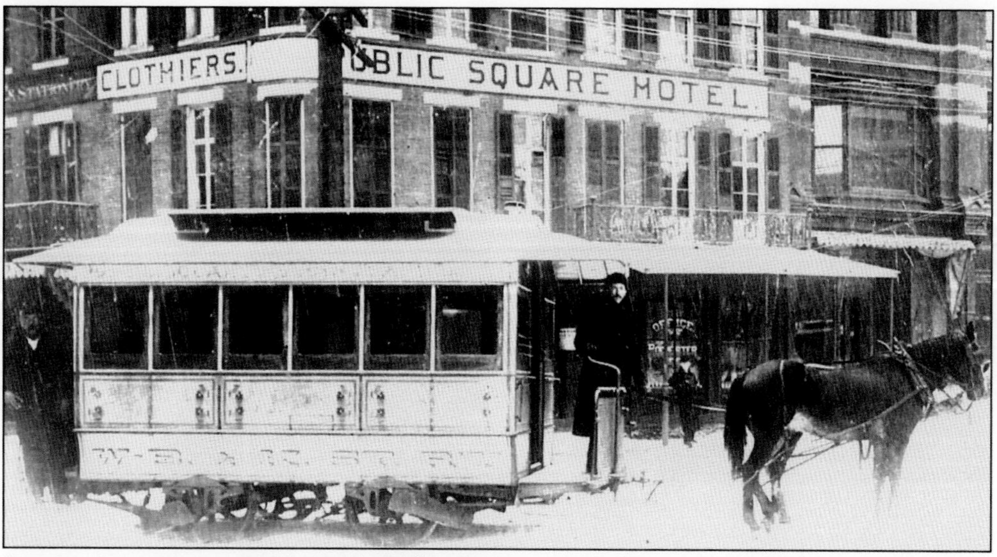

PUBLIC SQUARE, C. 1885–1892. Wilkes-Barre and Kingston Street Railway horse-drawn streetcar No. 10 is in front of the Public Square Hotel in Wilkes-Barre on the South Main Street line entering the west side of the public square. It served the public square and South Wilkes-Barre. The enclosed horse-drawn streetcar was built by the John Stephenson Company of New York in September 1885 with an open operator platform.

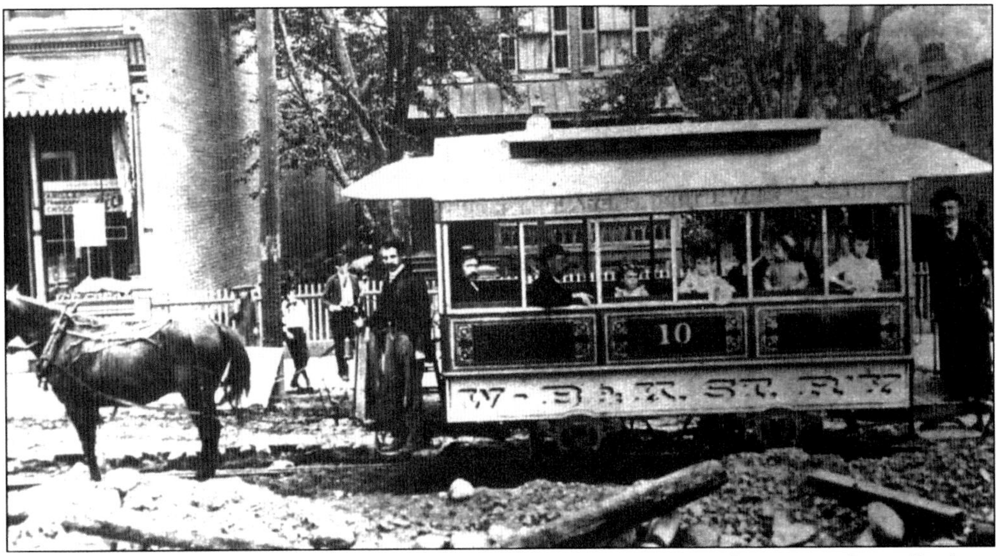

Wilkes-Barre, c. 1892. D. W. Barlow captured the Wilkes-Barre and Kingston Street Railway horse-drawn streetcar No. 10 in this photograph. The one-horse streetcar cost $700 to build in 1885. Horse-drawn streetcars in Wilkes-Barre were discontinued in 1893, and all trolleys were electrified. The first electric trolley in Wilkes-Barre ran on North Main Street on March 19, 1888. (NRHS North Jersey Chapter collection.)

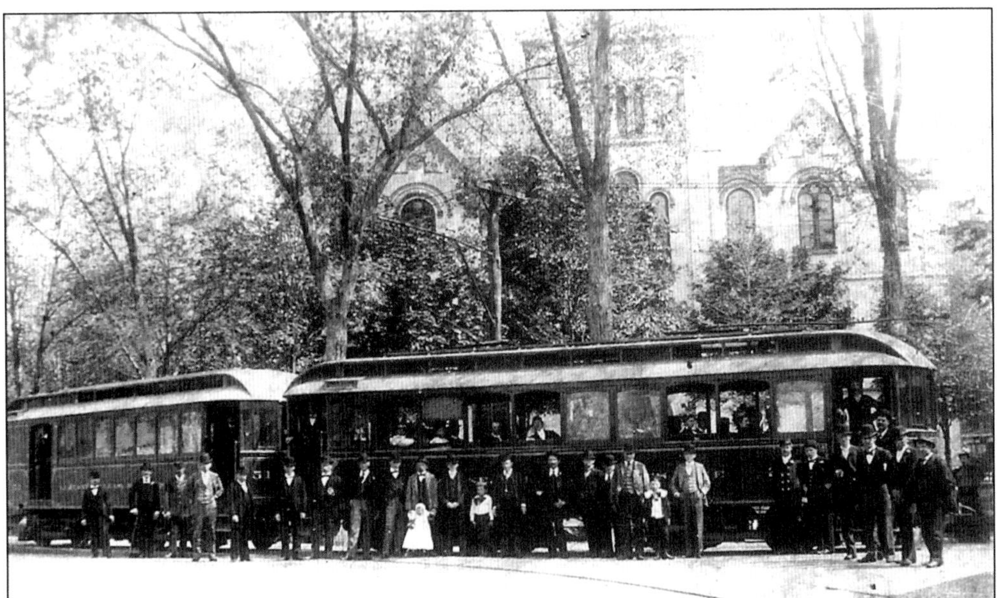

Public Square in Wilkes-Barre, 1898. Pictured here are Wilkes-Barre, Dallas and Harvey's Lake trolleys No. 51 and No. 2. The photograph was taken by D. W. Barlow in front of the old Luzerne County Courthouse. Both trolleys were built by Jackson and Sharp and were ordered on October 8, 1896. The Luzerne-to-Harvey's Lake line was hazardous and accident prone. Wilkes-Barre borough celebrated its centennial jubilee starting on May 10, 1906.

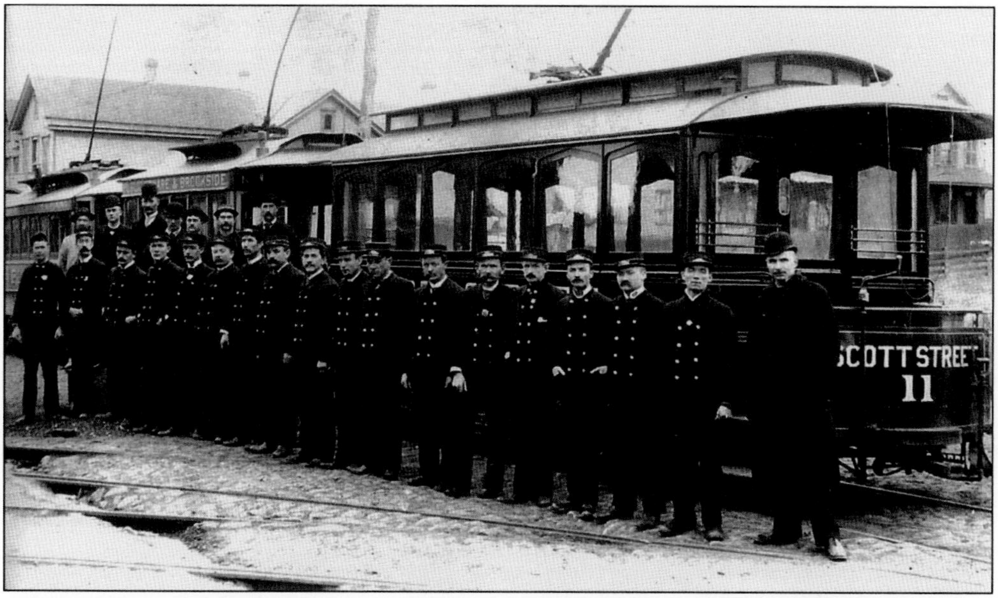

CANAL STREET TROLLEY BARN, C. 1891. The Wilkes-Barre and Suburban Street Railway trolleys No. 4, No. 5, and No. 6 and Scott Street trolley No. 11 are shown with railway employees in Wilkes-Barre. Trolley No. 11 was one of four trolleys ordered from the J. G. Brill Company in 1891. The *Evening Leader* newspaper dated Friday, December 4, 1891, stated that trolley No. 11 started service the previous day. (William Johns collection.)

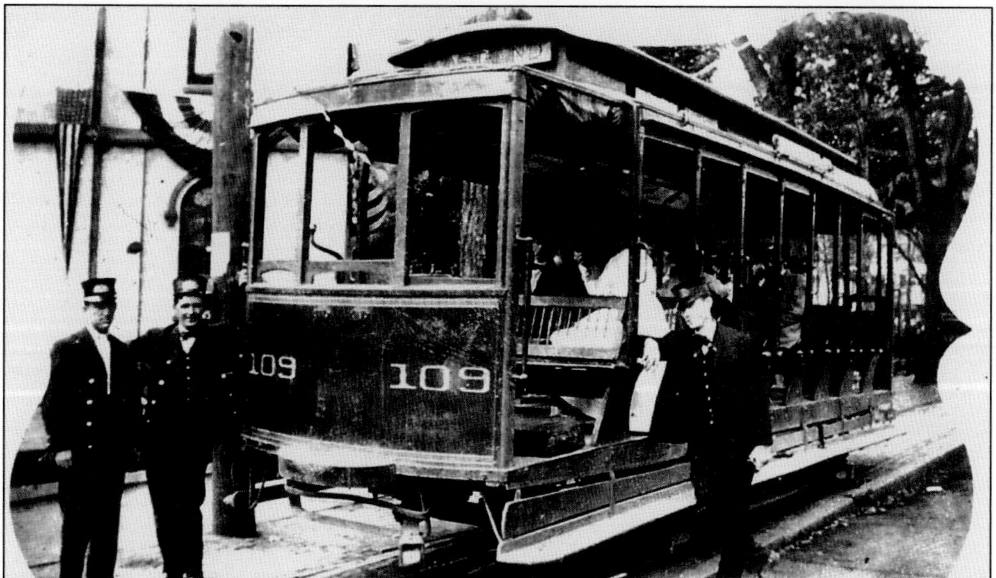

SCOTT STREET TROLLEY AT THE PUBLIC SQUARE, C. 1906. Wilkes-Barre and Wyoming Valley Traction Company trolley No. 109 is seen in Wilkes-Barre. The company was chartered on February 9, 1891, by G. Mortimer Lewis and financial backers John J. Patterson, Robert McMeen, J. Howard Neely, W. F. Sadler, and John Graham. The trolley was on the Scott Street line with the Luzerne County Courthouse in the background. The eight-bench trolley was built by the St. Louis Streetcar Company in 1893. Matthew Bilbow is the second from the left.

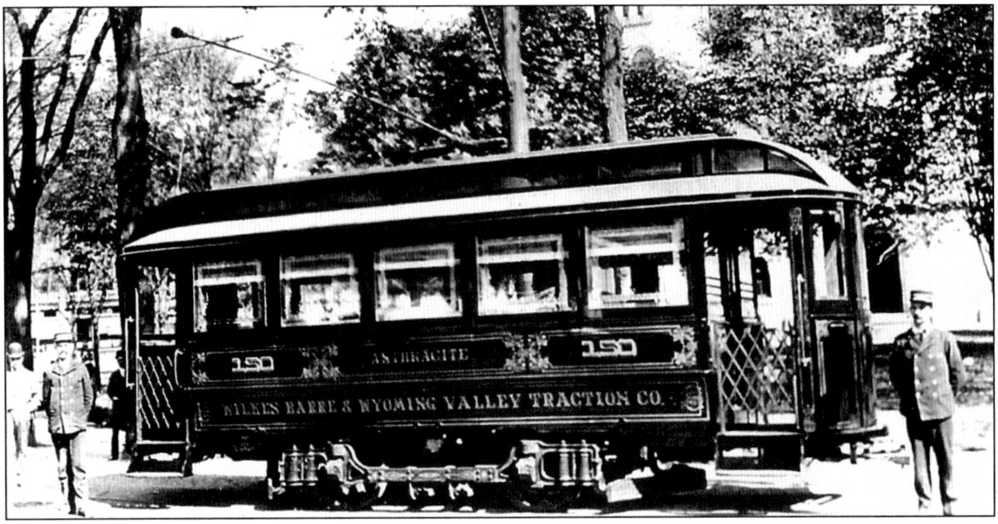

PARLOR CAR NO. 150 *ANTHRACITE* AT THE PUBLIC SQUARE, C. 1906. Wilkes-Barre and Wyoming Valley Traction Company trolley No. 150, shown in Wilkes-Barre, was built by the St. Louis Streetcar Company in 1893 for the traction company directors. It was delivered to the Wyoming Valley on April 27, 1893. The trolley was originally painted white with gold trim, but it was repainted dark green in 1894. The windows were heavy French plate glass with frosted edges, and the interior was finished mahogany.

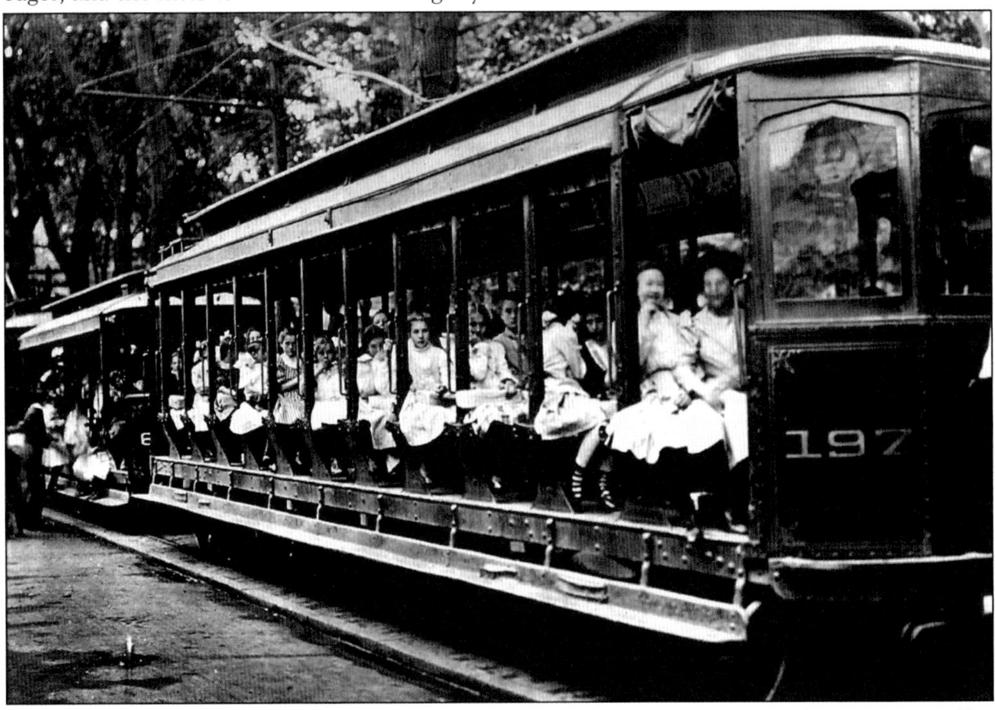

OPEN-CAR TROLLEYS AT THE PUBLIC SQUARE, C. 1906. Wilkes-Barre and Wyoming Valley Traction Company trolley No. 197 was photographed at the public square by D. W. Barlow during Wilkes-Barre's centennial. The 11-bench trolley was ordered from the J. G. Brill Company on February 29, 1896. The Wilkes-Barre and Wyoming Valley Traction Company was the only trolley company to use 11-bench open trolleys.

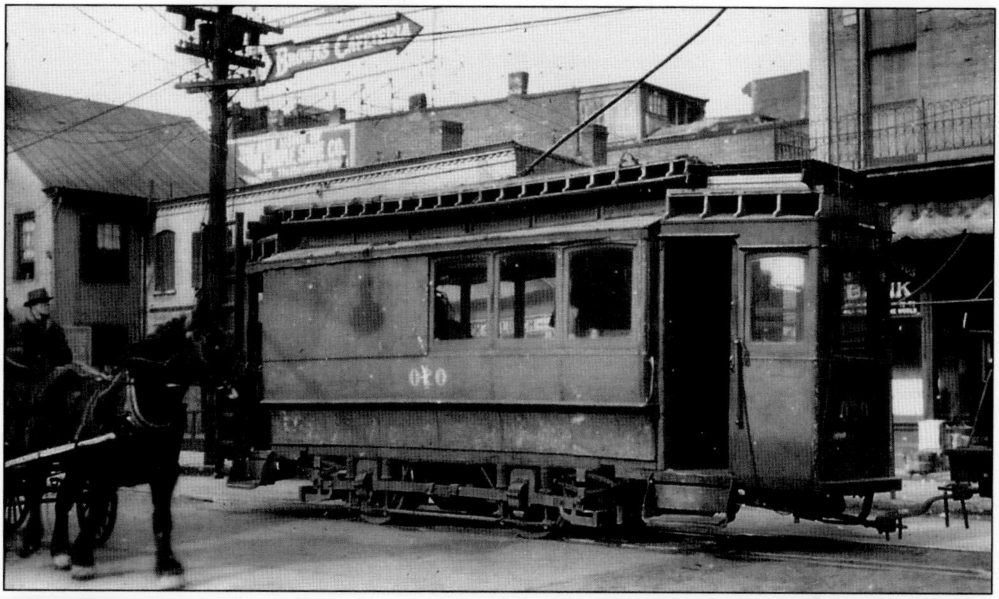

WORK TROLLEY IN WILKES-BARRE, C. 1924. Wilkes-Barre Railway work trolley No. 020 is close to the East Northampton Street trolley barn. The early work trolleys performed maintenance, made repairs, and removed snow from the tracks. Work trolley No. 020 was made from a passenger trolley that was built by the St. Louis Streetcar Company in the 1890s. (NRHS North Jersey Chapter collection.)

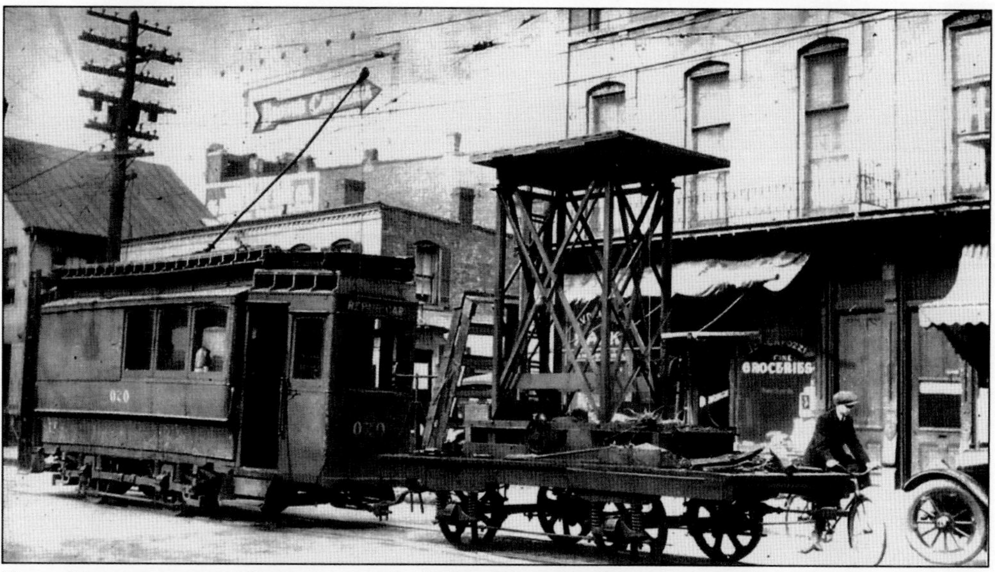

EAST NORTHAMPTON STREET, 1924. Wilkes-Barre Railway work trolley No. 020 and tower trailer No. 00L are in front of Percy Brown's store on Northampton Street in Wilkes-Barre. In 1928, the original work trolley No. 020 was replaced by a larger trolley that was rebuilt from a passenger trolley ordered from the J. G. Brill Company in the 1890s. Tower trailer No. 00L was made from a short wooden flatcar with a mounted pedestal.

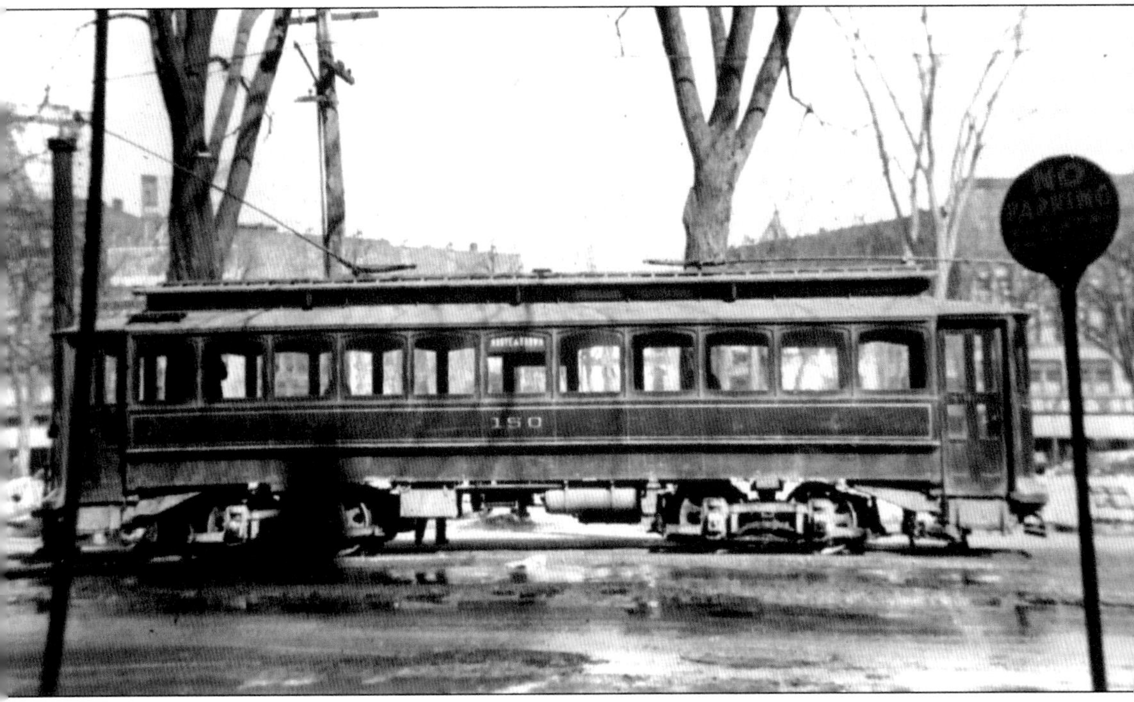

GROVE AND BROWN LINE TROLLEY AT THE PUBLIC SQUARE, 1920S. Wilkes-Barre Railway trolley No. 150 is between South Main Street and East Market Street in Wilkes-Barre. At nearly 33 feet long, trolley No. 150 was the longest spliced trolley owned by the Wilkes-Barre Railway. It was made in 1900 from two 18-foot trolleys ordered from the J. G. Brill Company. The Nesbitt Theater opened in Wilkes-Barre on October 29, 1897. (NRHS North Jersey Chapter collection.)

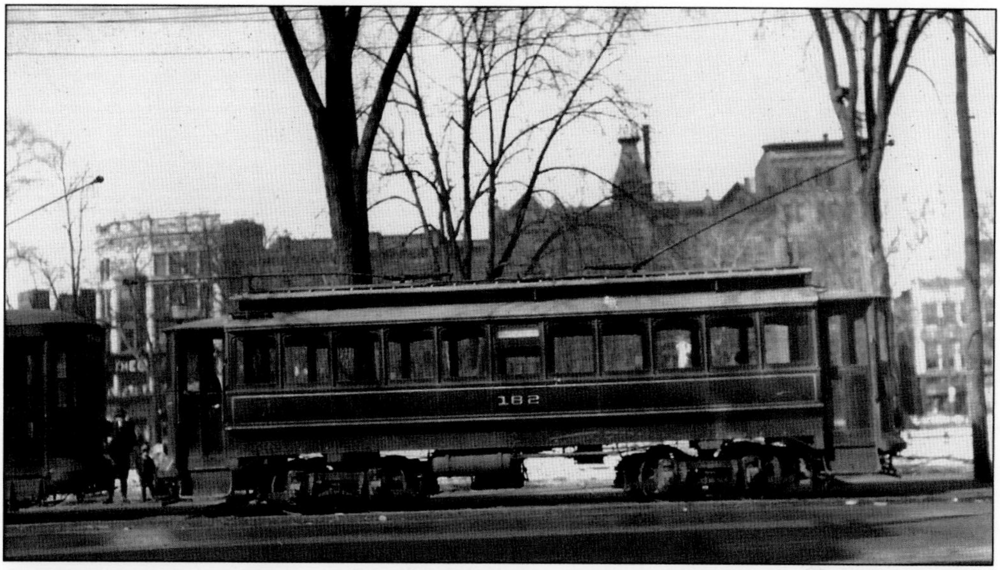

The Public Square, 1920s. Wilkes-Barre Railway trolley No. 182, seen between East Market Street and North Main Street in Wilkes-Barre, was ordered from the J. G. Brill Company in 1898. It was spliced together from the only two 16-foot trolleys operated in the Wyoming Valley. During World War I, trolley No. 182 was converted into a recruiting office for the U.S. Army. It made regular tours of the Wyoming Valley trolley system.

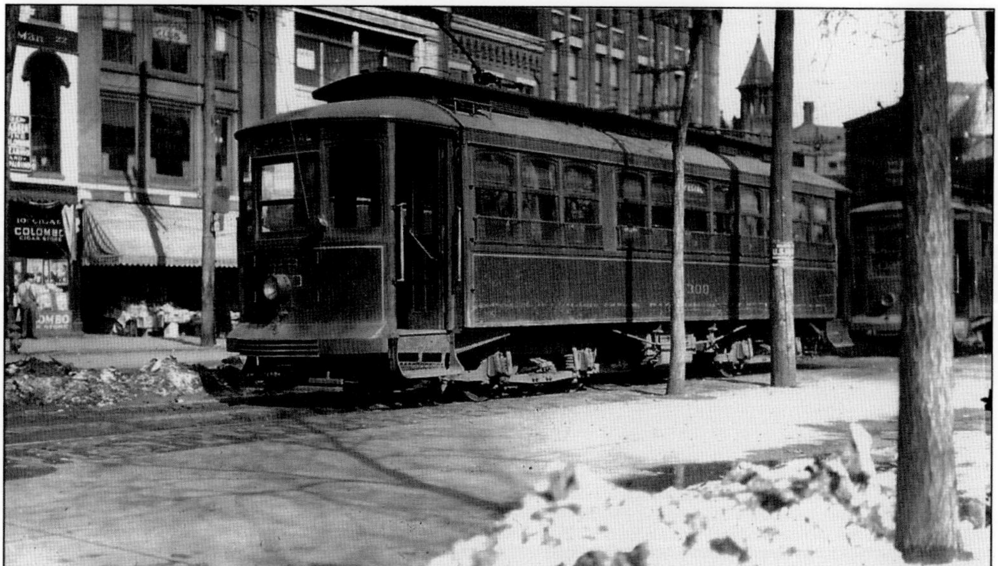

Funeral Car Parked at the Public Square. Wilkes-Barre Railway trolley No. 300 is near North Main Street. It was built in 1910 at the Northampton Street trolley barn in Wilkes-Barre. The funeral trolley was used to transport caskets along the trolley line. Visible in the photograph is the hinged door on the trolley's front center dash panel that was used to insert the casket into the trolley. (NRHS North Jersey Chapter collection.)

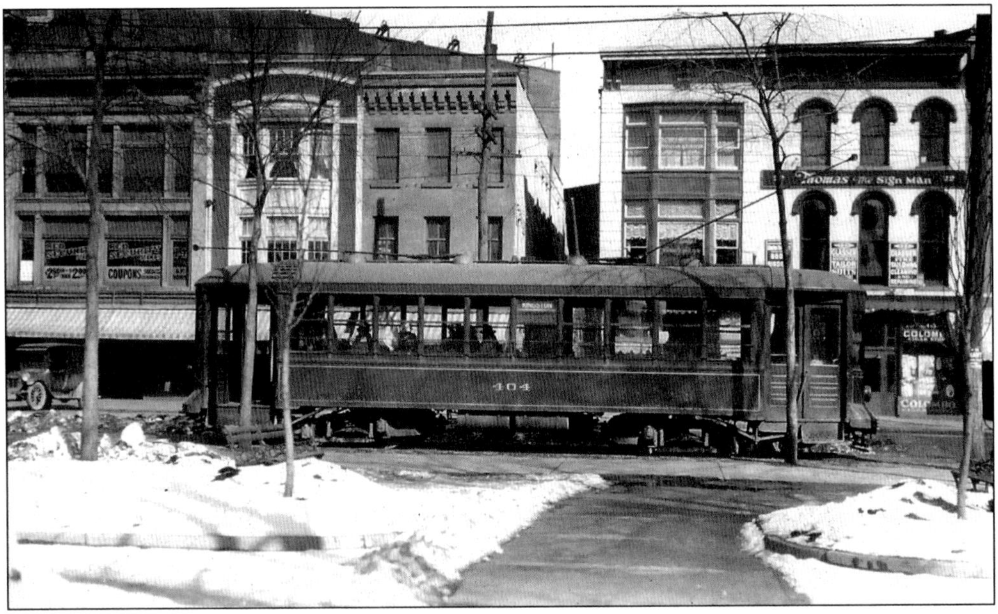

THE PUBLIC SQUARE IN WILKES-BARRE. Wilkes-Barre Railway trolley No. 404 is seen between North Main Street and West Market Street. The trolley was ordered from the J. G. Brill Company on February 20, 1913, and it was delivered to the Wilkes-Barre Railway in August 1913. It was used on the Kingston line until the trolley line was abandoned in 1937. Trolley No. 404 was scrapped in 1939.

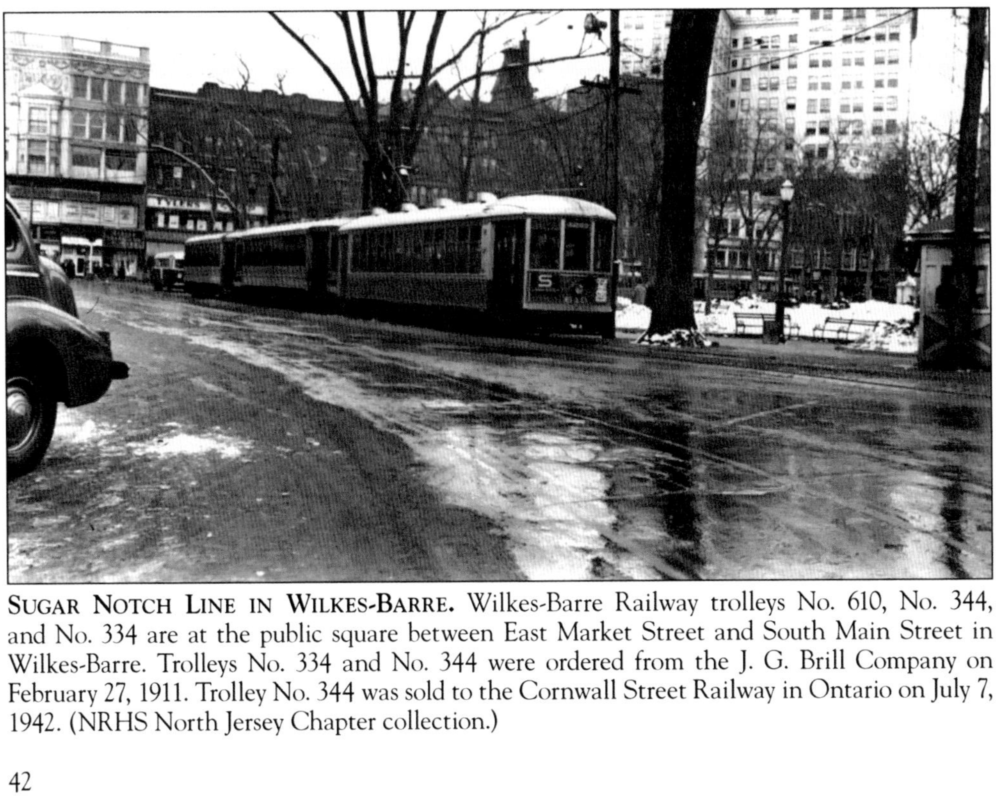

SUGAR NOTCH LINE IN WILKES-BARRE. Wilkes-Barre Railway trolleys No. 610, No. 344, and No. 334 are at the public square between East Market Street and South Main Street in Wilkes-Barre. Trolleys No. 334 and No. 344 were ordered from the J. G. Brill Company on February 27, 1911. Trolley No. 344 was sold to the Cornwall Street Railway in Ontario on July 7, 1942. (NRHS North Jersey Chapter collection.)

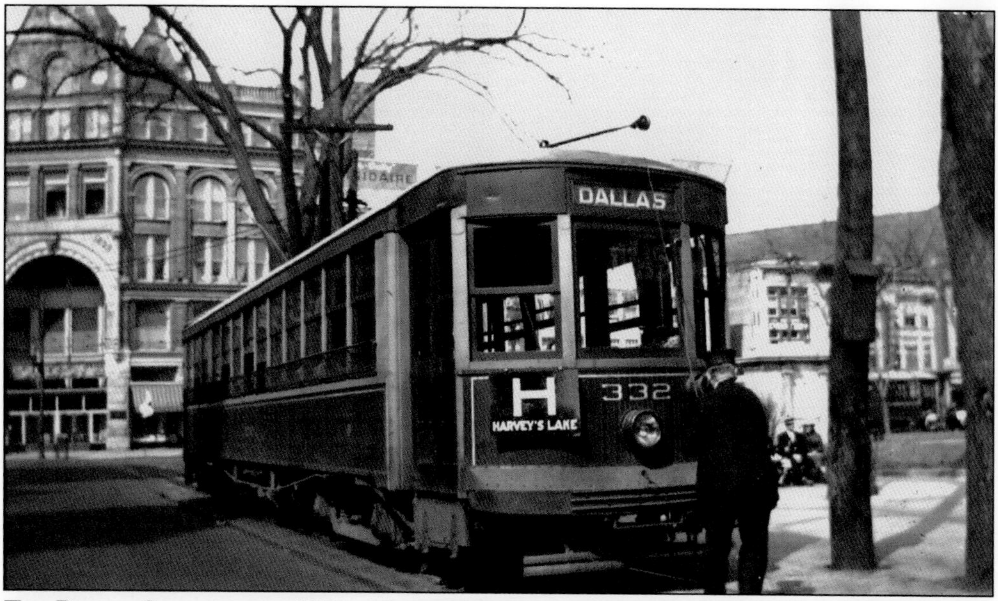

THE PUBLIC SQUARE NEAR WEST MARKET STREET, 1937. Wilkes-Barre Railway Corporation trolley No. 332 is in Wilkes-Barre on the Harvey's Lake line bound for Dallas on Sunday, April 18, 1937. The trolley was ordered from the J. G. Brill Company on February 27, 1911, and it was delivered in August 1911. The trolley was scrapped in 1939.

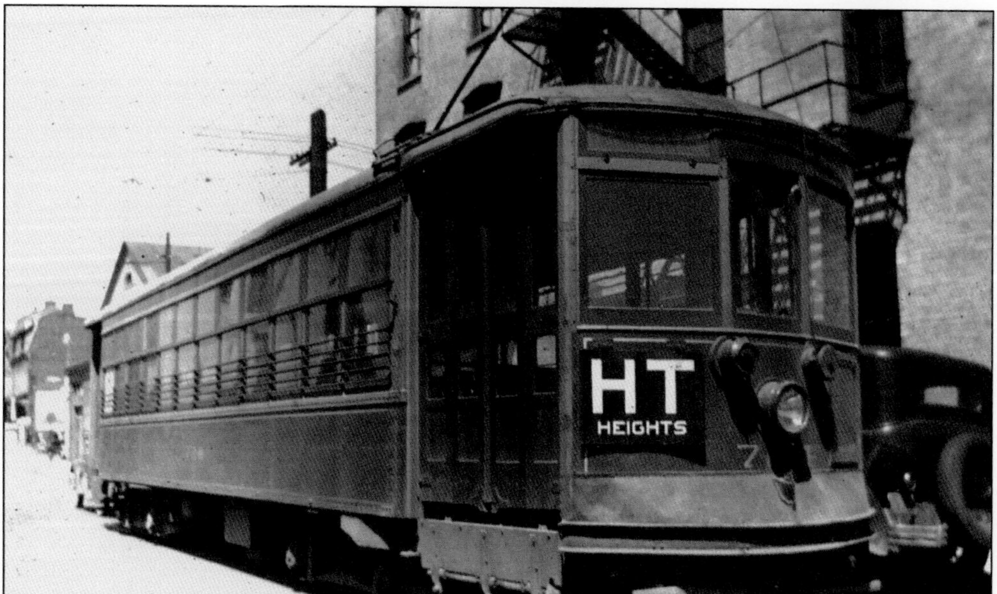

HEIGHTS LINE IN WILKES-BARRE, 1937. Wilkes-Barre Railway Corporation trolley No. 724 is pictured at South Main Street and South Street on Saturday, April 24, 1937. The trolley was ordered in October 1923 from the Wason Company. The Heights line started in 1895–1896, and it was discontinued on Saturday, October 1, 1938. The trolley was scrapped in 1948.

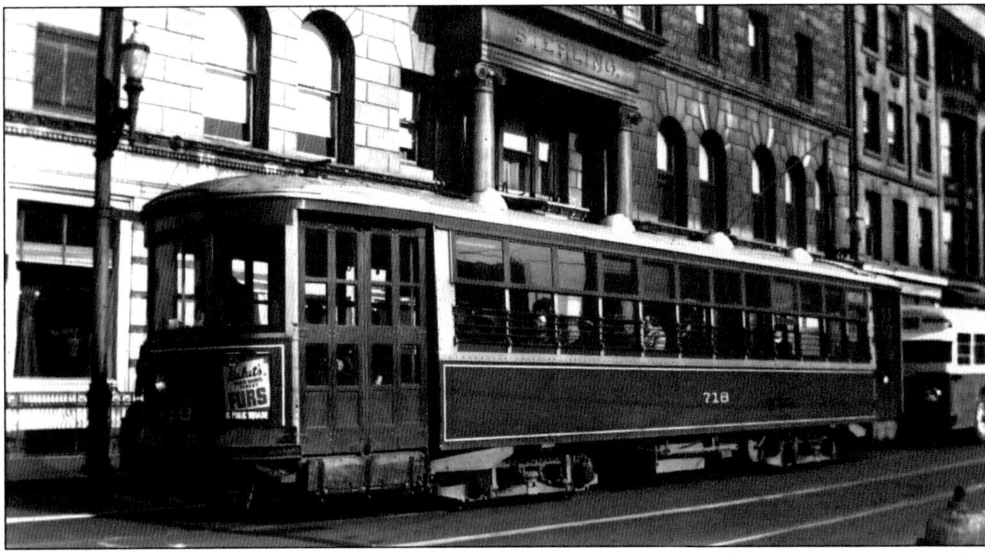

WEST MARKET STREET AT RIVER STREET, 1937. Wilkes-Barre Railway Corporation trolley No. 718 is seen in front of the Sterling Hotel in Wilkes-Barre on Sunday, October 17, 1937. The trolley was ordered from the J. G. Brill Company in 1923. Trolley No. 718 was sold in February 1942, and it became San Diego Electric Railway trolley No. 1024. The trolley was scrapped in May 1947.

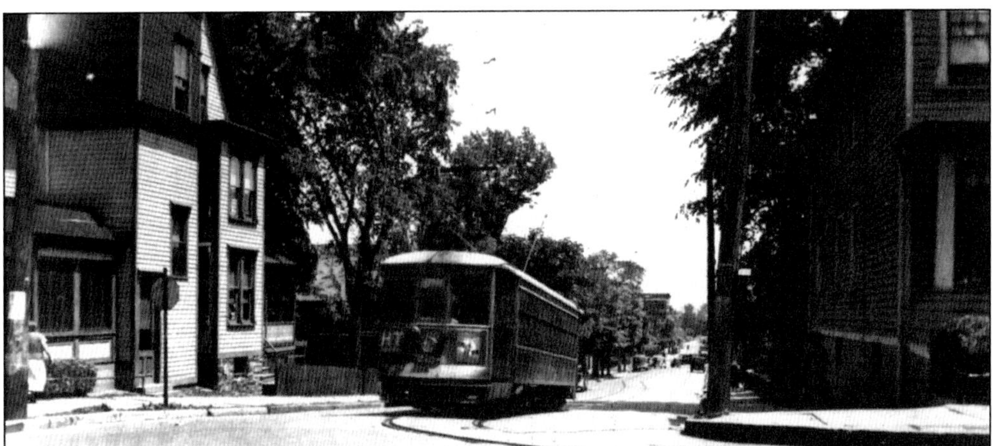

SOUTH HANCOCK STREET AT EAST NORTHAMPTON STREET, 1938. Wilkes-Barre Railway Corporation trolley No. 724 works on the Heights line in Wilkes-Barre on Monday, May 30, 1938. The trolley was built for the Sistersville and New Martinsville Traction Company in West Virginia, and it was later sold to the Wilkes-Barre Railway. After the Heights line was abandoned in 1938, the trolley was used on the Georgetown line. It was scrapped in 1948 after the Georgetown line was discontinued.

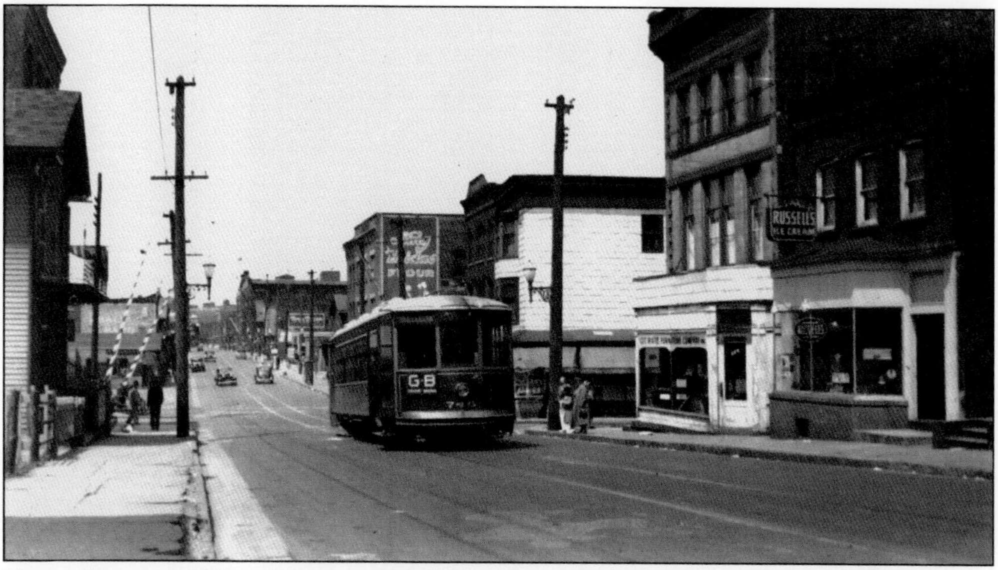

HAZLE STREET AT HIGH STREET, 1938. Wilkes-Barre Railway Corporation trolley No. 746 is in Wilkes-Barre on the Grove and Brown line on Monday, May 30, 1938. The track on Hazle Street at High Street, which was a branch off the Grove and Brown line, was built for the old Coalville horse-drawn streetcar barn on the Hazle Street hill.

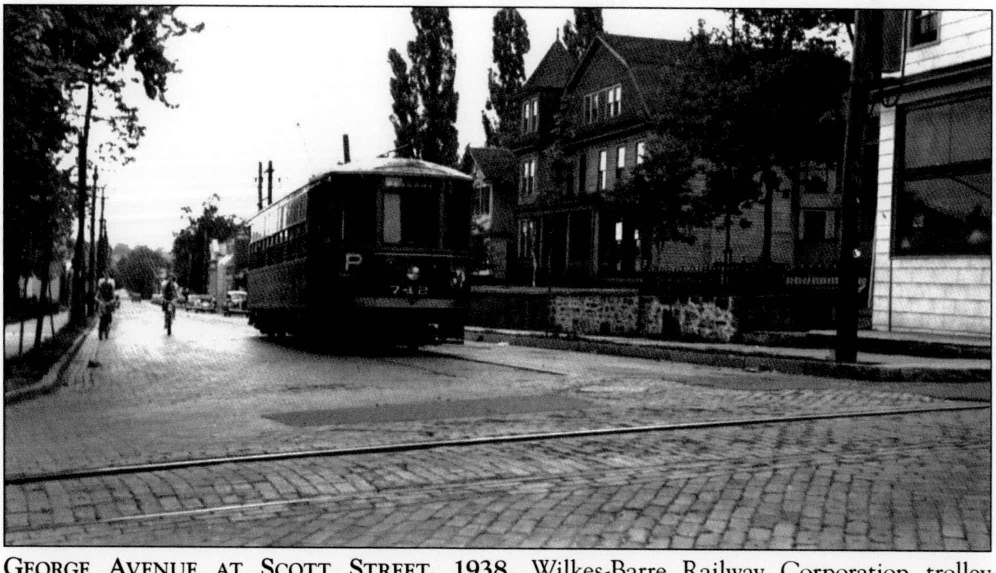

GEORGE AVENUE AT SCOTT STREET, 1938. Wilkes-Barre Railway Corporation trolley No. 742 is seen at the end of the Parsons line in Wilkes-Barre on Sunday, June 19, 1938. Regular passenger service on the trolley line started on George Avenue in 1891. The final day of trolley service on the Parsons line was Monday, September 15, 1941.

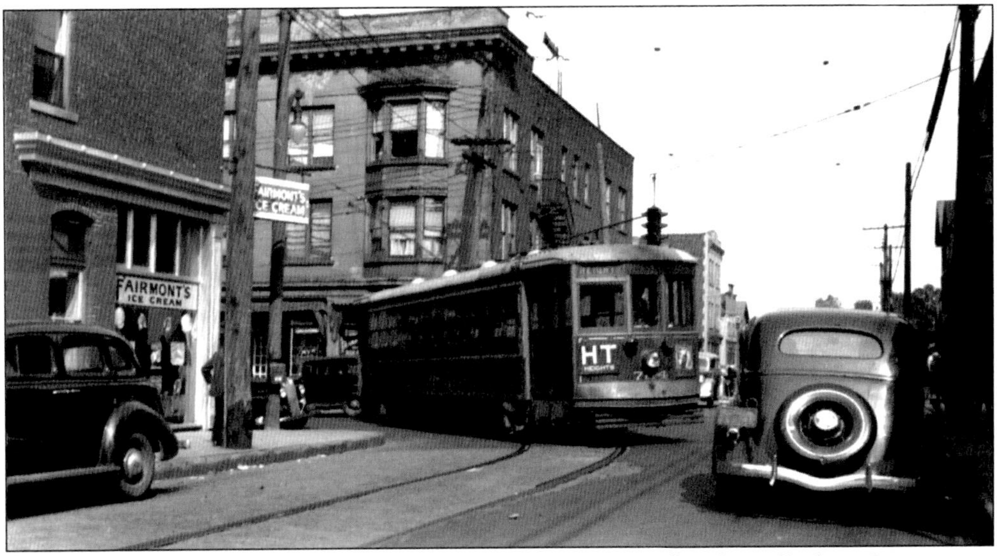

SOUTH HANCOCK STREET AT EAST MARKET STREET, 1938. Wilkes-Barre Railway Corporation trolley No. 724 is shown on the last day of service on the Heights line and the Grove and Brown line on Saturday, October 1, 1938. The trolley was delivered to the Wilkes-Barre Railway on December 29, 1925. Trolley No. 724 was later in service on the Georgetown line, and it was scrapped in 1948.

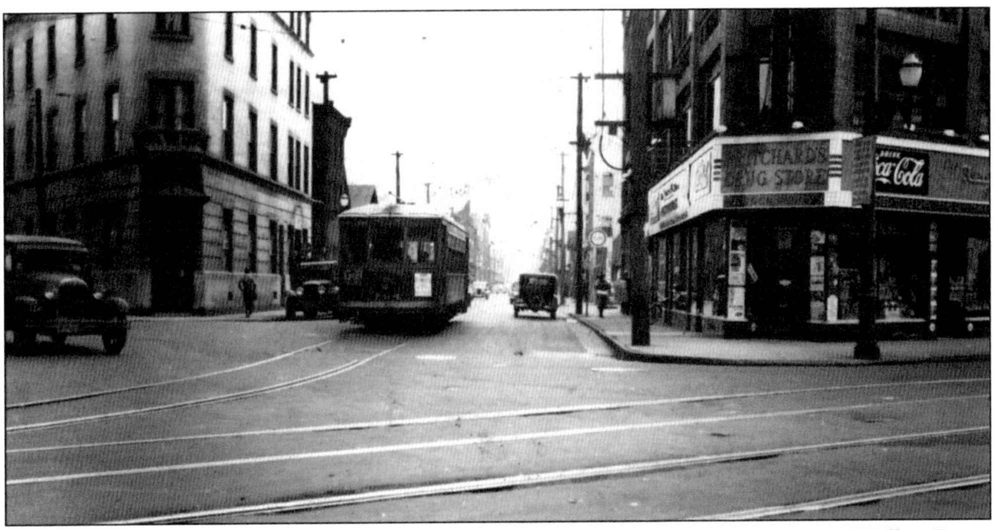

HAZLE AVENUE AT SOUTH MAIN STREET AND ROSS STREET, 1938. Wilkes-Barre Railway Corporation trolley No. 754 works on the last day of the Grove and Brown line in Wilkes-Barre on Saturday, October 1, 1938. Trolley No. 754 was originally ordered from the J. G. Brill Company in 1924 for the Coast Cities Railway of Asbury Park, New Jersey. In 1932, the trolley was purchased secondhand by the Wilkes-Barre Railway.

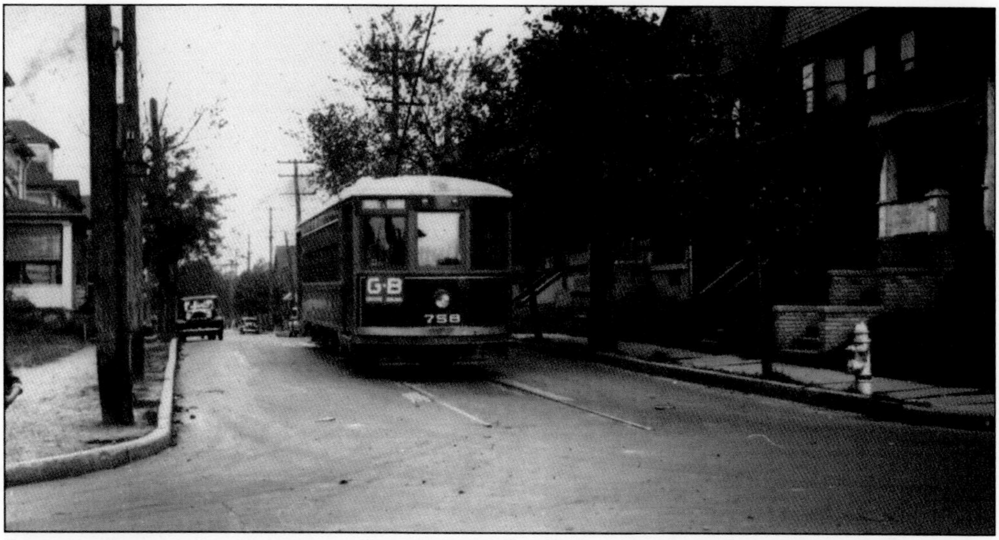

Brown Street at Gilligan Street, 1938. Wilkes-Barre Railway Corporation trolley No. 758 is seen in Wilkes-Barre on Saturday, October 1, 1938, the last day of service on the Grove and Brown line. The trolley was ordered from the J. G. Brill Company on October 28, 1924. It was delivered secondhand to the Wilkes-Barre Railway on March 29, 1932.

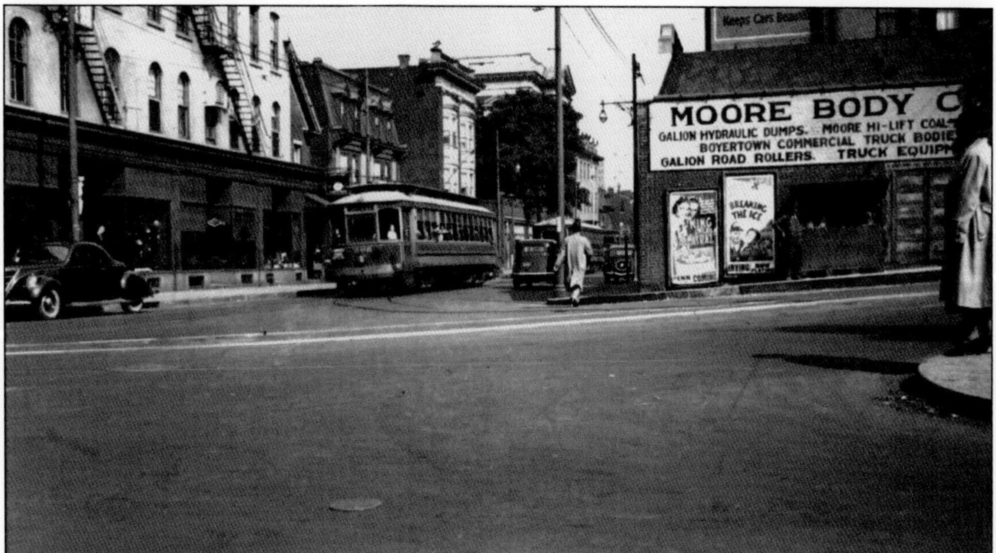

South Washington Street at South Street, 1938. The Wilkes-Barre Railway Corporation trolley No. 286 special is shown in Wilkes-Barre on Wednesday, October 5, 1938. The trolley was chartered by the Hanover school system. It was ordered on December 12, 1903, from the J. G. Brill Company. The 19-ton trolley was equipped with manually operated doors, and it was rebuilt with Westinghouse motors. Trolley No. 286 was in service until 1939.

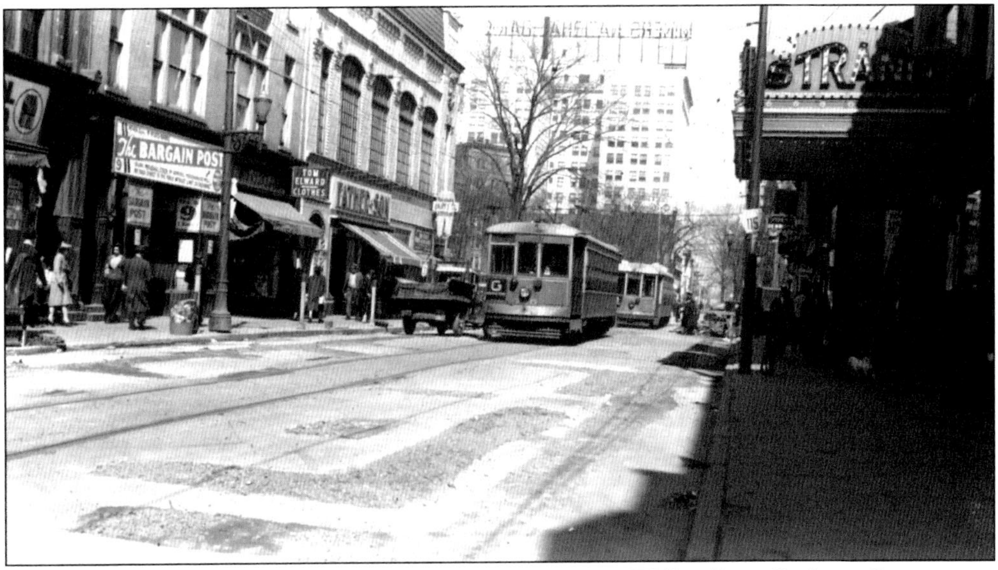

EAST MARKET STREET NEAR THE PUBLIC SQUARE, 1939. Wilkes-Barre Railway Corporation trolleys No. 720 and No. 606 work on the Georgetown line in Wilkes-Barre on Friday, April 21, 1939. Trolley No. 606 was built in 1918, and it was purchased by the Wilkes-Barre Railway in the 1920s. It was scrapped in March 1948. Trolley No. 720 was originally ordered from the J. G. Brill Company in 1923 for the Sistersville and New Martinsville Traction Company in West Virginia. It was bought by the Wilkes-Barre Railway two years later.

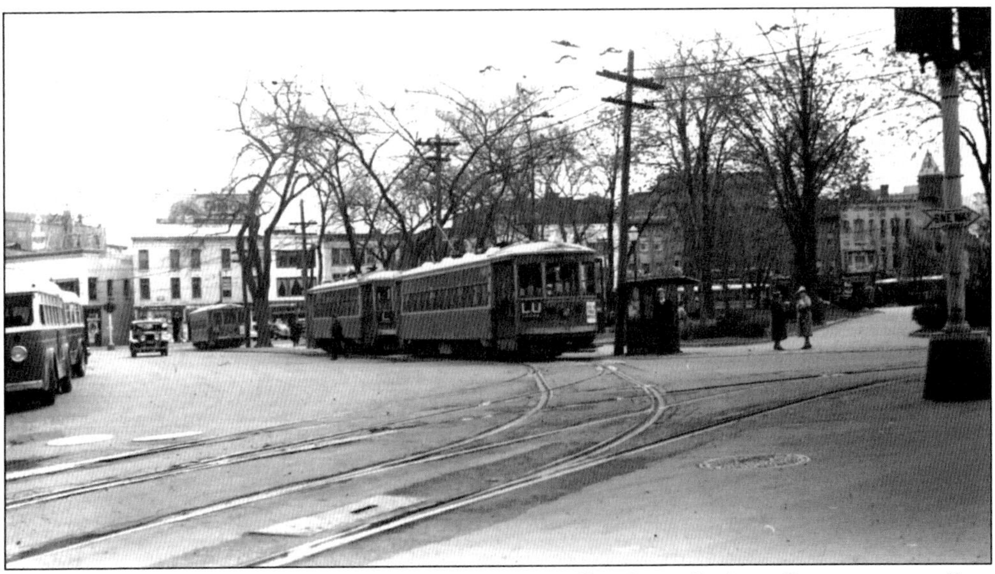

TROLLEYS PARKED AT THE PUBLIC SQUARE, 1939. Wilkes-Barre Railway Corporation trolleys No. 742, No. 776, and No. 728 are pictured at West Market Street in Wilkes-Barre on the Luzerne line on Sunday, April 30, 1939, their last day of service. Regular passenger service on the Luzerne trolley line began on December 9, 1889.

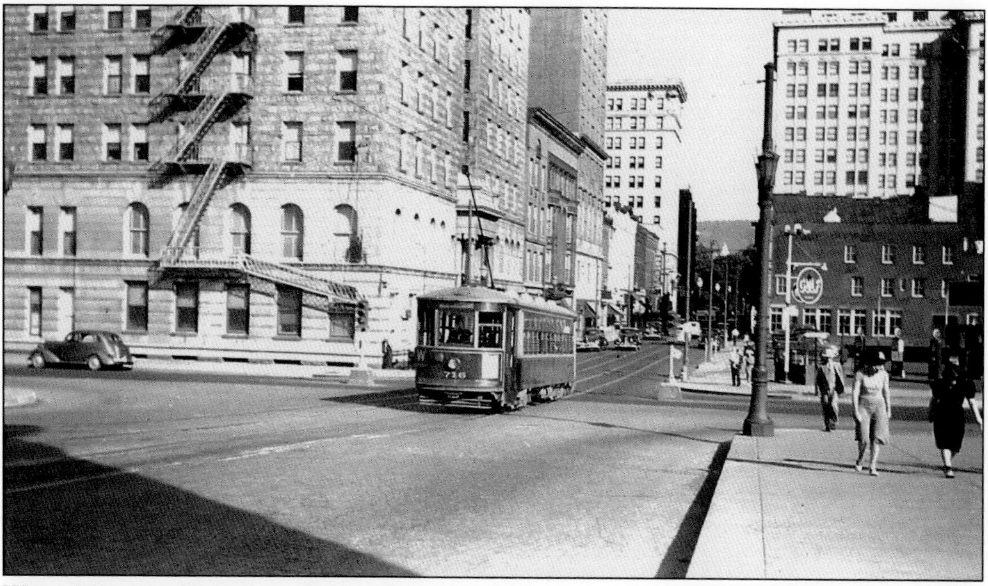

West Market Street at River Street, 1939. Wilkes-Barre Railway Corporation trolley No. 716 is seen from the Market Street bridge entrance onto River Street in Wilkes-Barre on the West Pittston line on Sunday, June 4, 1939. The Sterling Hotel is on the left. The West Pittston line was one of the most heavily traveled trolley lines in the Wyoming Valley.

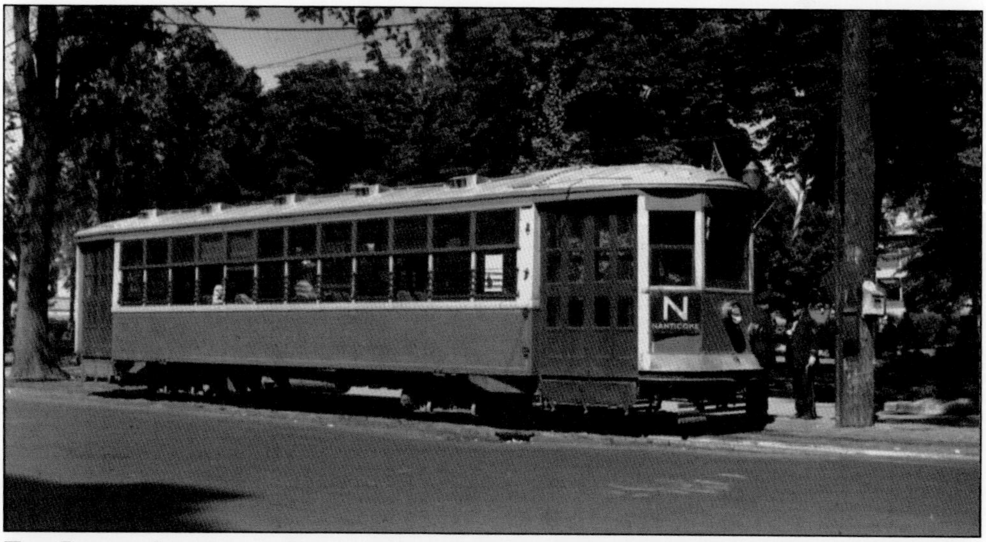

The Public Square at South Main Street, 1939. Wilkes-Barre Railway Corporation trolley No. 774 is in Wilkes-Barre on the Nanticoke line on Sunday, June 4, 1939. The 45-foot trolley was ordered from the J. G. Brill Company in Philadelphia. In 1933, it was purchased secondhand by the Wilkes-Barre Railway. Trolley No. 774 was scrapped in 1950.

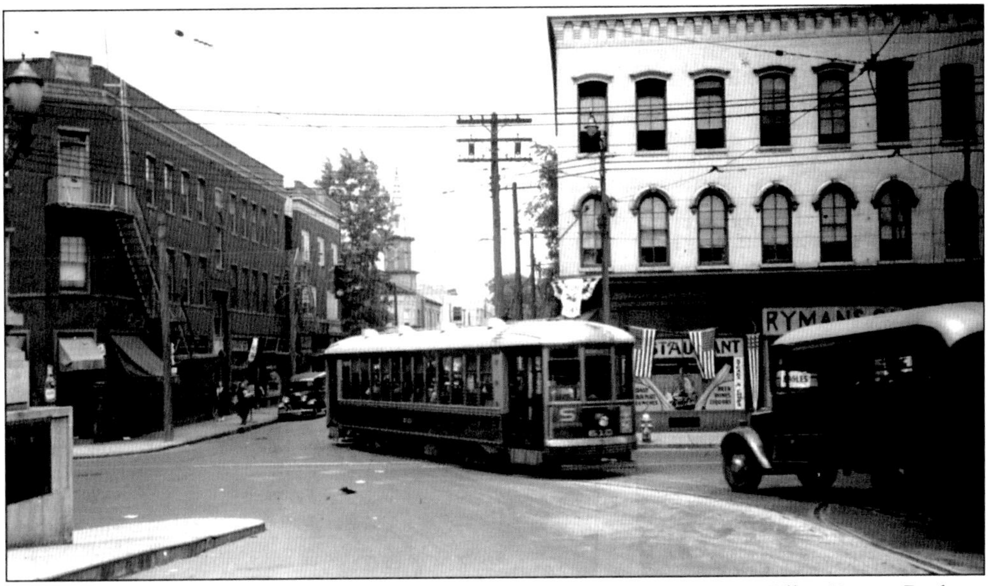

East South Street at South Washington Street, 1939. Wilkes-Barre Railway Corporation trolley No. 610 is seen in Wilkes-Barre on the Sugar Notch line on Friday, June 16, 1939. The trolley was ordered from the J. G. Brill Company in 1918 for service at the Hog Island shipyard in Philadelphia. It was delivered to the Wilkes-Barre Railway on April 19, 1921. The last day of service on the Sugar Notch trolley line was Monday, August 5, 1946.

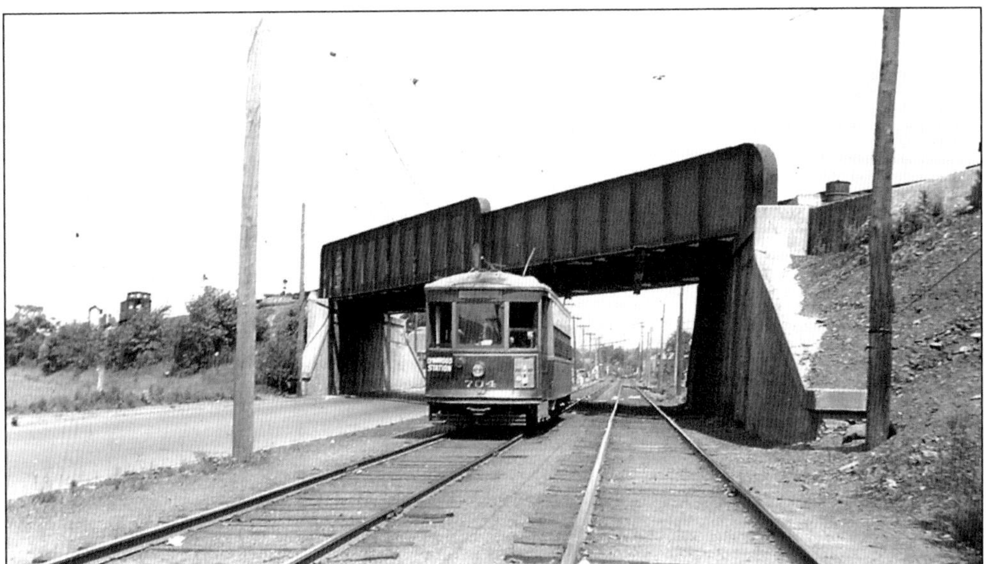

West End Road, 1939. Wilkes-Barre Railway Corporation trolley No. 704 is at the Wilkes-Barre connecting railroad bridge in Hanover on the Plymouth line on Friday, June 16, 1939. The 45-foot trolley was equipped with air-operated doors, and it was ordered from the J. G. Brill Company on March 22, 1923. Trolley No. 704 was scrapped in 1947.

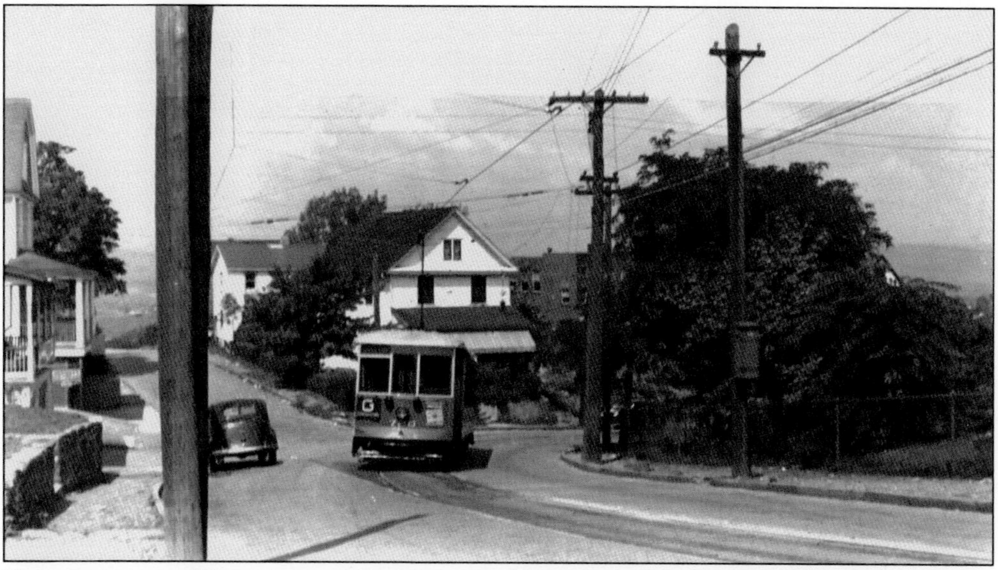

DERAILMENT AT NORTHAMPTON STREET AND LEHIGH STREET, 1939. Wilkes-Barre Railway Corporation trolley No. 720 was derailed on the Georgetown line in Wilkes-Barre on Sunday, August 27, 1939. Regular passenger service on the Georgetown line began on September 2, 1895. The trolley line went from the public square to the Central Railroad of New Jersey crossing at Northampton Street and Diamond Street.

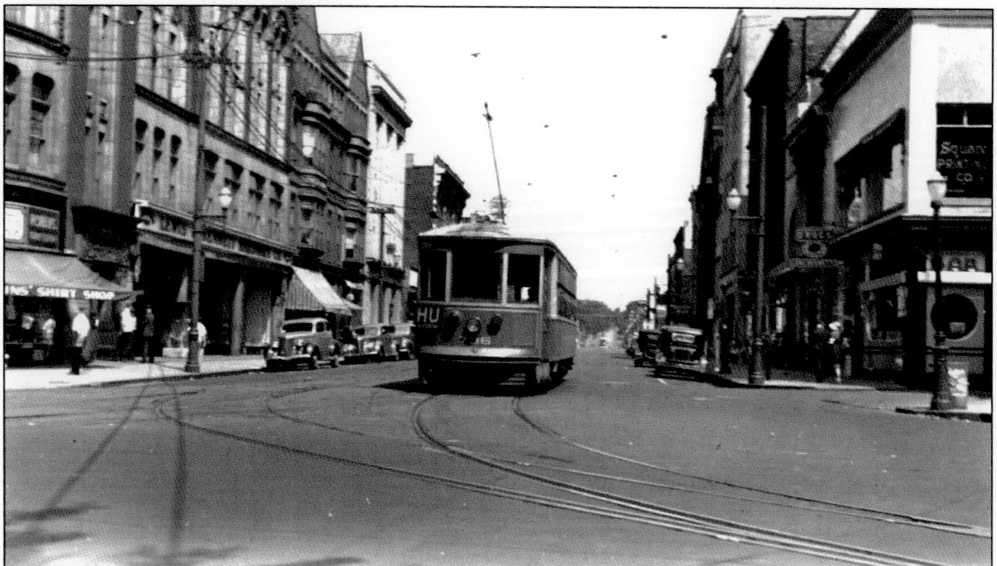

NORTH MAIN STREET AT THE PUBLIC SQUARE, 1939. Wilkes-Barre Railway Corporation trolley No. 736 works on the Hudson line in Wilkes-Barre on Sunday, August 27, 1939. The trolley was ordered from the J. G. Brill Company on May 3, 1926. Trolley No. 736 was sent to San Diego, California, in February 1942, and it was scrapped in 1947.

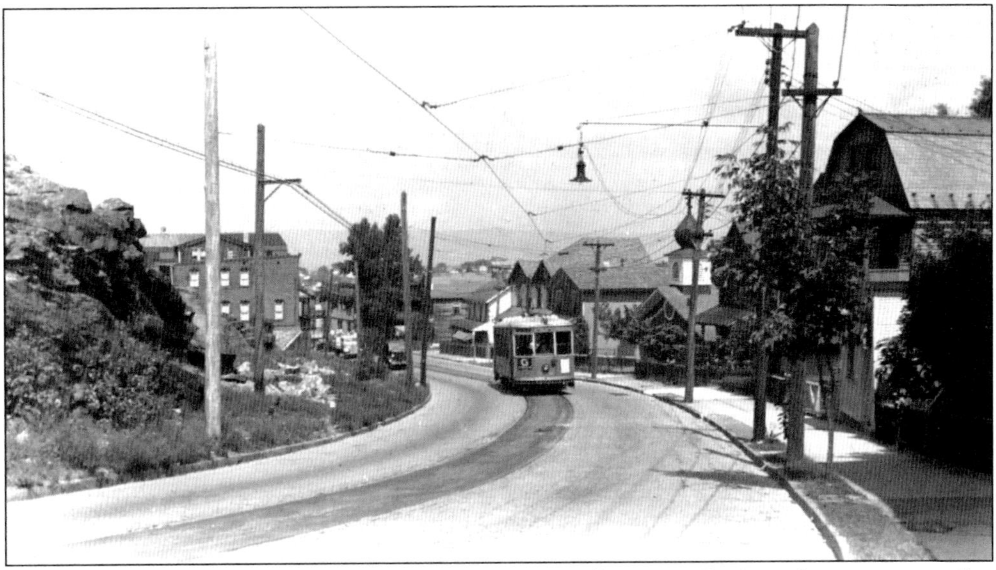

NORTHAMPTON STREET AT SPENCER STREET, 1939. Wilkes-Barre Railway Corporation trolley No. 754 is in Wilkes-Barre on the Georgetown line on Sunday, August 27, 1939. The last day of the Georgetown line was Wednesday, April 30, 1947. The 40-foot trolley was the last trolley on the Plymouth line, which was abandoned on August 31, 1947.

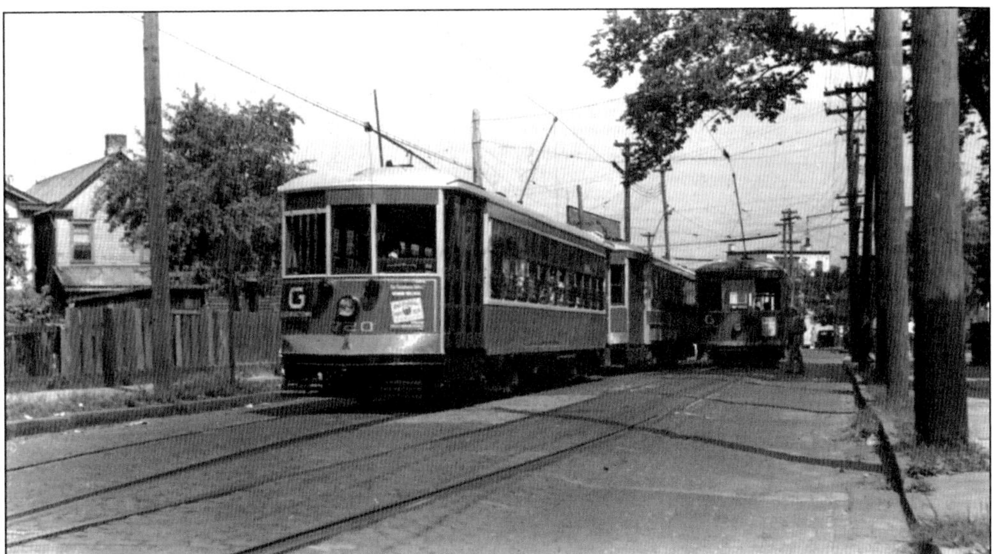

HILLSIDE STREET SWITCH AT EAST MARKET STREET, 1939. Wilkes-Barre Railway Corporation trolleys No. 720, No. 354, and No. 754 are seen in Wilkes-Barre on the Georgetown line on Sunday, August 27, 1939. Trolley No. 354 was ordered on February 27, 1911, from the J. G. Brill Company. The trolley was updated with Westinghouse motors from a 500-series trolley that was scrapped in 1935.

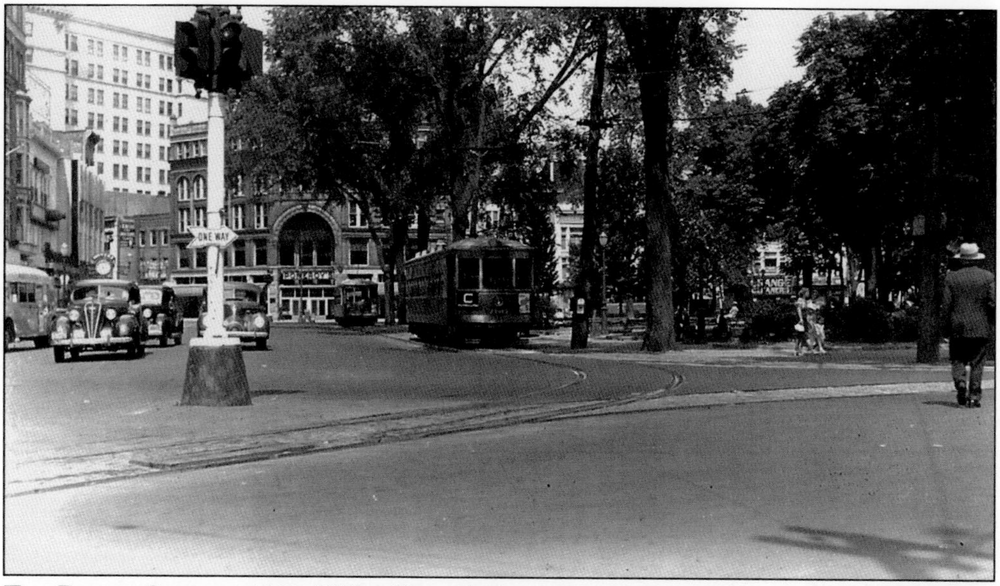

THE PUBLIC SQUARE, 1939. Wilkes-Barre Railway Corporation trolleys No. 780 and No. 714 are between South Main Street and West Market Street in Wilkes-Barre on the Plymouth line on Sunday, August 27, 1939. Both trolleys were equipped with Westinghouse motors. Trolley No. 714 was 45 feet long, and it was ordered from the J. G. Brill Company on March 22, 1923, for the Wilkes-Barre Railway.

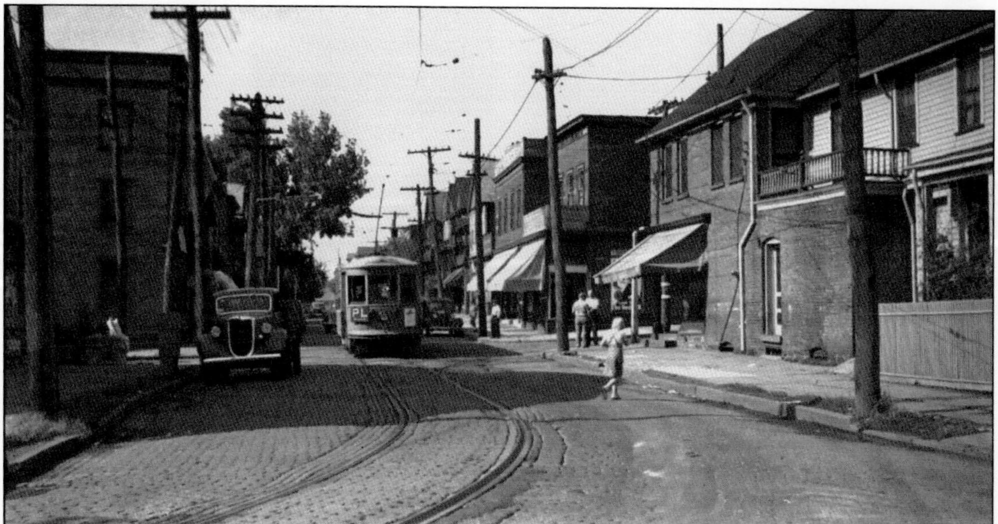

NORTH WASHINGTON STREET AT CHESTNUT STREET, 1939. Wilkes-Barre Railway Corporation trolley No. 734, pictured in Wilkes-Barre on the Plains line on Saturday, September 9, 1939, was built in 1926. The last day of service on the Plains line was Saturday, October 19, 1940, and the trolley line was replaced by bus service. Trolley No. 734 was sold to the Virginia Electric and Power Company in 1940.

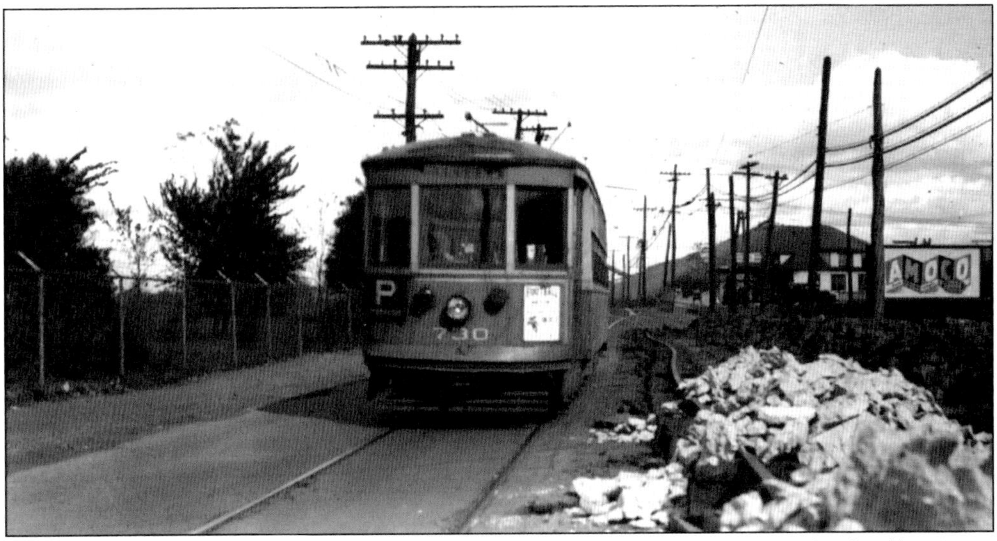

NORTH WASHINGTON STREET NEAR GEORGE AVENUE, 1939. This photograph of Wilkes-Barre Railway Corporation trolley No. 730 in Wilkes-Barre on the Parsons line on Saturday, October 14, 1939, shows the tracks and roadway being repaired and leveled off after mine subsidence. The 45-foot trolley was ordered from the J. G. Brill Company on May 3, 1926, for the Wilkes-Barre Railway.

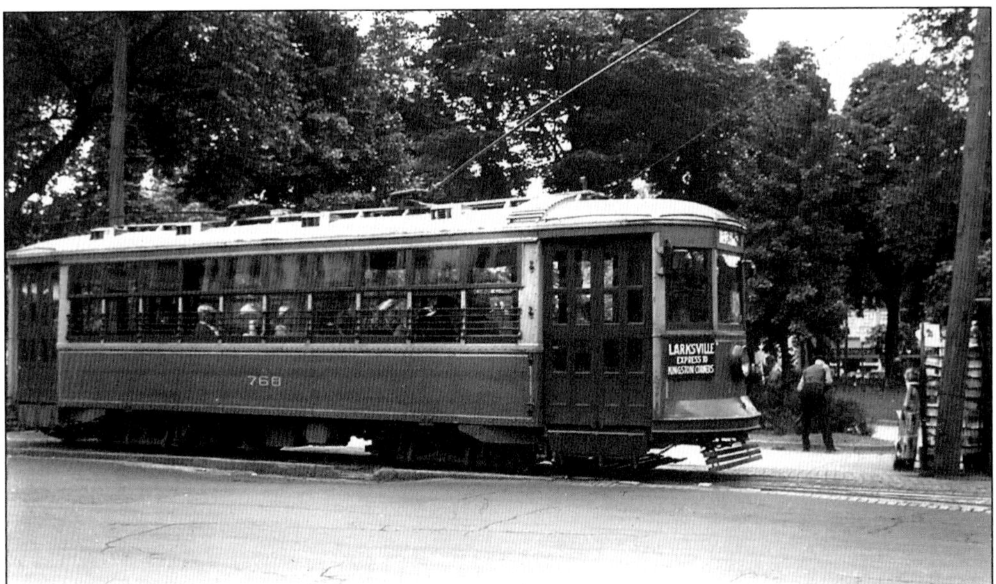

THE PUBLIC SQUARE AT WEST MARKET STREET, 1940. Wilkes-Barre Railway Corporation trolley No. 768 was the Larksville line express to Kingston Corners in Wilkes-Barre. The trolley was ordered from the J. G. Brill Company for the Eastern Pennsylvania Railway. It was delivered to the Wilkes-Barre Railway in September 1933. The last day of service on the Larksville line was Tuesday, August 10, 1948.

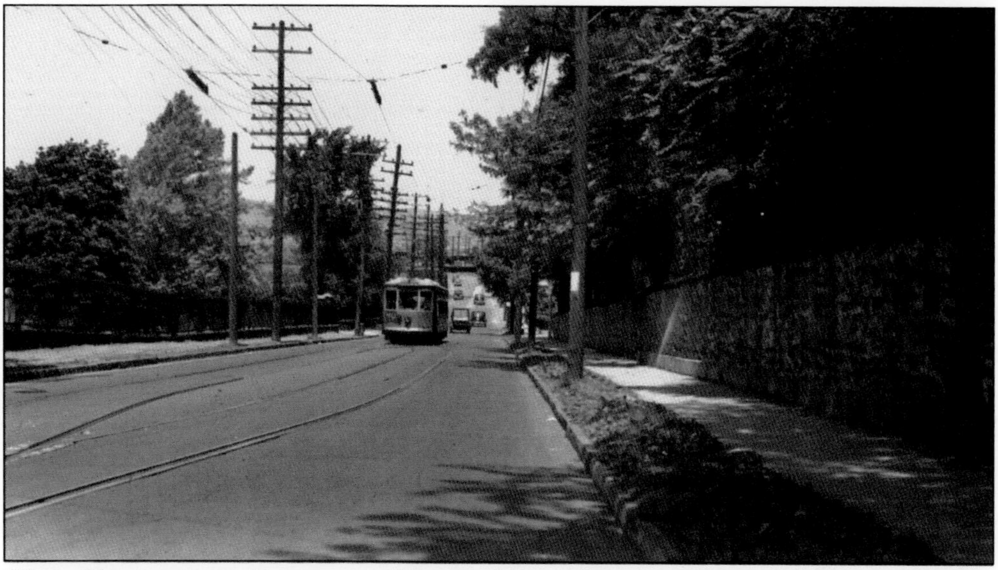

WEST HOLLENBACK AVENUE AT NORTH MAIN STREET, 1940. Wilkes-Barre Railway Corporation trolley No. 712 works on the Hudson line in Wilkes-Barre on Saturday, February 3, 1940. The trolley was ordered from the J. G. Brill Company in 1923, and it was equipped with Westinghouse motors. In 1942, the trolley was sold to the San Diego Electric Railway, and it remained in service until 1947.

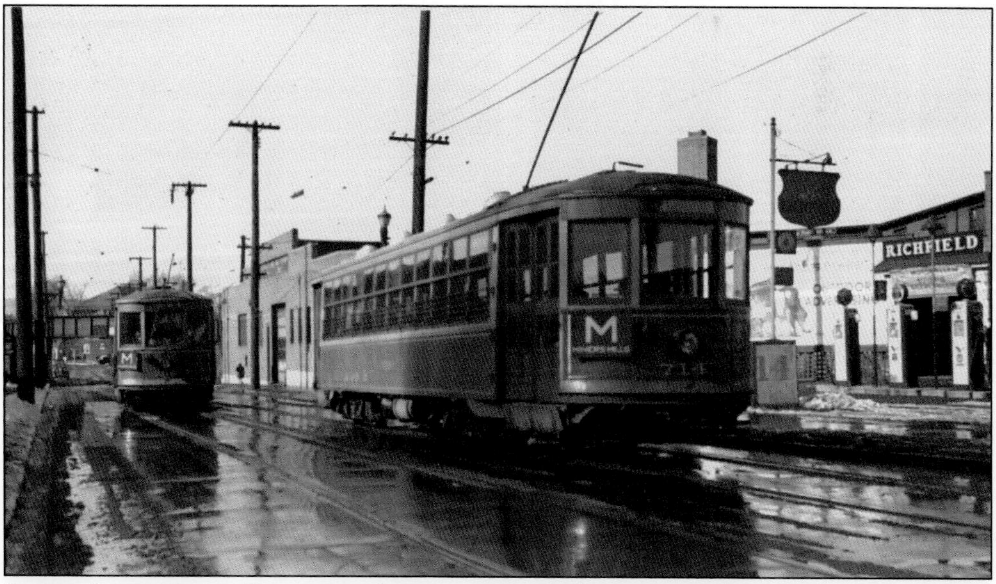

SCOTT STREET NEAR DELAWARE STREET, 1940. Wilkes-Barre Railway Corporation trolleys No. 714 and No. 706 are busy on the Miners Mills line at the Delaware and Hudson Railroad crossing in Wilkes-Barre on Saturday, February 3, 1940. The 45-foot trolleys were ordered from the J. G. Brill Company on March 22, 1923. The last day of service on the Miners Mills line was October 19, 1940.

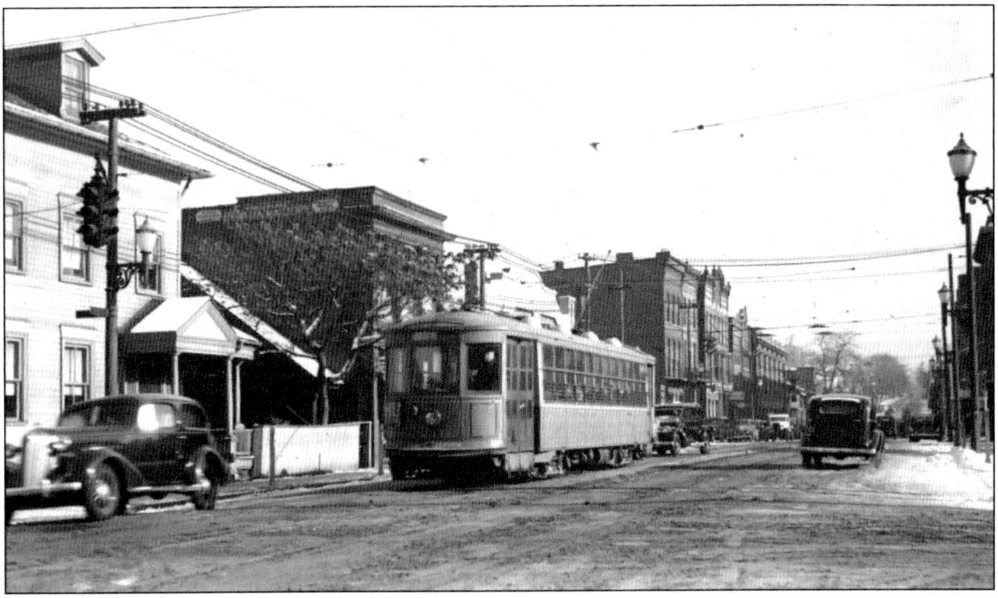

NORTH MAIN STREET AT UNION STREET, 1940. Wilkes-Barre Railway Corporation trolley No. 718 works on the Hudson line in Wilkes-Barre on Saturday, February 3, 1940. The 45-foot trolley was built in 1923 with Westinghouse motors. The last day of service on the Hudson line was Monday, September 15, 1941. The trolley line was temporarily replaced with buses until trackless trolleys began service on December 1, 1941.

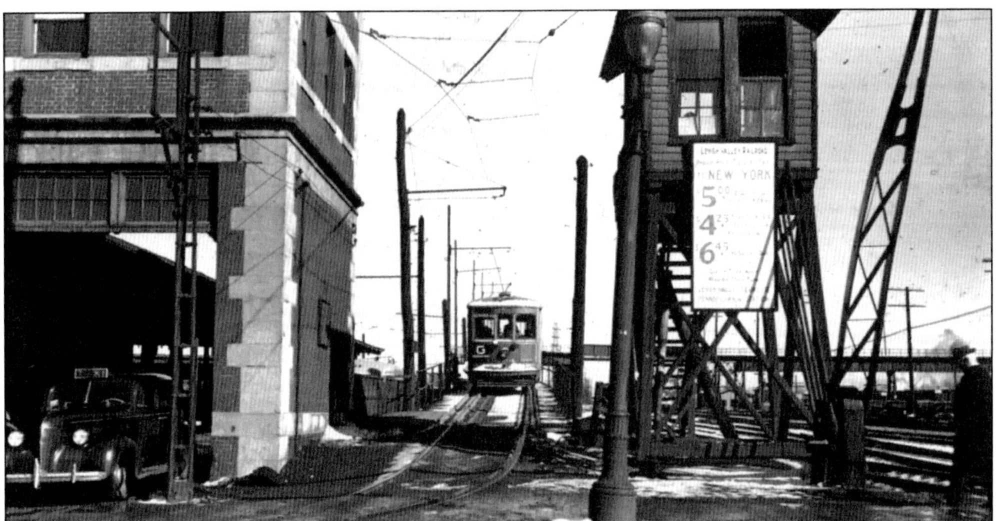

TRESTLE AT EAST MARKET STREET, 1940. Wilkes-Barre Railway Corporation trolley No. 724 is on the Georgetown line trestle over the Lehigh Valley Railroad in Wilkes-Barre on Saturday, February 3, 1940. The last day of service on the Georgetown line was Wednesday, April 30, 1947. The trolley line was replaced by trackless trolley on June 9, 1947.

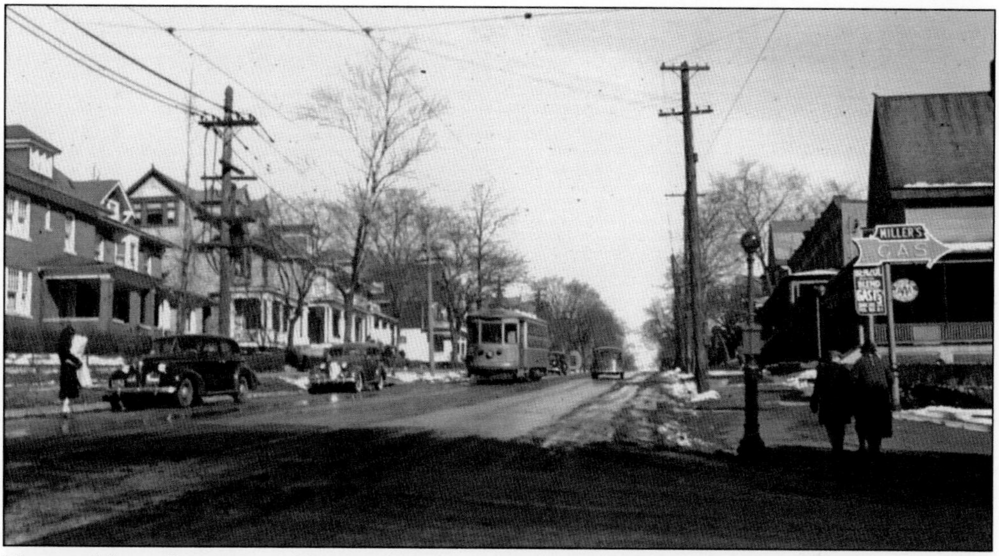

NORTH MAIN STREET AT NORTH STREET, 1940. Wilkes-Barre Railway Corporation trolley No. 730 is seen on the Parsons line in Wilkes-Barre on Saturday, February 3, 1940. The trolley was built with Westinghouse motors, and it was purchased by the Wilkes-Barre Railway in 1926. In July 1940, the trolley was sold to the Virginia Electric and Power Company.

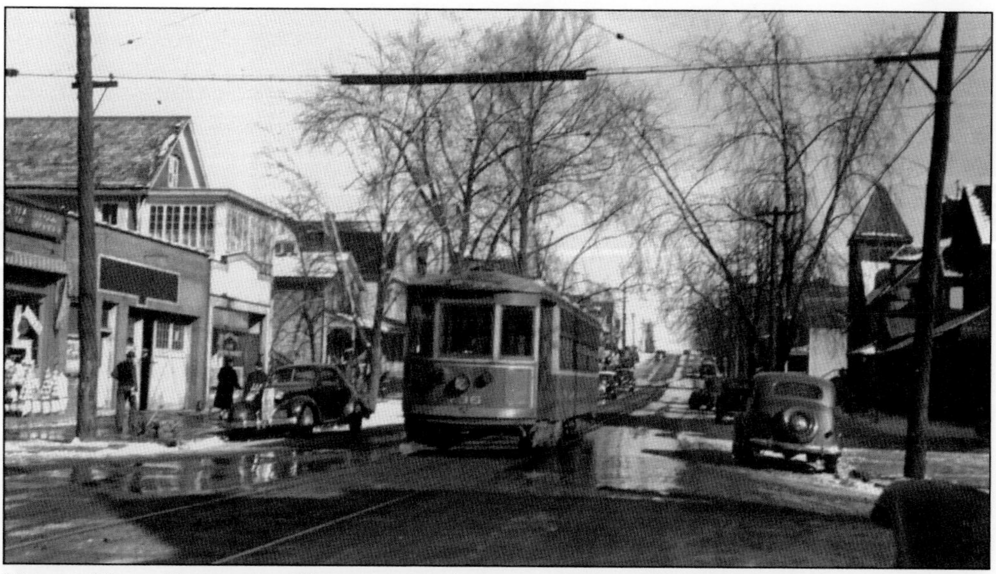

NORTH MAIN STREET AT HOLLENBACK AVENUE, 1940. Wilkes-Barre Railway Corporation trolley No. 736 works on the Parsons line in Wilkes-Barre on Saturday, February 3, 1940. The 45-foot trolley was ordered from the J. G. Brill Company with Westinghouse motors on May 3, 1926. Trolley No. 736 was sold to the San Diego Electric Railway in 1942.

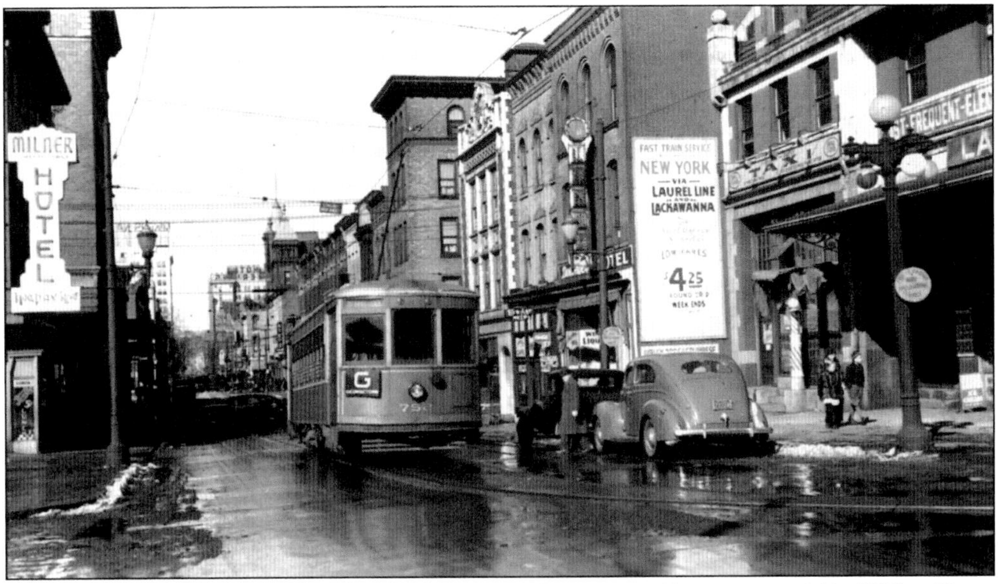

EAST MARKET STREET AT THE LEHIGH VALLEY RAILROAD CROSSING, 1940. Wilkes-Barre Railway Corporation trolley No. 752 is at the Lehigh Valley Railroad crossing on the Georgetown line in Wilkes-Barre on Saturday, February 3, 1940. The 40-foot trolley was ordered from the J. G. Brill Company on October 28, 1924, for the Coast Cities Railway in New Jersey. It was delivered to the Wilkes-Barre Railway on March 29, 1932.

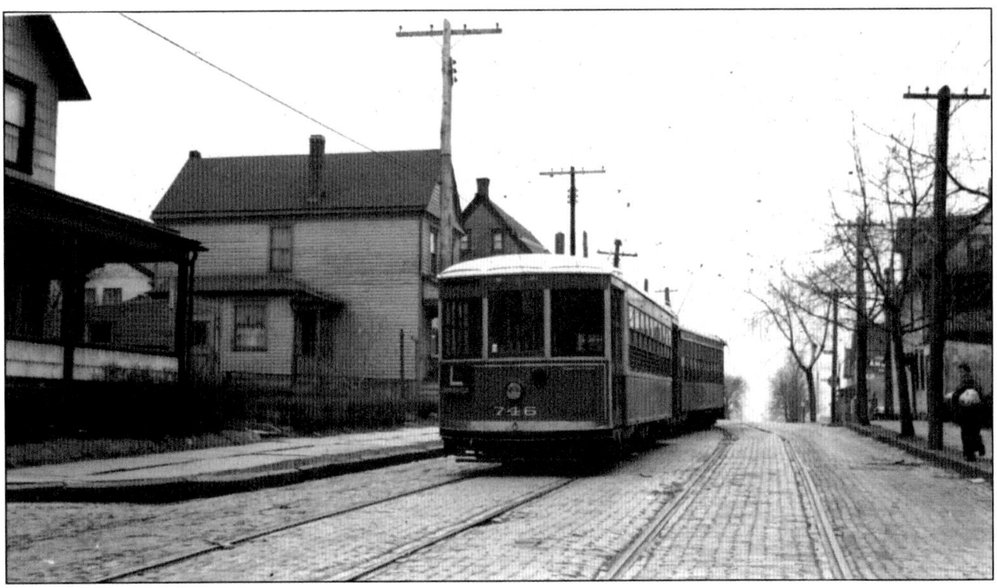

SOUTH SHERMAN STREET NEAR EAST SOUTH STREET, 1940. Wilkes-Barre Railway Corporation trolleys No. 746 and No. 722, both from the Larksville line, are seen in Wilkes-Barre on Wednesday, April 3, 1940. Both trolleys were parked there during the April 1940 flood. Trolley No. 722 was ordered from the Wason Company in 1923 for the Sistersville and New Martinsville Traction Company in West Virginia. Trolley No. 746 was ordered from the J. G. Brill Company in 1924 for the Coast Cities Railway.

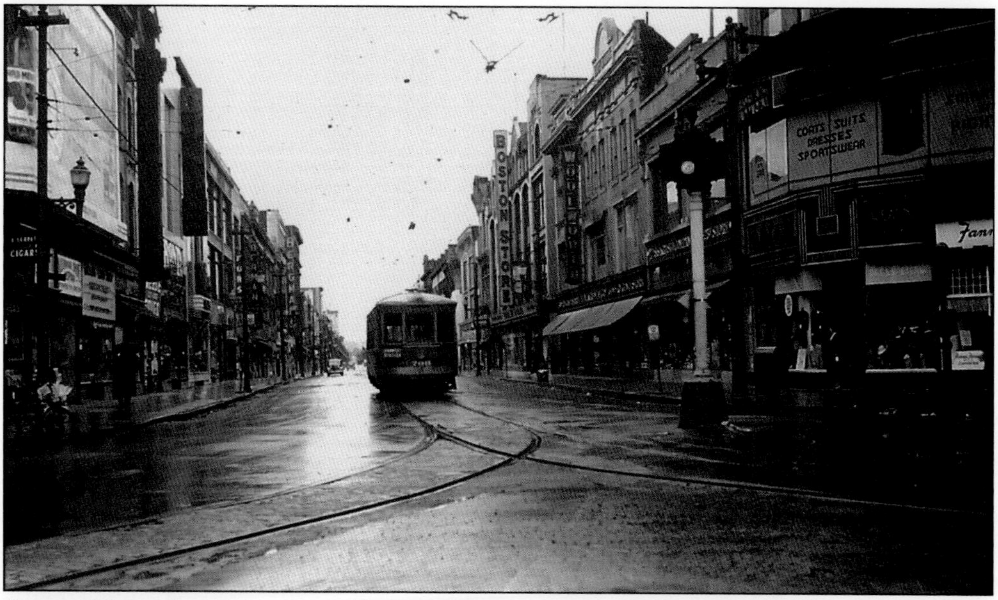

SOUTH MAIN STREET AT THE PUBLIC SQUARE, 1940. Wilkes-Barre Railway Corporation trolley No. 788 travels on the Plymouth line in Wilkes-Barre on Sunday, April 21, 1940. The trolley was ordered from the J. G. Brill Company on April 2, 1924, for the Eastern Pennsylvania Railway in Pottsville. It was delivered to the Wilkes-Barre Railway in September 1933.

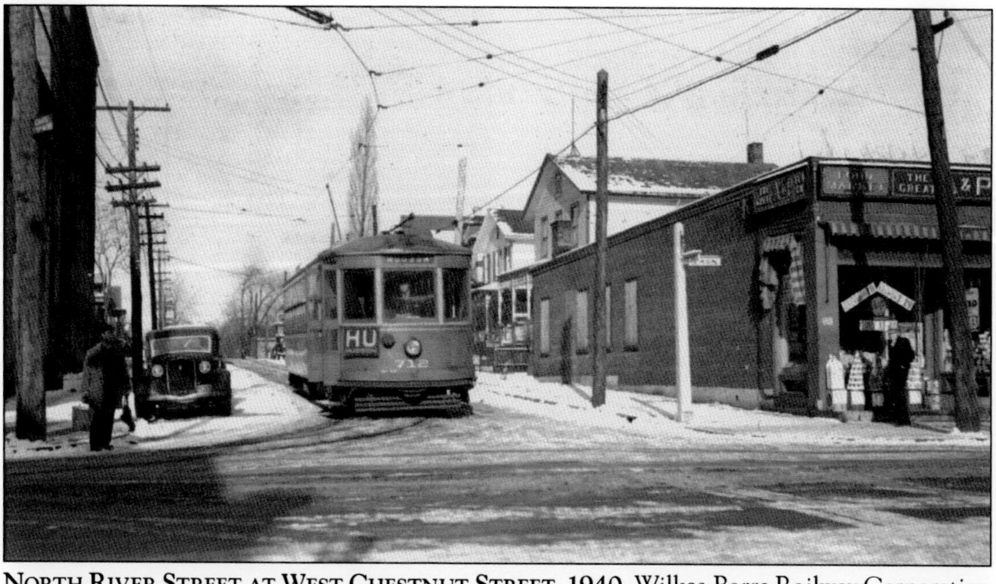

NORTH RIVER STREET AT WEST CHESTNUT STREET, 1940. Wilkes-Barre Railway Corporation trolley No. 712 travels on the Hudson line in Wilkes-Barre on Friday, July 5, 1940. The trolley ran to Forty Fort and West Pittston. It was sold to the San Diego Electric Railway in 1942. The trolley was in service in California until 1947.

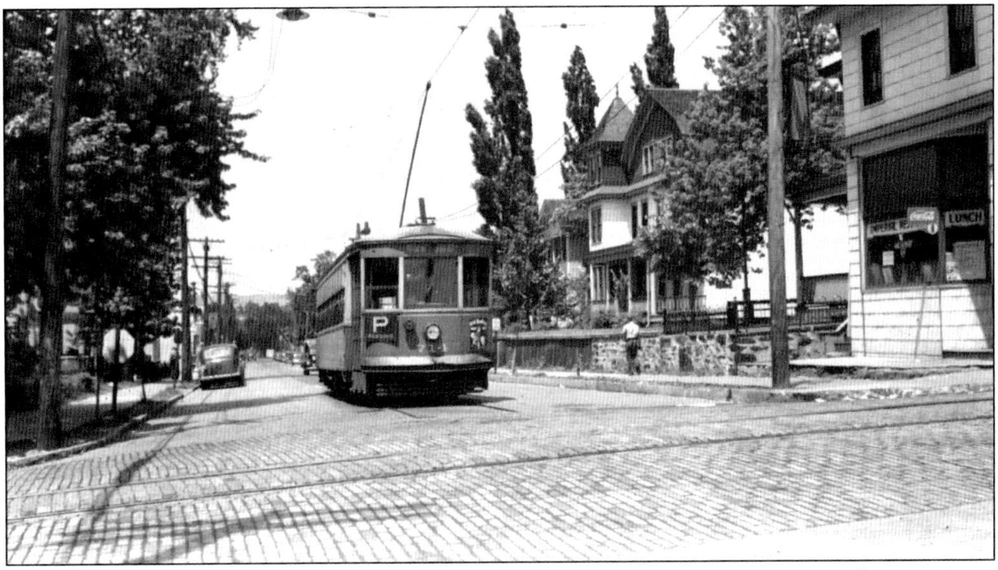

GEORGE AVENUE AT SCOTT STREET, 1940. Wilkes-Barre Railway Corporation trolley No. 714 is seen on the Parsons line in Wilkes-Barre on Friday, July 5, 1940. The 45-foot trolley was ordered with Westinghouse motors from the J. G. Brill Company in Philadelphia on March 22, 1923. It was equipped with air-operated doors that could be opened from the motorman's station.

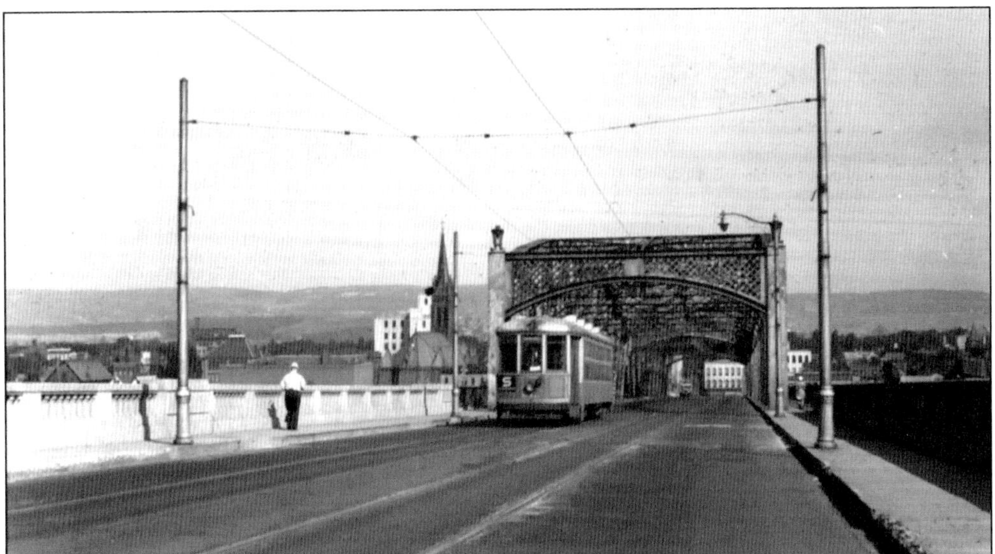

SOUTH STREET BRIDGE, 1940. Wilkes-Barre Railway Corporation trolley No. 616 travels on the Sugar Notch line in Wilkes-Barre on Saturday, August 3, 1940. The trolley was ordered on April 23, 1918, and it served at the Hog Island shipyard in Philadelphia before being delivered to the Wilkes-Barre Railway in the 1920s. The South Street Bridge closed on Wednesday, August 6, 1941, and it reopened on Monday, September 1, 1942. Trolley No. 616 was scrapped in 1948.

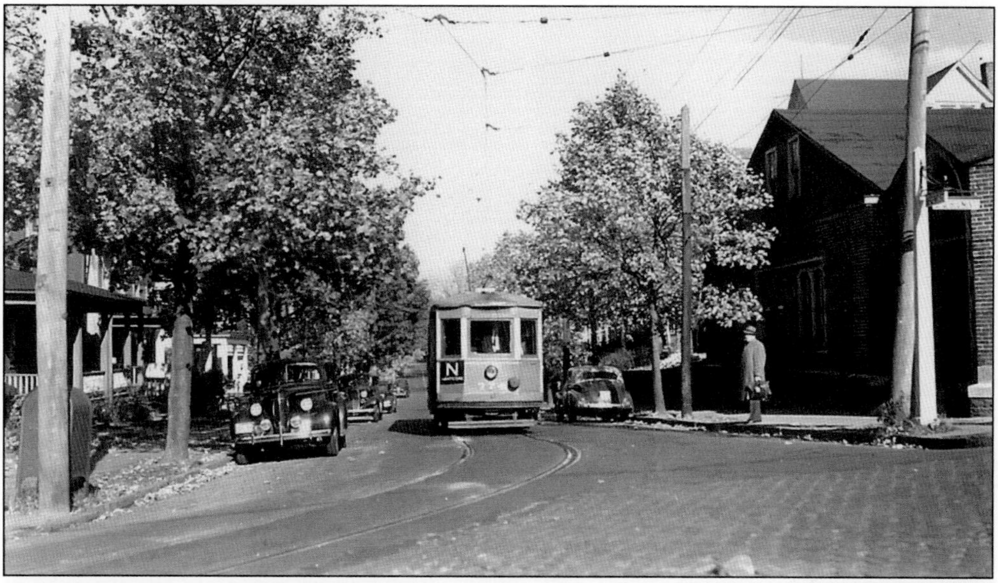

REGENT STREET AT DIVISION STREET, 1940. Wilkes-Barre Railway Corporation trolley No. 774 is shown on the Nanticoke line in Wilkes-Barre on Thursday, October 17, 1940. The former Eastern Pennsylvania Railway trolley No. 301 was ordered from the J. G. Brill Company. The 45-foot trolley was scrapped in 1950 after the Nanticoke line was abandoned on Saturday October 14, 1950.

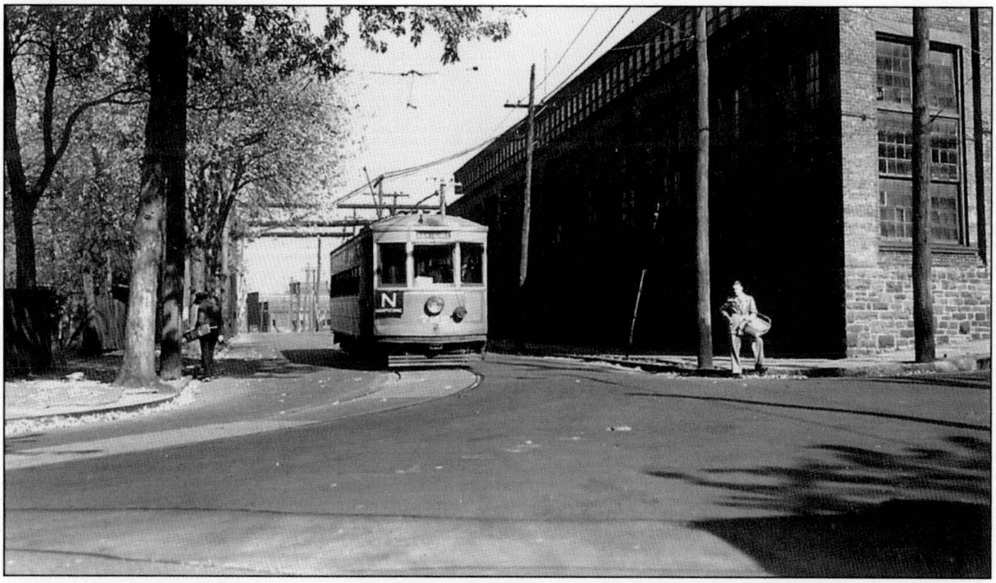

SOUTH FRANKLIN STREET AT HARTON STREET, 1940. Wilkes-Barre Railway Corporation trolley No. 788 works on the Nanticoke line in Wilkes-Barre on Thursday, October 17, 1940. Trolley No. 788 was the last trolley on the Nanticoke line on October 14, 1950. It left the public square in Wilkes-Barre that morning with an estimated 200 people operated by motorman Robert Cipriani. Bus service replaced the trolley line.

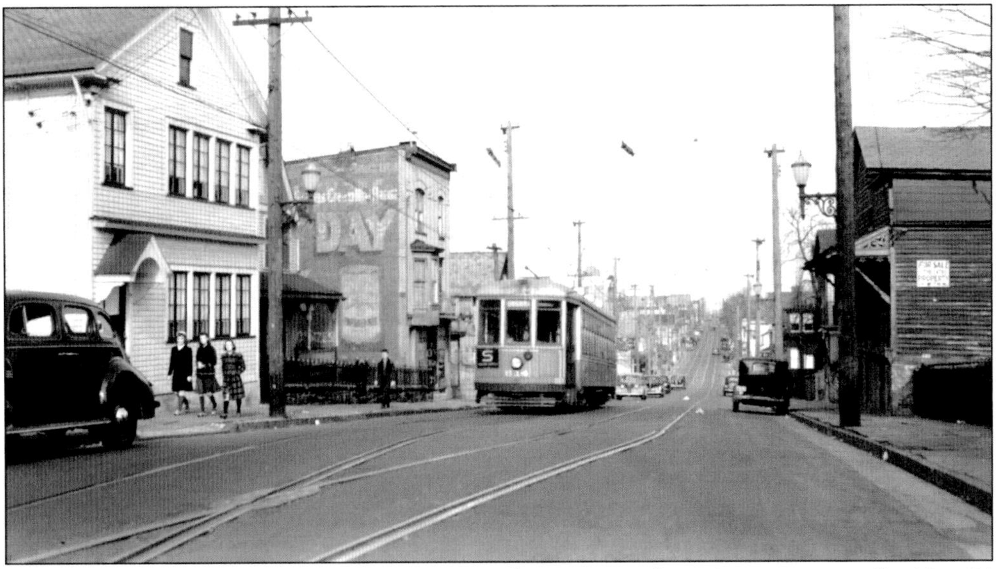

HAZLE STREET AT SOLOMON STREET, 1940. Wilkes-Barre Railway Corporation trolley No. 614 is on the Sugar Notch line in Wilkes-Barre on Friday, November 22, 1940. The Ashley and Sugar Notch lines went from South Main Street in Wilkes-Barre to Maffett Patch Switch in Ashley. The last day of service on the Sugar Notch line was Monday, August 5, 1946, and the Ashley line was discontinued one month later.

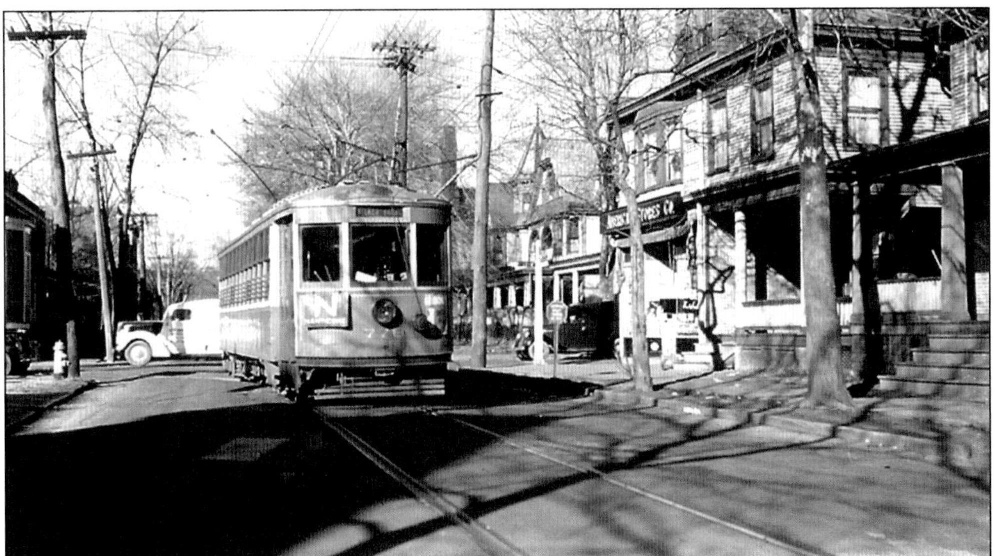

HANOVER STREET AT BARNEY STREET, 1940. Wilkes-Barre Railway Corporation trolley No. 778 is on the Nanticoke line in Wilkes-Barre on Monday, December 22, 1940. The trolley was built for the Eastern Pennsylvania Railway in 1924, and it was delivered to the Wilkes-Barre Railway in 1933. Trolley No. 778 was rebuilt with Westinghouse motors in 1942, and it was in service until October 1950.

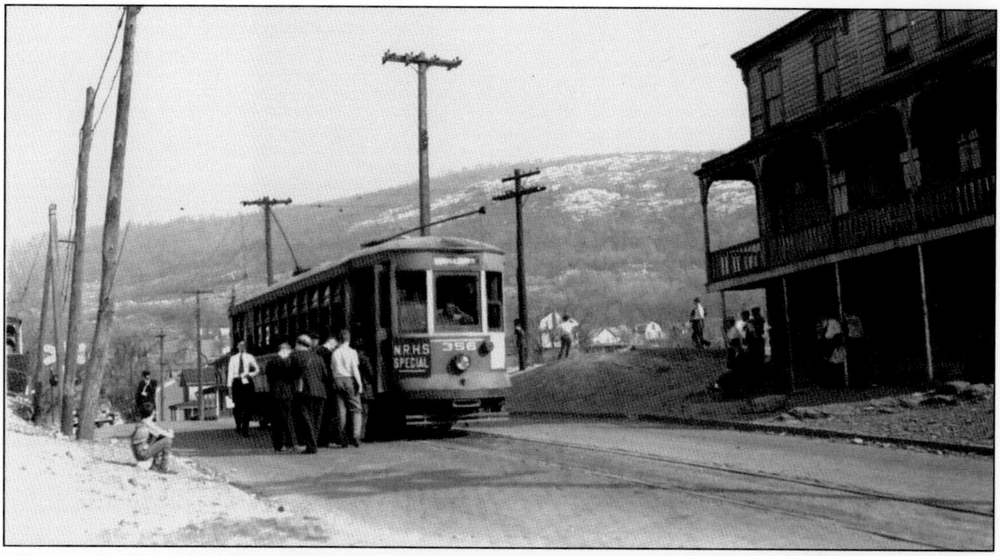

NORTHAMPTON STREET, 1941. The Wilkes-Barre Railway Corporation trolley No. 356 special is seen at the Central Railroad of New Jersey crossing on Sunday, April 20, 1941. The photograph was taken at the end of the Georgetown line in Wilkes-Barre with Laurel Run Borough in the background. The trolley was chartered by the New Jersey chapter of the NRHS. In 1939, the trolley collided with an automobile in Kingston Township on the last day of service to Dallas.

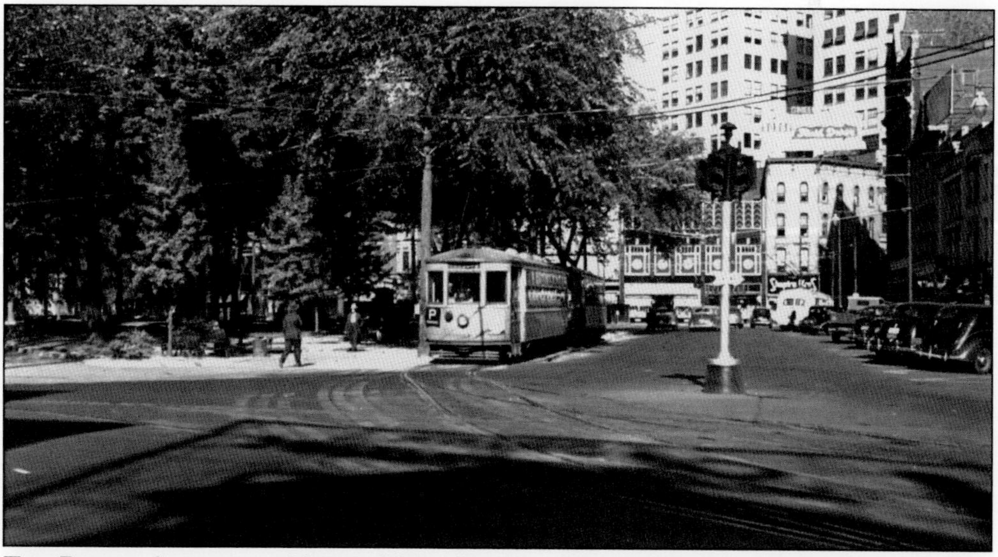

THE PUBLIC SQUARE AT NORTH MAIN STREET, 1941. Wilkes-Barre Railway Corporation trolley No. 706 from the Parsons line and trolley No. 728 on the Hudson line are photographed in Wilkes-Barre on Friday, May 30, 1941. Both trolleys were ordered from the J. G. Brill Company. Trolley No. 706 was built in 1923, and trolley No. 728 was built in 1926.

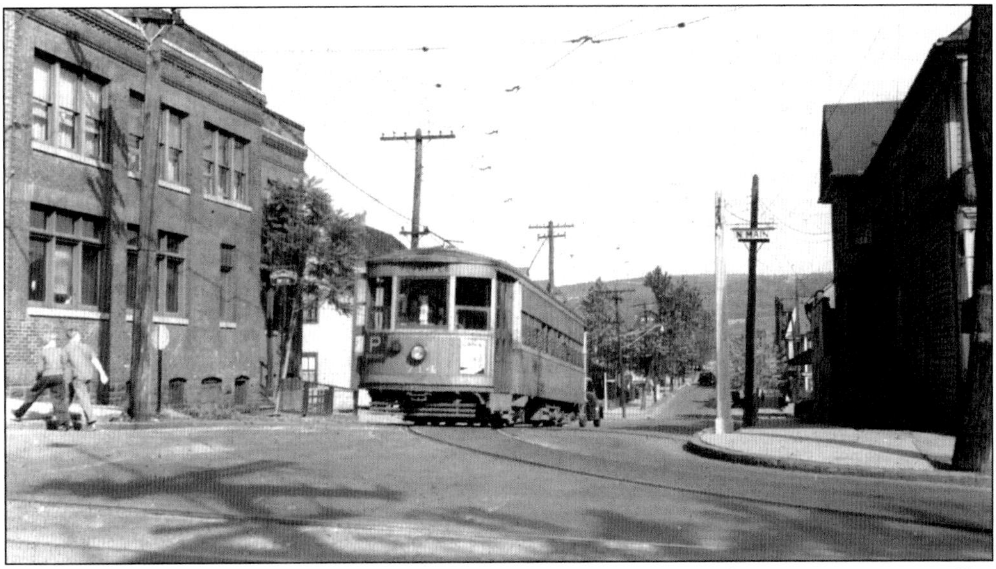

ELM STREET AT NORTH MAIN STREET, 1941. Wilkes-Barre Railway Corporation trolley No. 714 is on the Parsons line on Friday, May 30, 1941. The final day of trolley service on the Parsons line in Wilkes-Barre was Monday, September 15, 1941. The trolleys on the Parsons line were replaced by buses until trackless trolleys went into service on June 8, 1945.

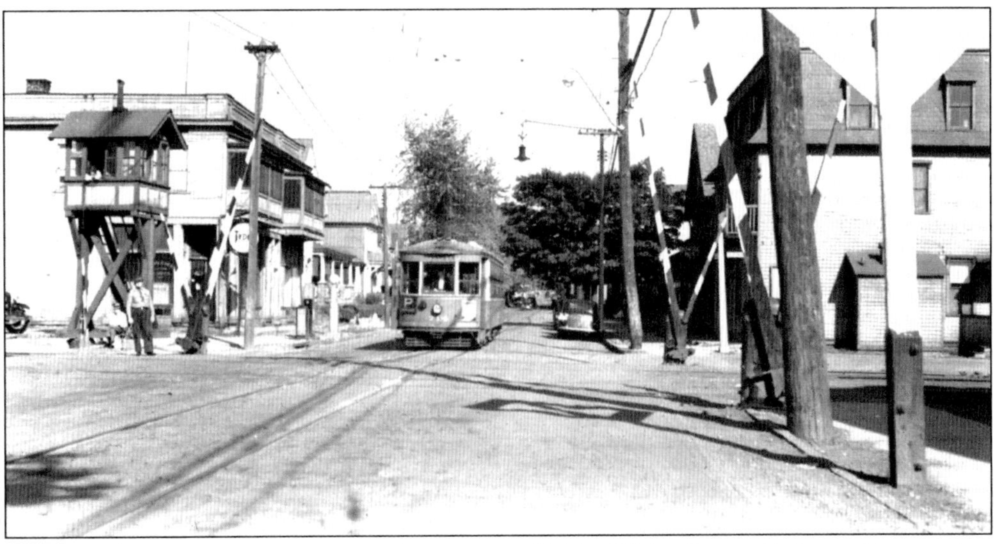

GEORGE AVENUE AT RAILROAD CROSSING, 1941. Wilkes-Barre Railway Corporation trolley No. 714 is seen at the Delaware and Hudson Railroad crossing on the Parsons line in Wilkes-Barre on Friday, May 30, 1941. The trolley was in service on the Plymouth line until 1940. Trolleys began running on the Parsons line from George Avenue to the Delaware and Hudson Railroad crossing on October 7, 1891.

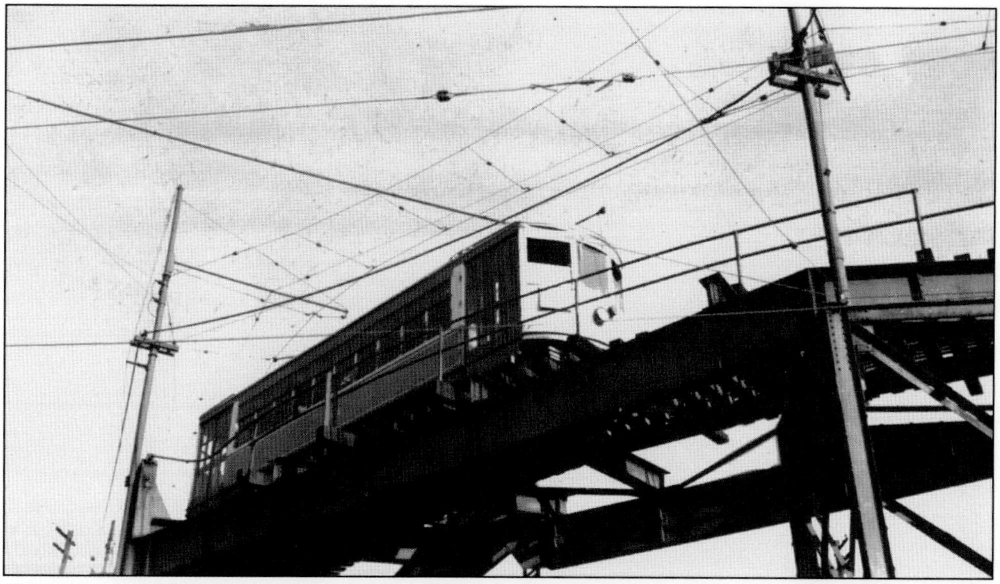

GEORGETOWN TRESTLE, 1941. Wilkes-Barre Railway Corporation trolley No. 754 is at the Lackawanna and Wyoming Valley Railroad station and the Lehigh Valley Railroad on the Georgetown line in Wilkes-Barre on Friday, May 30, 1941. The trolley was ordered from the J. G. Brill Company for the Coast Cities Railway of Asbury Park, New Jersey. Trolley No. 754 was scrapped in March 1950.

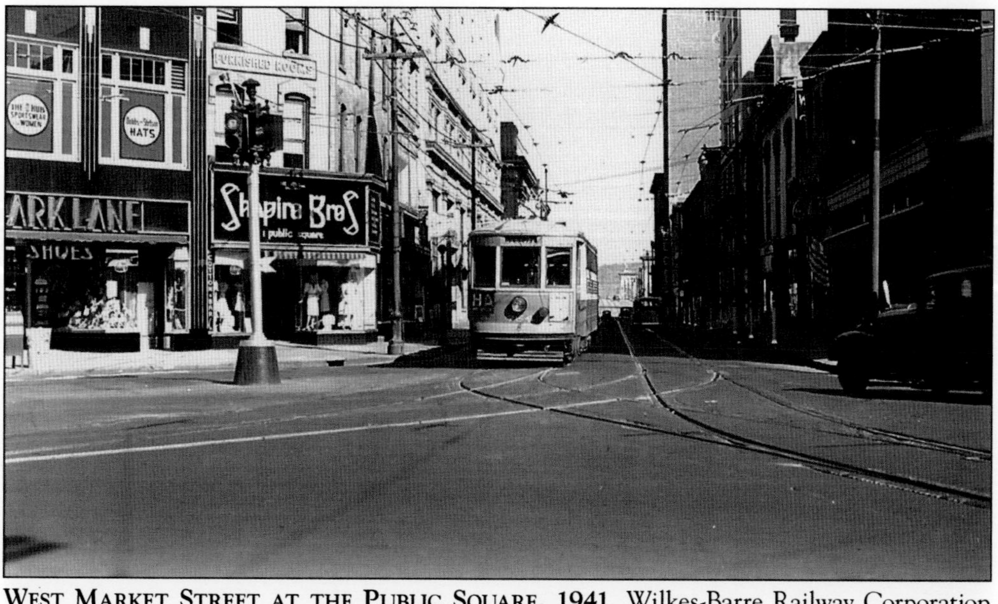

WEST MARKET STREET AT THE PUBLIC SQUARE, 1941. Wilkes-Barre Railway Corporation trolley No. 764 travels on the Hanover line in Wilkes-Barre on Friday, May 30, 1941. The removal of trolley tracks between the public square and the Kingston courthouse started on Monday, September 11, 1950. The last day of service on the Hanover line was Saturday, October 14, 1950.

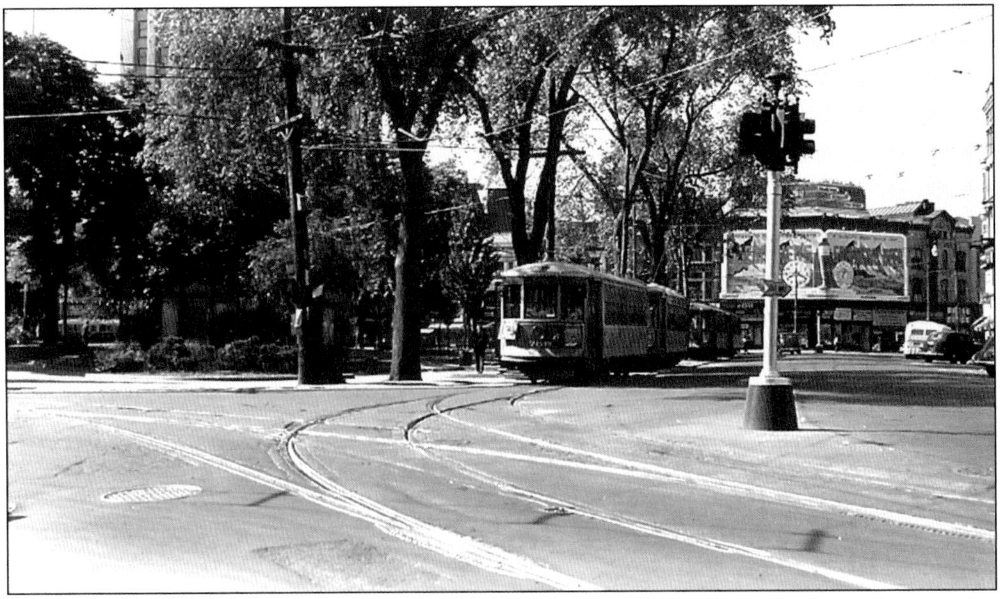

THE PUBLIC SQUARE AT WEST MARKET STREET, 1941. Wilkes-Barre Railway Corporation trolley No. 768 on the Edwardsville line, trolley No. 756 on the Luzerne line, trolley No. 764 on the Hanover line, and trolley No. 790 on the Nanticoke line are all seen in Wilkes-Barre on Friday, May 30, 1941. The trolleys were ordered from the J. G. Brill Company in 1924 and were purchased secondhand by the Wilkes-Barre Railway.

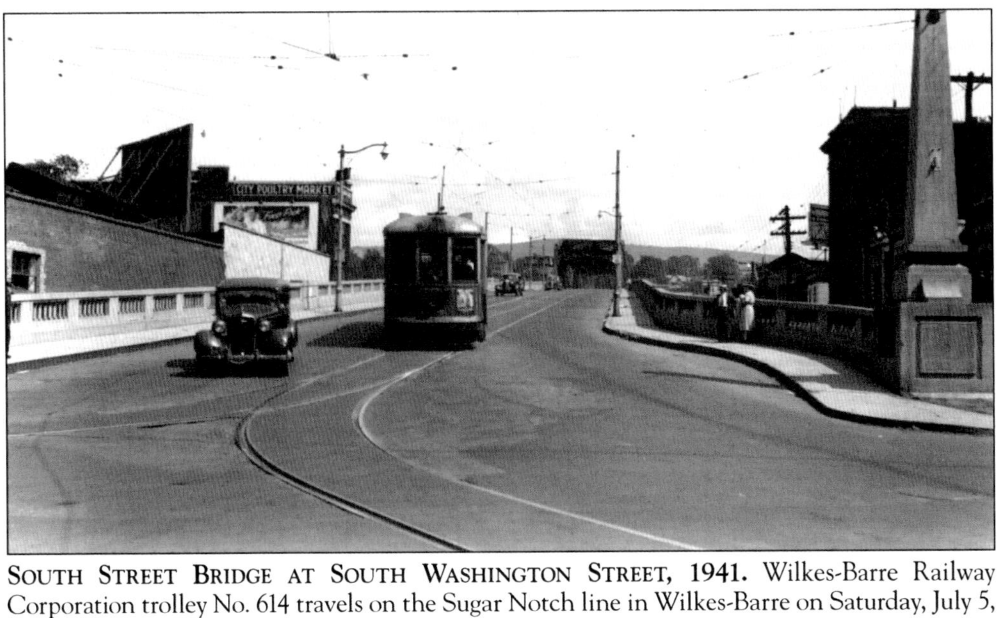

SOUTH STREET BRIDGE AT SOUTH WASHINGTON STREET, 1941. Wilkes-Barre Railway Corporation trolley No. 614 travels on the Sugar Notch line in Wilkes-Barre on Saturday, July 5, 1941. The trolley was built in 1918 for service at the Hog Island shipyard in Philadelphia, and it was delivered to the Wilkes-Barre Railway in the 1920s.

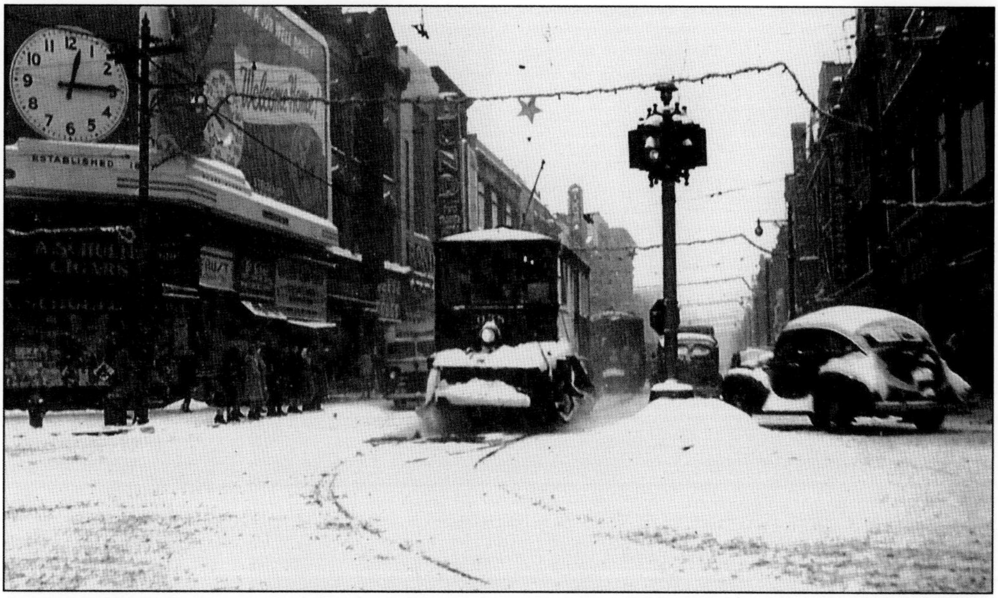

SOUTH MAIN STREET AT THE PUBLIC SQUARE, 1945. Wilkes-Barre Railway Corporation sweeper trolley No. 038 works on the Nanticoke line in Wilkes-Barre on a snowy Wednesday, December 19, 1945. The sweeper trolley was ordered from the J. G. Brill Company for the Wilkes-Barre, Dallas and Harvey's Lake Railway on August 7, 1899. It was in service until 1949.

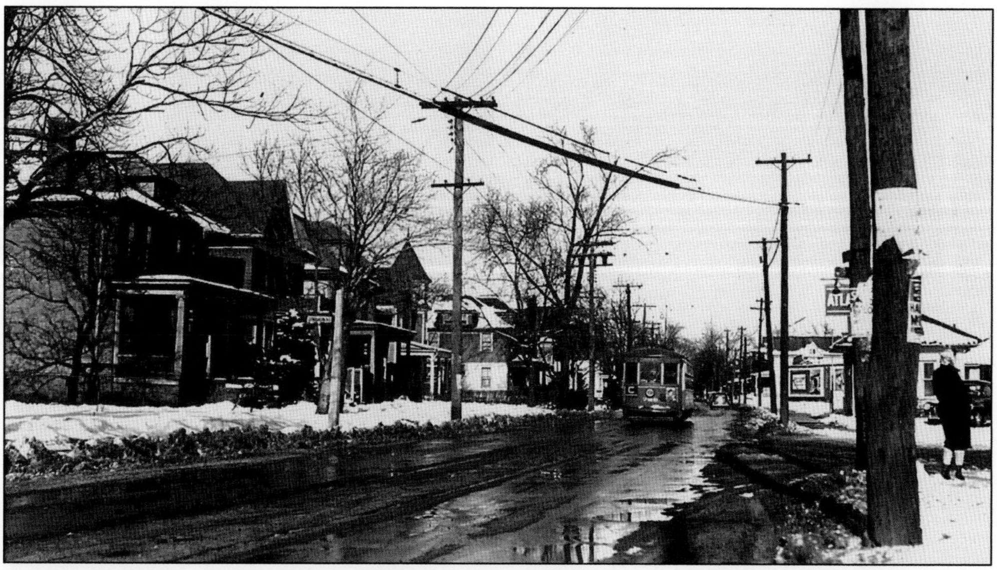

CAREY AVENUE AT DIVISION STREET, 1946. Wilkes-Barre Railway Corporation trolley No. 788 is on the Plymouth line in Wilkes-Barre on Thursday, February 21, 1946. The trolley was ordered in 1924 for the Eastern Pennsylvania Railway in Pottsville. In 1933, it was purchased by the Wilkes-Barre Railway. The final day of service on the Plymouth line was Sunday, August 31, 1947. Trolley No. 788 was scrapped in November 1950.

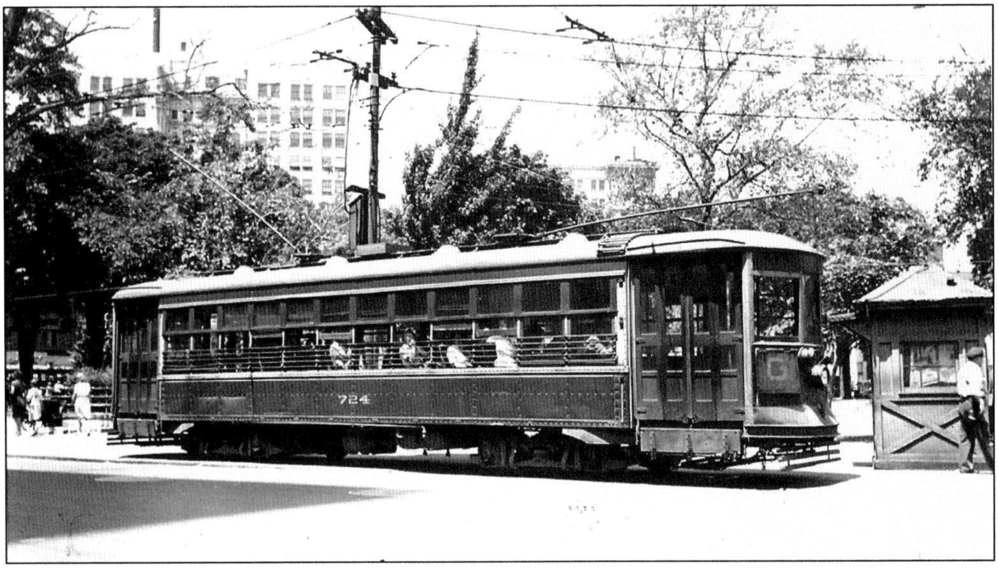

The Public Square, 1946. Wilkes-Barre Railway Corporation trolley No. 724 travels on the Georgetown line in Wilkes-Barre on Thursday, May 30, 1946. It was ordered from the Wason Company in 1923 for the Sistersville and New Martinsville Traction Company in West Virginia. The trolley was delivered to the Wilkes-Barre Railway on December 29, 1925. Trolley No. 724 was scrapped on August 7, 1948.

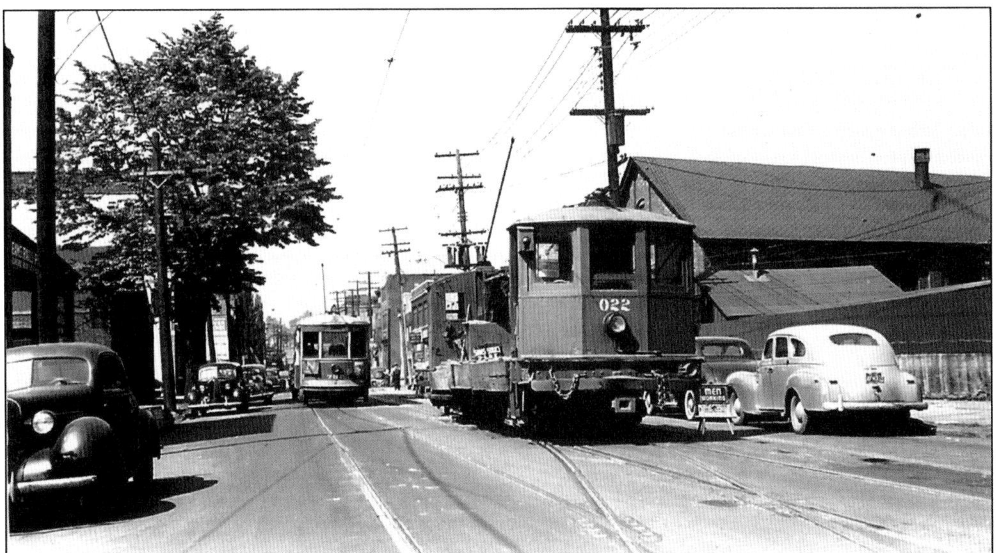

South Main Street at the Wood Street Barn, 1946. Wilkes-Barre Railway Corporation trolley No. 782, work trolley No. 022, and flatbed trailer No. 08 on the Nanticoke line are all shown in Wilkes-Barre on Friday, May 31, 1946. Trolley No. 782 was scrapped after the final day of service on the Nanticoke line in 1950. Work trolley No. 022 was used at the Market Street trolley yard in Kingston after Wyoming Valley trolley service was discontinued in 1950. It was scrapped in March 1952.

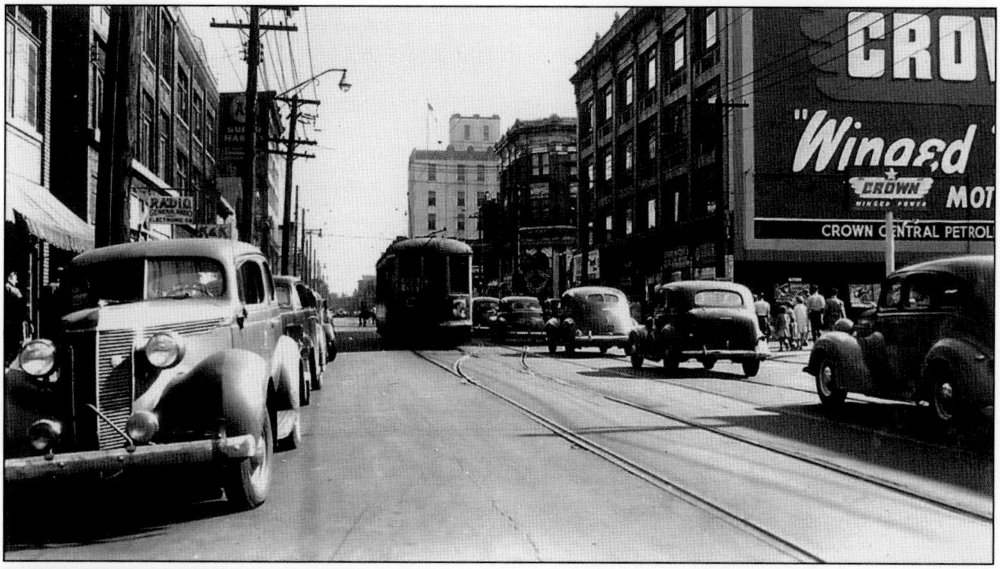

South Main Street at Hazle Avenue, 1946. Wilkes-Barre Railway Corporation trolley No. 602 is on the Plymouth line in Wilkes-Barre on Wednesday, September 11, 1946. The trolley was delivered to the Wilkes-Barre Railway in April 1920. Trolley No. 602 was updated for single motorman operation, and it was equipped with air-operated folding front doors. The trolley was in service until 1948.

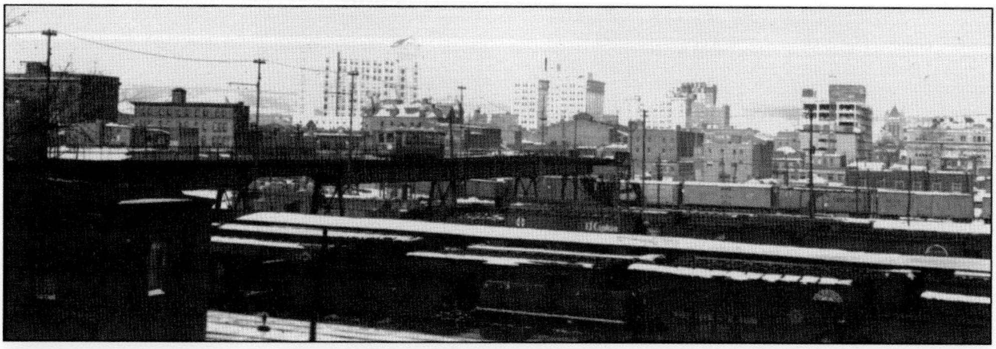

Georgetown Trestle, 1947. Wilkes-Barre Railway Corporation trolley No. 754 is on the Georgetown trestle over the Lehigh Valley Railroad and the Central Railroad of Pennsylvania on the Georgetown line in Wilkes-Barre on Sunday, February 23, 1947. The trolley was equipped with Westinghouse motors. It was on the Coast Cities Railway before it was delivered to the Wilkes-Barre Railway on March 29, 1932.

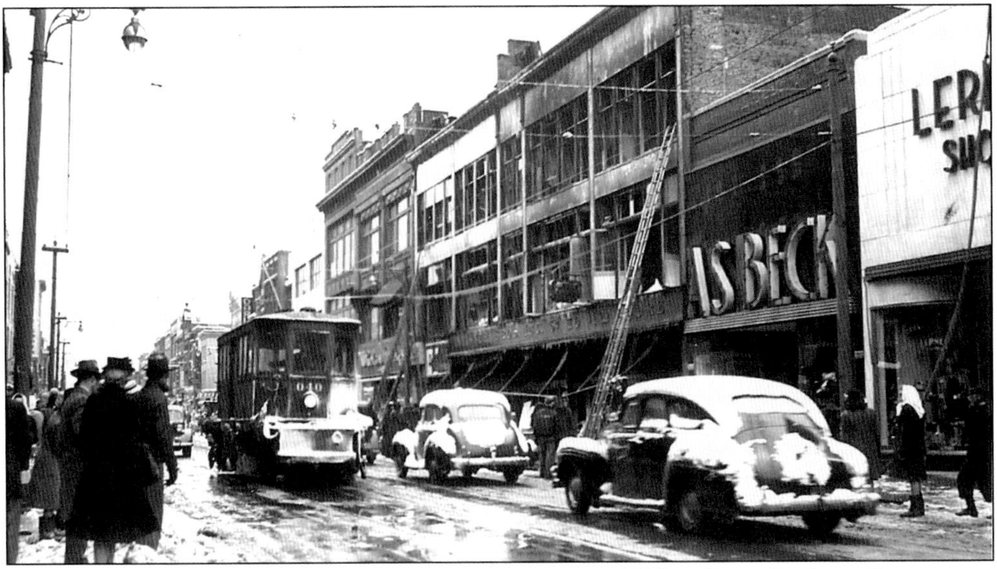

SOUTH MAIN STREET AT THE PUBLIC SQUARE, 1947. Wilkes-Barre Railway Corporation sweeper trolley No. 040 is shown on the Nanticoke line in Wilkes-Barre on Monday, March 3, 1947. The trolley was purchased by the Wilkes-Barre, Dallas and Harvey's Lake Railway in 1899. Sweeper trolley No. 040 was in service until the Nanticoke line was discontinued, and it was scrapped in 1950.

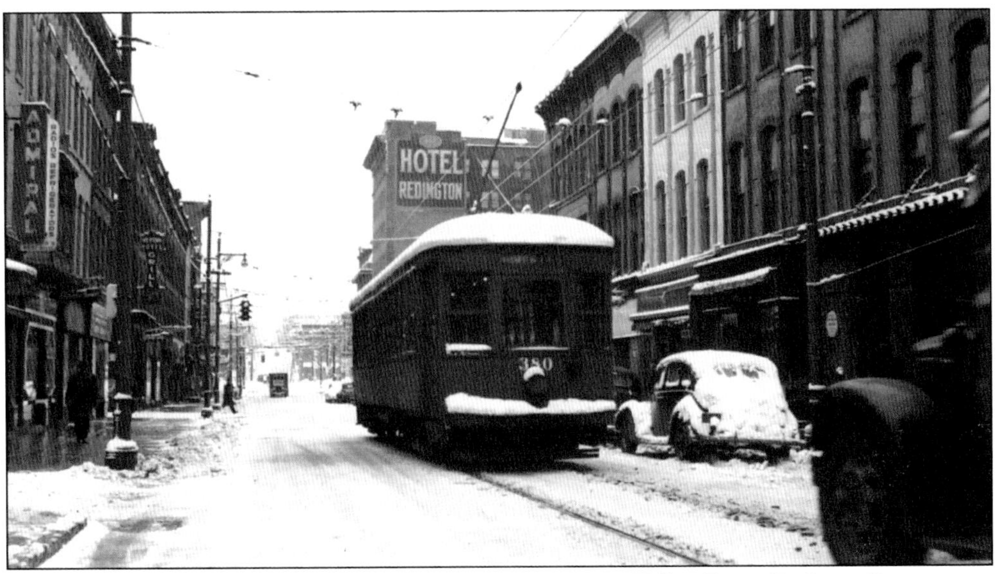

EAST MARKET STREET AT WASHINGTON STREET, 1947. Wilkes-Barre Railway Corporation trolley No. 380 is in Wilkes-Barre on the Georgetown line on Monday, March 3, 1947. At 27 tons, trolley No. 380 was too heavy for regular trolley service in the Wyoming Valley. The trolley was in service on the Harvey's Lake line until 1931, and it was on the Dallas line until 1939.

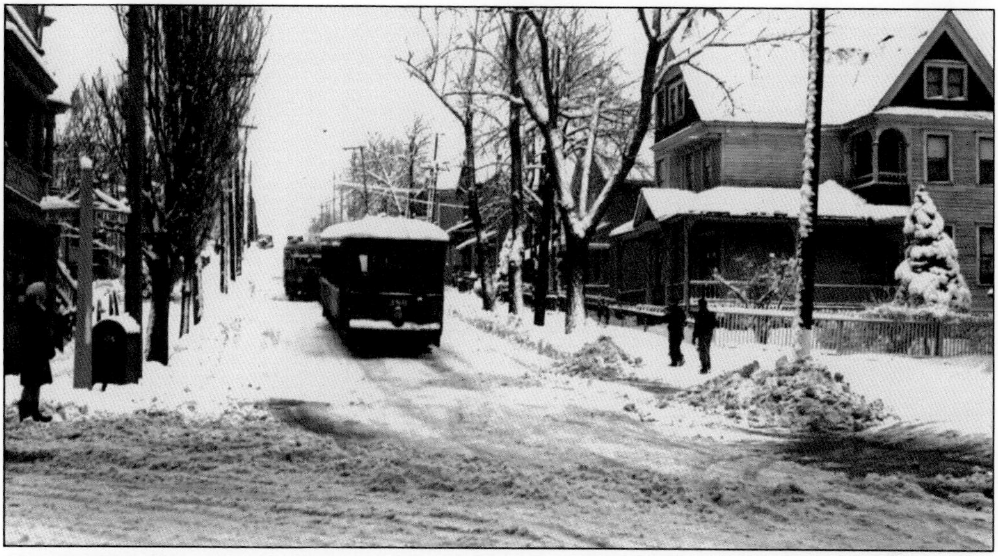

Hillside Street at East Northampton Street, 1947. Wilkes-Barre Railway Corporation trolley No. 380 travels on the Georgetown line in Wilkes-Barre on Monday, March 3, 1947. The trolley was equipped with only two Westinghouse motors when it was delivered to the Wilkes-Barre Railway in 1913, but it was rebuilt with four motors in 1914.

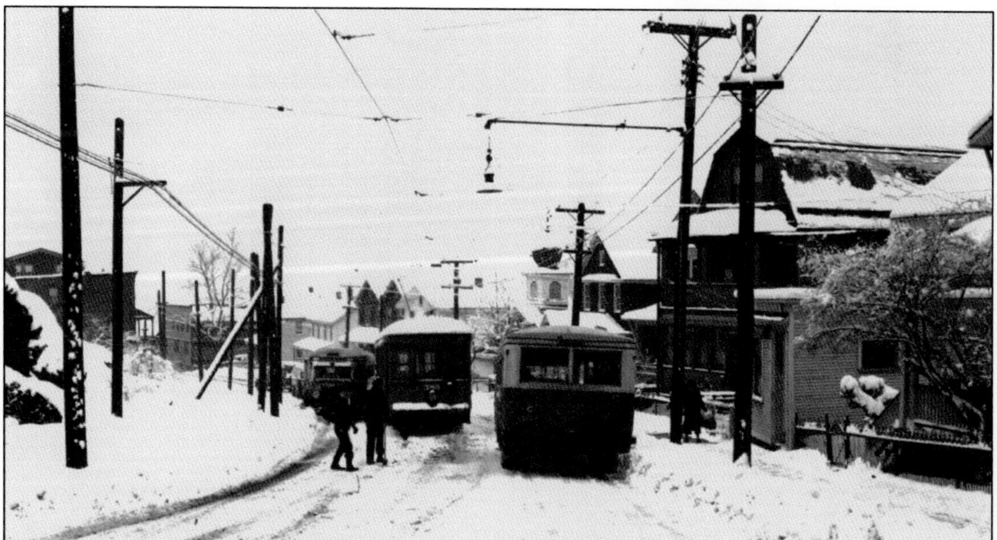

Northampton Street at Spencer Street, 1947. Wilkes-Barre Railway Corporation trolley No. 380 and a bus on the Georgetown line are seen in Wilkes-Barre on Monday, March 3, 1947. In front of the trolley, Joseph Vanderhoff and Mr. Pettinger are preparing to salt the tracks. Buses were used when the trolley line was blocked by snow or ice.

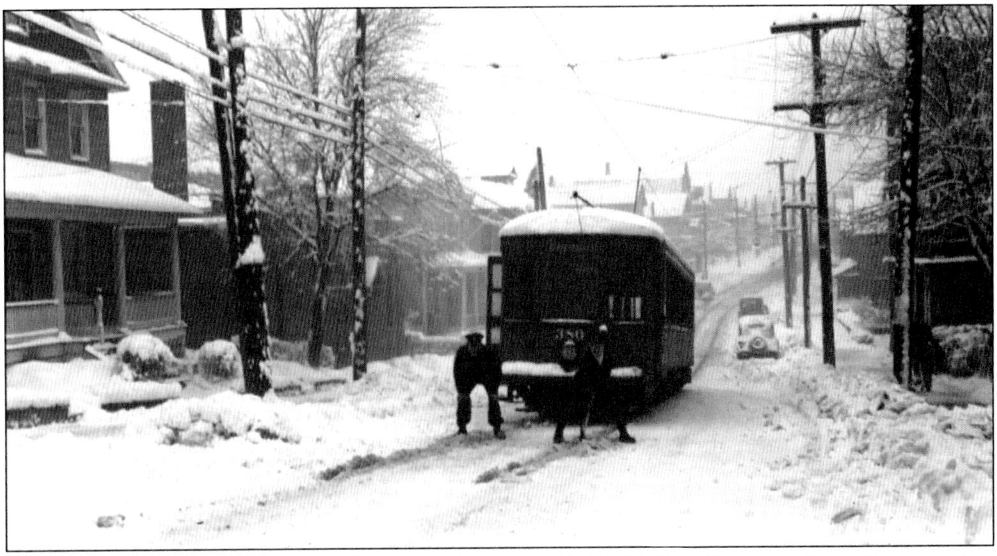

Northampton Street near Walnut Street, 1947. Wilkes-Barre Railway Corporation trolley No. 380 works on the Georgetown line in Wilkes-Barre on Monday, March 3, 1947. Regular service on the Georgetown line was extended past Walnut Street on May 29, 1908. Joseph Vanderhoff and Mr. Pettinger are salting the trolley tracks. The trolley is off the tracks.

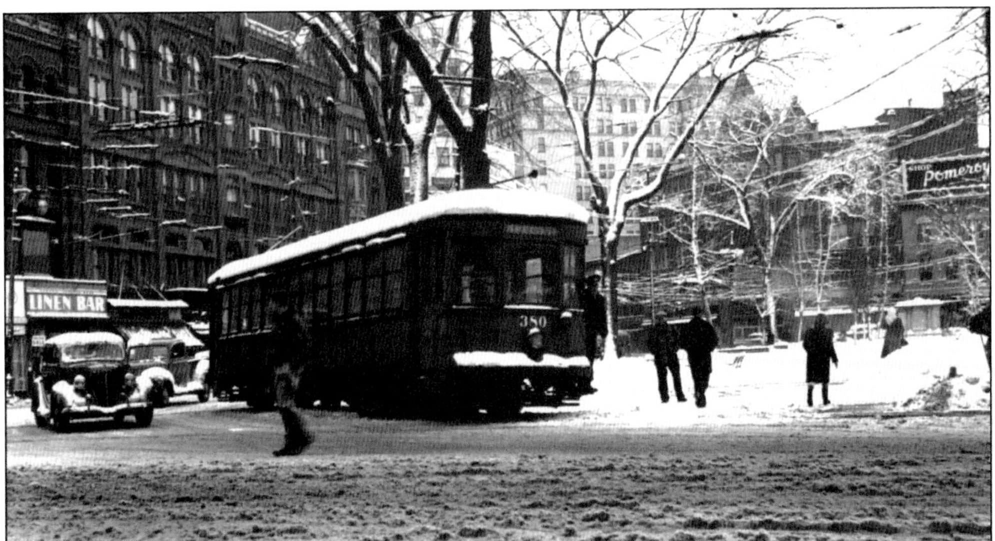

The Public Square at South Main Street, 1947. Wilkes-Barre Railway Corporation salt trolley No. 380 works on the Georgetown line in Wilkes-Barre on Monday, March 3, 1947. Regular passenger trolley service from the public square started on September 2, 1895. Trolley No. 380 was converted into a salt car in 1943, and it was scrapped in May 1950.

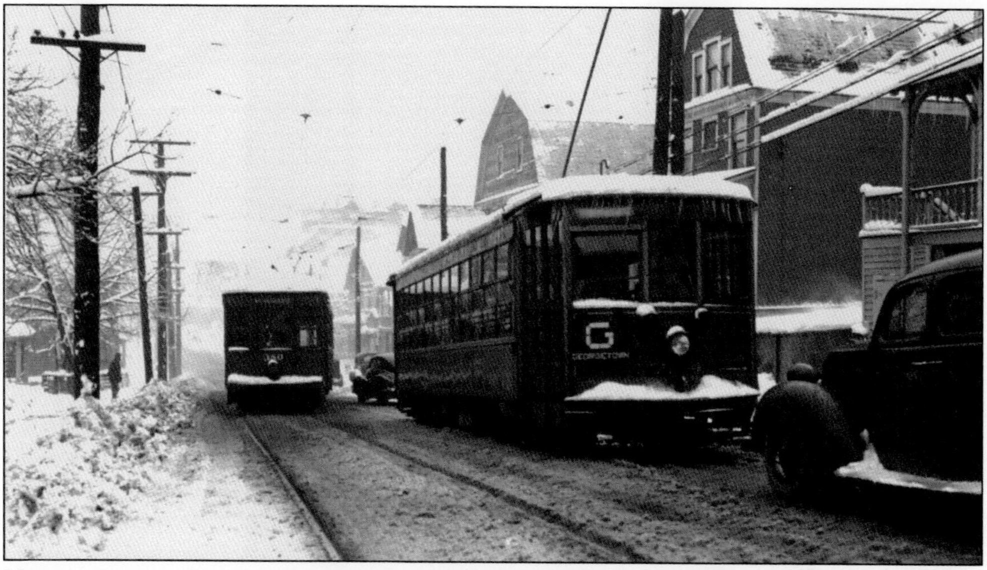

NORTHAMPTON STREET NEAR CASEY AVENUE, 1947. Wilkes-Barre Railway Corporation trolleys No. 380 and No. 724 are on the Georgetown line in Wilkes-Barre on Monday, March 3, 1947. On Memorial Day 1908, a record number of approximately 1,600 passengers took the Georgetown trolley to see the Giant's Despair automobile race up the mountain. The final day of service on the Georgetown line was Wednesday, April 30, 1947.

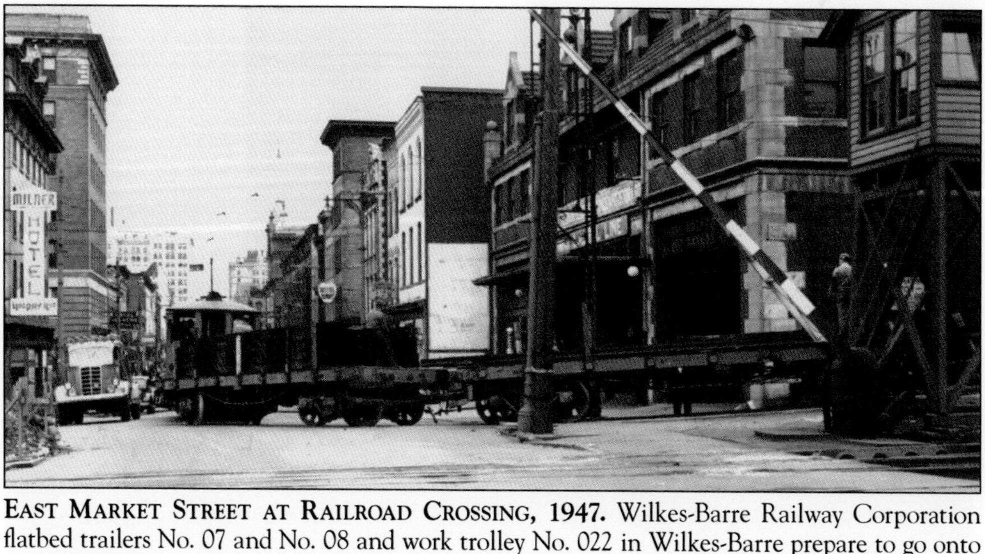

EAST MARKET STREET AT RAILROAD CROSSING, 1947. Wilkes-Barre Railway Corporation flatbed trailers No. 07 and No. 08 and work trolley No. 022 in Wilkes-Barre prepare to go onto the Georgetown trestle over the Lehigh Valley Railroad and Central Railroad of Pennsylvania on Thursday, May 15, 1947. This photograph shows the removal of tracks after the Georgetown line was abandoned.

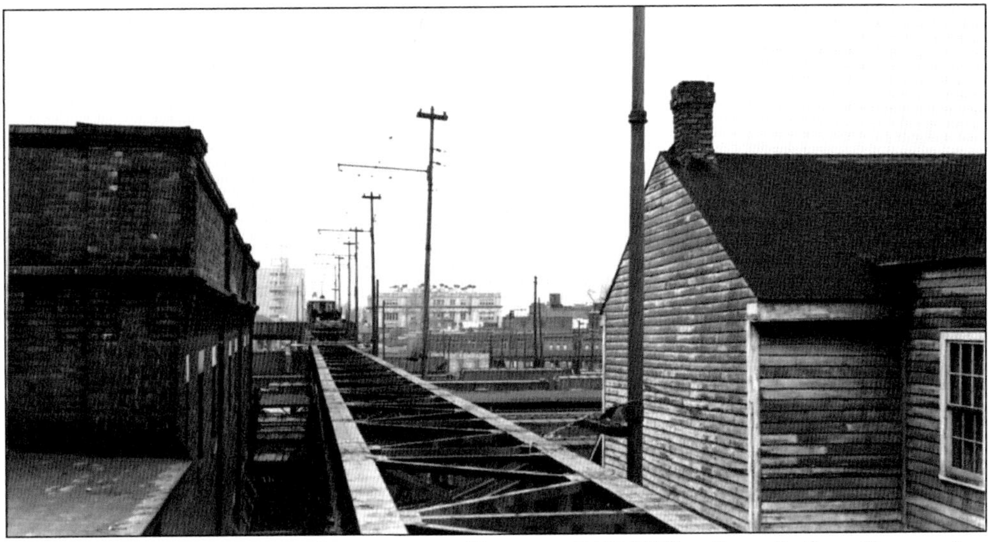

Removing Track from the Georgetown Trestle, 1947. Wilkes-Barre Railway Corporation trailers No. 07 and No. 08 and work trolley No. 022 remove track from the abandoned Georgetown line trestle over the Lehigh Valley Railroad and the Central Railroad of Pennsylvania near East Market Street in Wilkes-Barre on Thursday, May 15, 1947. Buses temporarily provided service along the abandoned trolley line and were replaced by trackless trolleys on June 9, 1947.

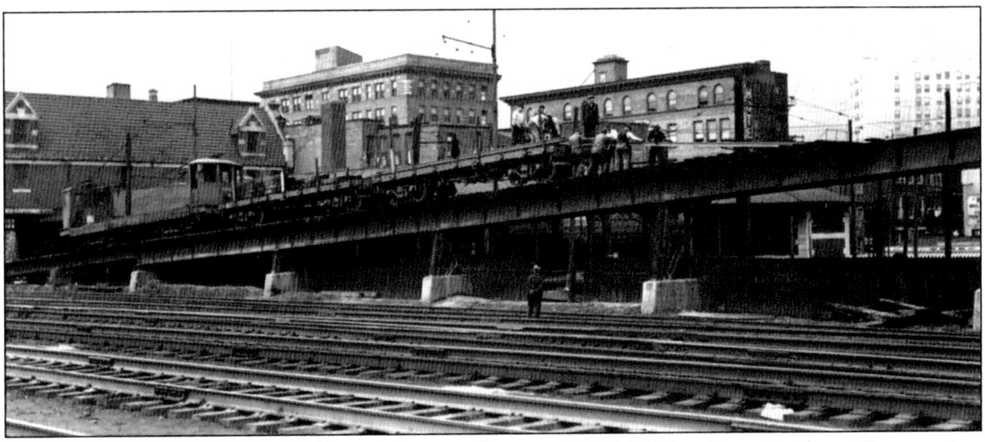

Georgetown Trestle near East Market Street, 1947. Wilkes-Barre Railway Corporation work trolley No. 022 and flatbed trailers No. 07 and No. 08 are on the Georgetown trestle above the Lehigh Valley Railroad and the Central Railroad of Pennsylvania removing trolley tracks near East Market Street in Wilkes-Barre on Wednesday, May 15, 1947. The trolley tracks were removed two weeks after the Georgetown line was abandoned.

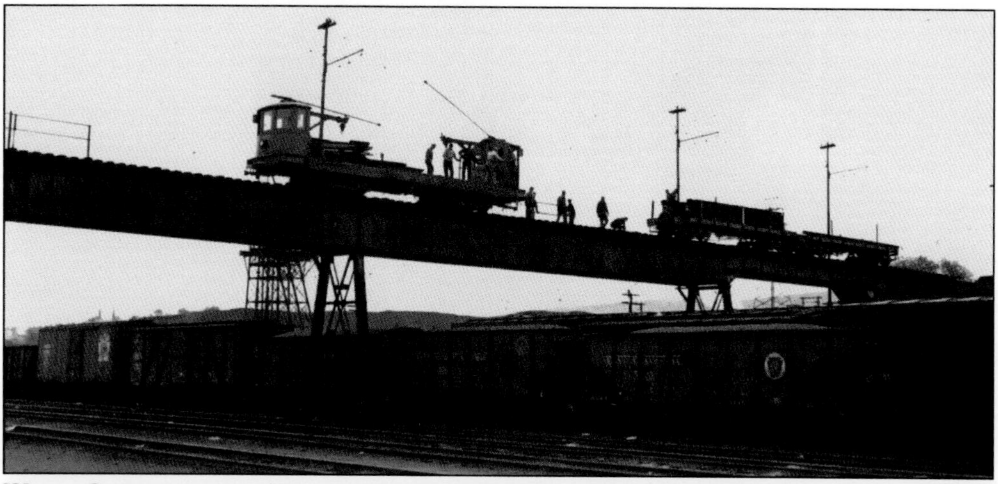

Work Crew on the Abandoned Georgetown Trestle, 1947. Wilkes-Barre Railway Corporation work trolley No. 022 and flatbed trailers No. 07 and No. 08 are on the Georgetown line near East Market Street in Wilkes-Barre on Wednesday, May 21, 1947. Flatbed trailers No. 07 and No. 08 were both built in 1912. The trailers were scrapped at the Wood Street trolley yard in 1950.

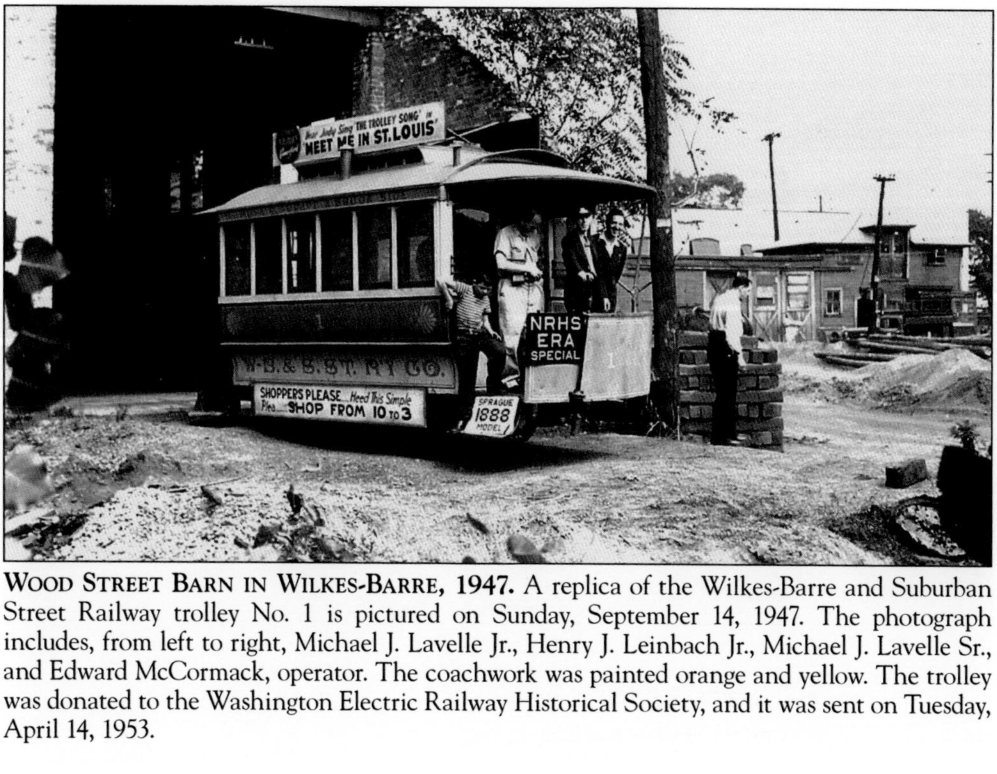

Wood Street Barn in Wilkes-Barre, 1947. A replica of the Wilkes-Barre and Suburban Street Railway trolley No. 1 is pictured on Sunday, September 14, 1947. The photograph includes, from left to right, Michael J. Lavelle Jr., Henry J. Leinbach Jr., Michael J. Lavelle Sr., and Edward McCormack, operator. The coachwork was painted orange and yellow. The trolley was donated to the Washington Electric Railway Historical Society, and it was sent on Tuesday, April 14, 1953.

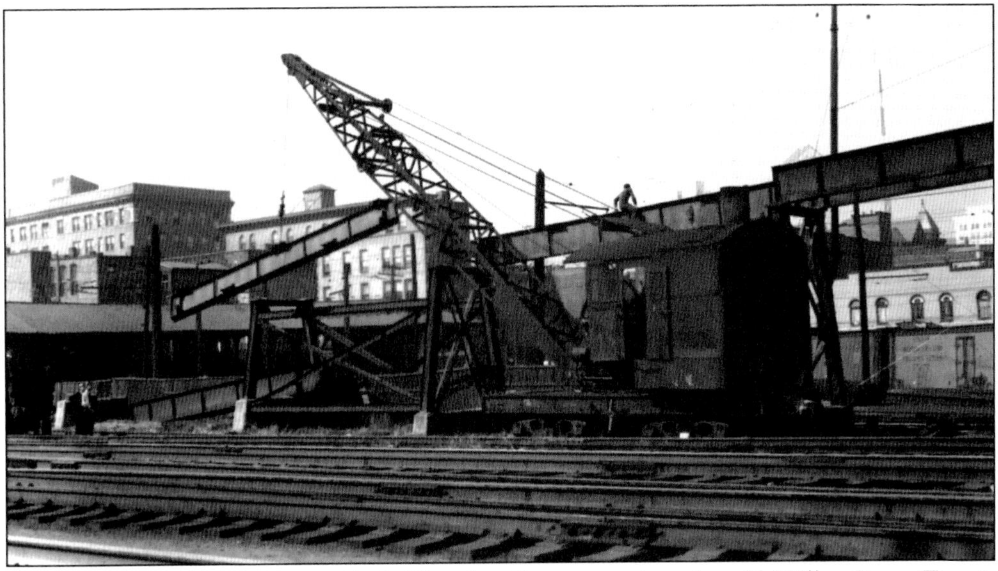

DISMANTLING THE TRESTLE, 1947. The derrick is removing the old Wilkes-Barre Transit Corporation trestle at the Delaware and Hudson Railroad and East Market Street on the interchange track of the Lehigh Valley Railroad in Wilkes-Barre in October 1947. The derrick belonged to Mayer Pollock, a scrap iron dealer in Pottstown. The derrick was built by Industrial Works in Bay City, Michigan.

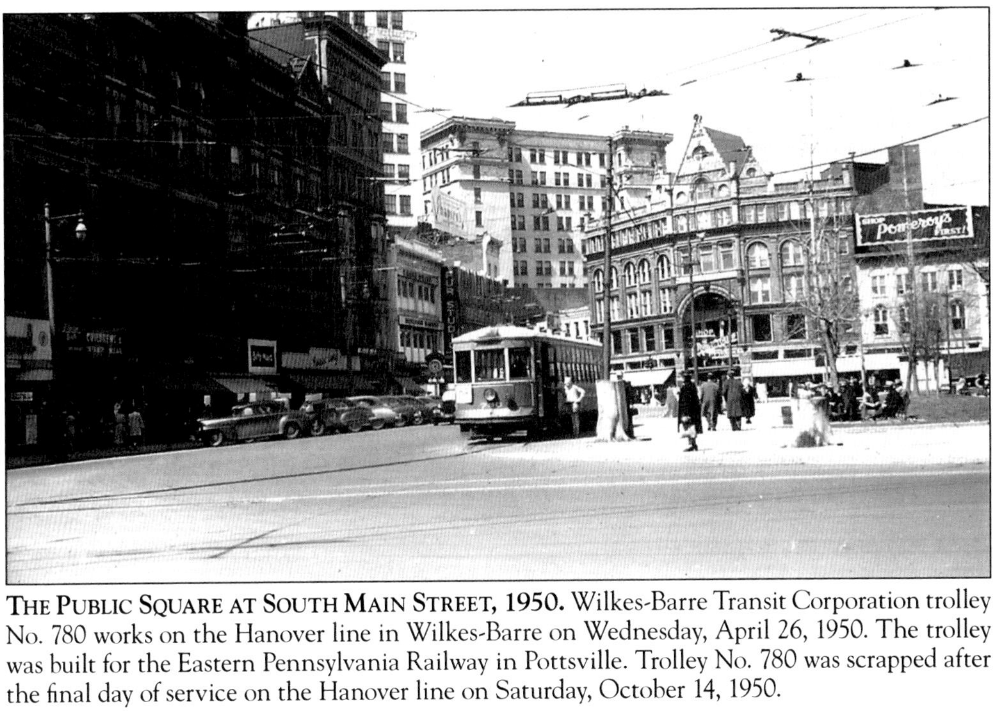

THE PUBLIC SQUARE AT SOUTH MAIN STREET, 1950. Wilkes-Barre Transit Corporation trolley No. 780 works on the Hanover line in Wilkes-Barre on Wednesday, April 26, 1950. The trolley was built for the Eastern Pennsylvania Railway in Pottsville. Trolley No. 780 was scrapped after the final day of service on the Hanover line on Saturday, October 14, 1950.

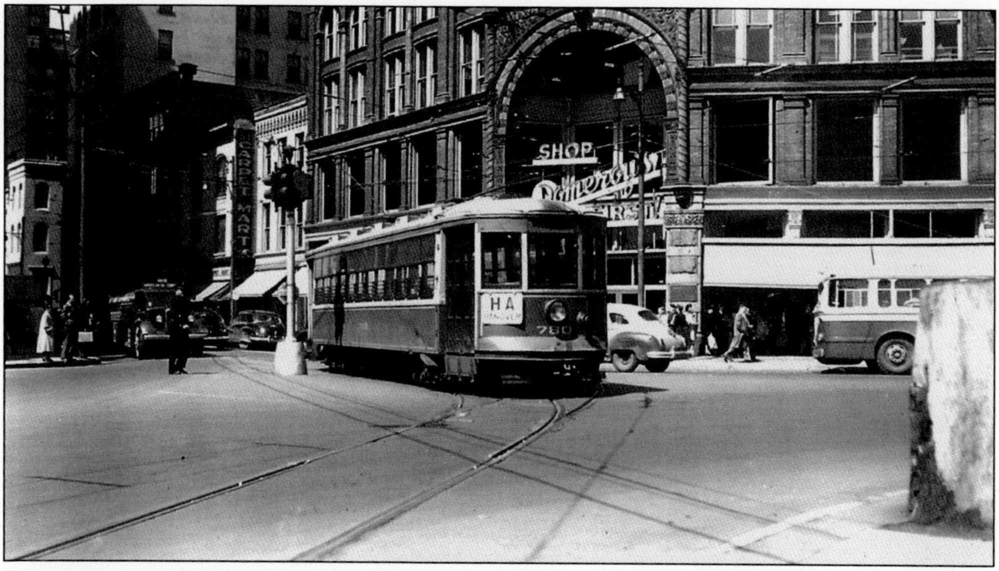

ENTERING THE PUBLIC SQUARE FROM WEST MARKET STREET, 1950. Wilkes-Barre Transit Corporation trolley No. 780 is on the Hanover line in Wilkes-Barre on Wednesday, April 26, 1950. The trolley was ordered from the J. G. Brill Company on April 2, 1924, and it was purchased secondhand by the Wilkes-Barre Railway in 1933. This photograph was taken when the trolley was coming from the Kingston Courthouse to start afternoon trips.

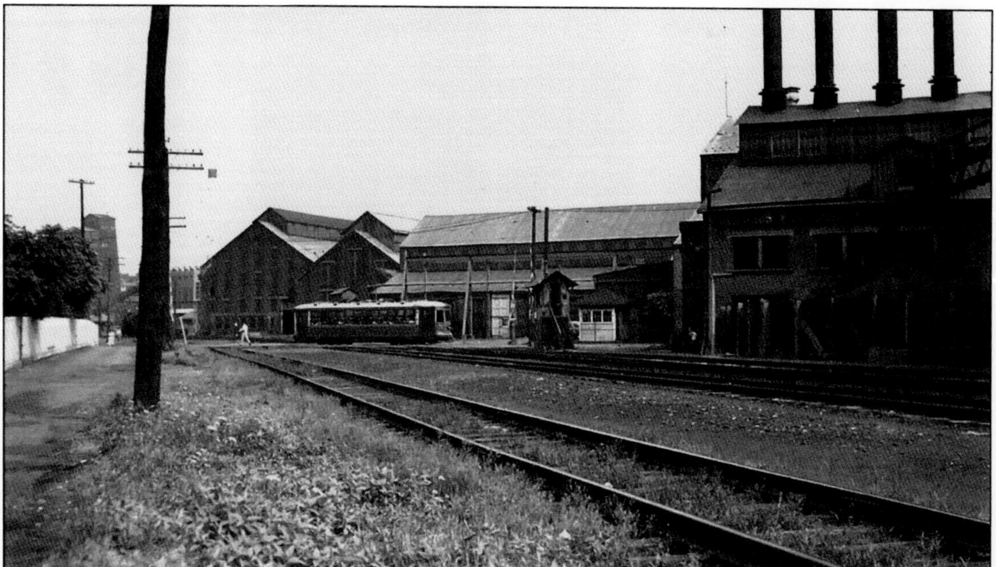

SOUTH FRANKLIN STREET, 1950. Wilkes-Barre Transit Corporation trolley No. 782 is pictured at the Pennsylvania Railroad crossing on the Nanticoke line in Wilkes-Barre on Thursday, August 3, 1950. The trolley was in service on the final day of the Nanticoke line on Saturday, October 14, 1950, and it was scrapped one month later. Franklin Street was the first street in Wilkes-Barre paved with asphalt in April 1886.

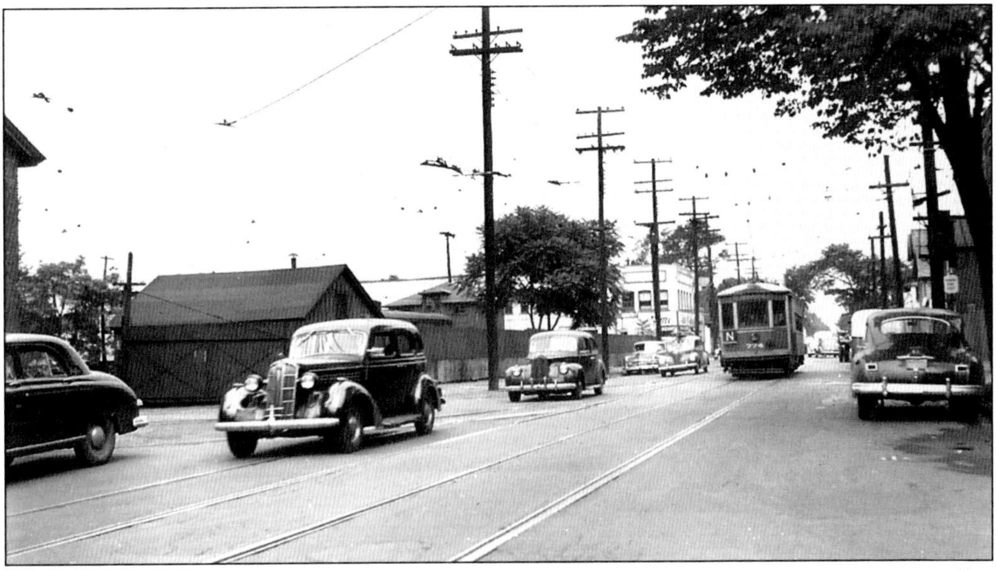

South Main Street at Wood Street, 1950. Wilkes-Barre Transit Corporation trolley No. 774 works on the Nanticoke line in Wilkes-Barre on Wednesday, September 27, 1950. The 45-foot trolley was ordered from the J. G. Brill Company with General Electric motors for the Eastern Pennsylvania Railway in Pottsville. It was delivered to the Wilkes-Barre Railway in 1933.

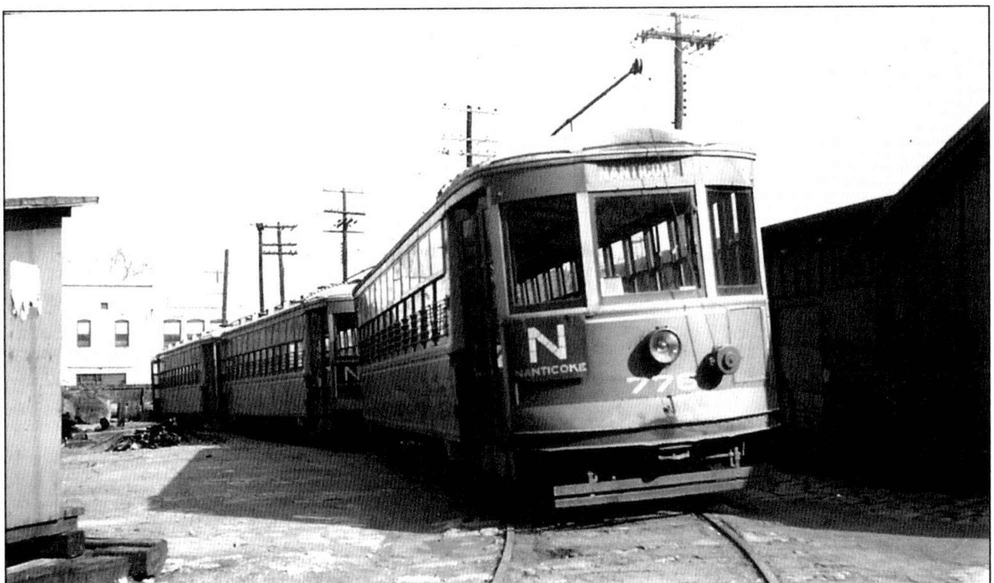

South Main Street at the Wood Street Yard, 1950. Wilkes-Barre Transit Corporation trolleys No. 776, No. 786, and No. 774 are seen in Wilkes-Barre on Wednesday, October 25, 1950. Trolley No. 786 was ordered from the J. G. Brill Company with General Electric motors on April 2, 1924, for the Eastern Pennsylvania Railway. The trolleys were scrapped in 1950.

Three

Upper Valley

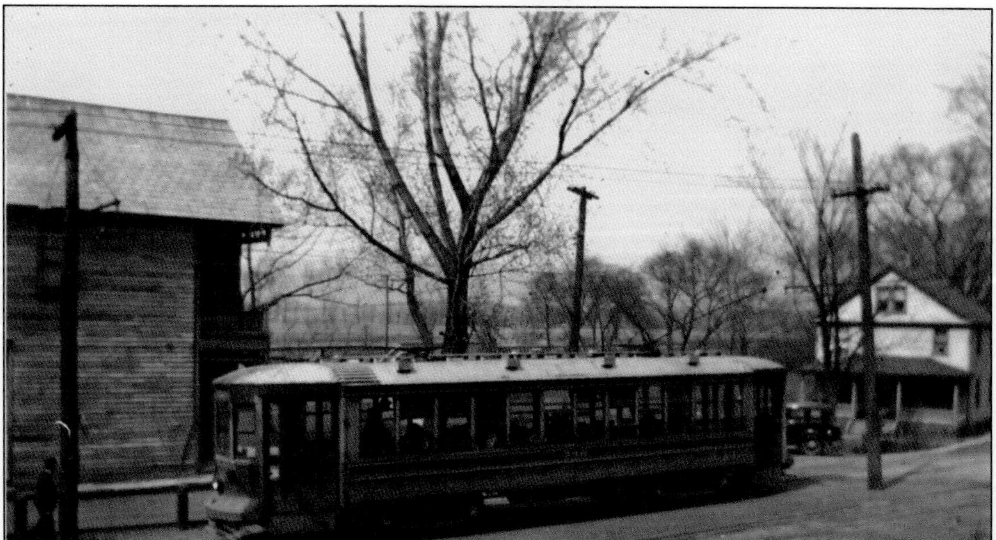

Courtright Street in Plains, 1937. Wilkes-Barre Railway Corporation trolley No. 346 is heading southbound to Wilkes-Barre at the Central Railroad of New Jersey crossing on the Pittston line on Sunday, April 18, 1937. Trolley No. 346 was stopped while the motorman was collecting fares. The trolley was delivered in 1911, and it was later used on the Sugar Notch line before it was scrapped in 1948.

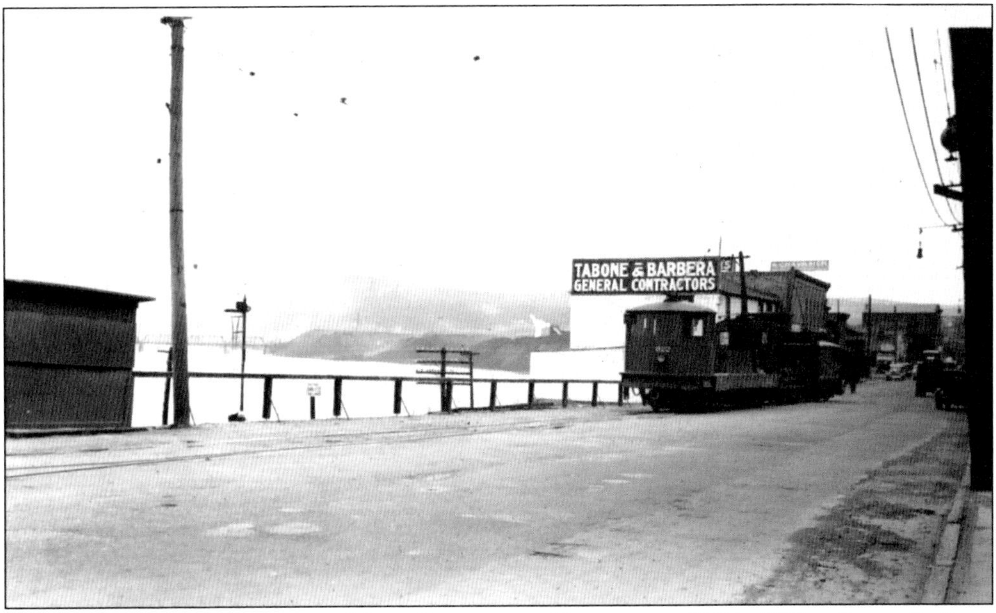

NORTH MAIN STREET NEAR MILL STREET IN PITTSTON, 1937. Wilkes-Barre Railway Corporation work trolleys No. 022 and No. 020 and tower trailer No. 00L are seen on Monday, April 26, 1937. The 43-foot work trolley No. 022 was ordered from the J. G. Brill Company on May 6, 1912, and it was equipped with a steel crane.

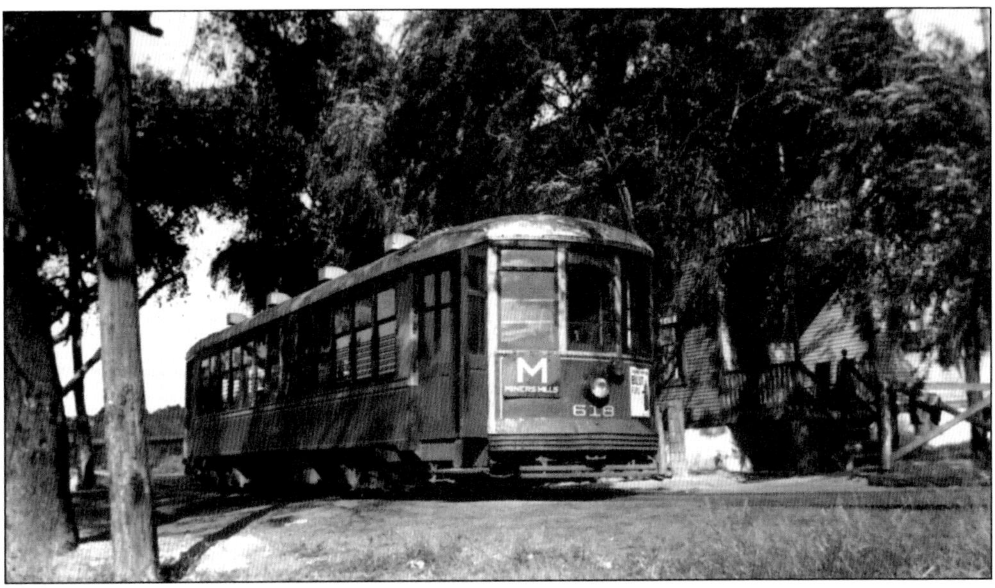

CLEVELAND STREET NEAR NORTH STREET IN PLAINS, 1937. Wilkes-Barre Railway Corporation trolley No. 618 is pictured at the end of the Miners Mills line on Sunday, September 19, 1937. The trolley was ordered on April 23, 1918, for the Hog Island shipyard in Philadelphia. It was purchased by the Wilkes-Barre Railway in the 1920s. The final day of service on the Miners Mills line was October 19, 1940.

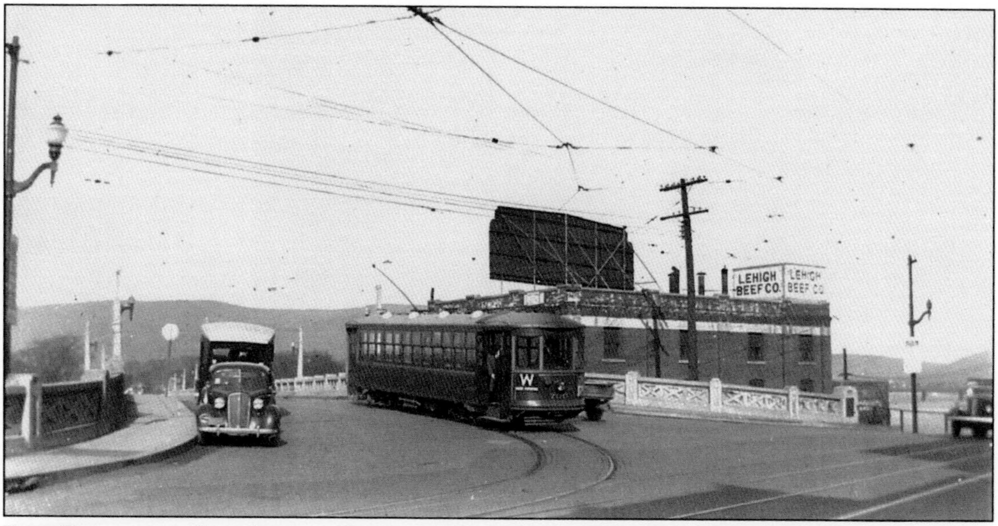

EAST END OF THE FORT JENKINS BRIDGE IN PITTSTON, 1938. Wilkes-Barre Railway Corporation trolley No. 700 is at North Main Street on the West Pittston line on Thursday, March 3, 1938. The 45-foot trolley was ordered from the J. G. Brill Company on March 22, 1923. The final day of service on the West Pittston line was Christmas Day 1939.

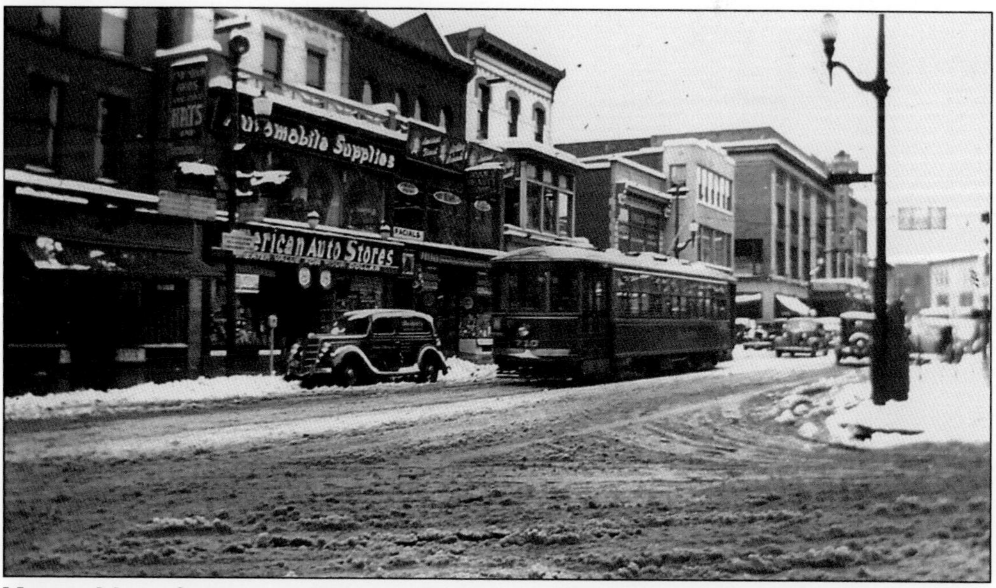

NORTH MAIN STREET AT WILLIAM STREET IN PITTSTON, 1938. Wilkes-Barre Railway Corporation trolley No. 710 travels on the West Pittston line on Thursday, April 7, 1938. The trolley was delivered to the Wilkes-Barre Railway in 1923. The interior was finished in stained mahogany. Trolley No. 710 was sold to the San Diego Electric Railway in 1942.

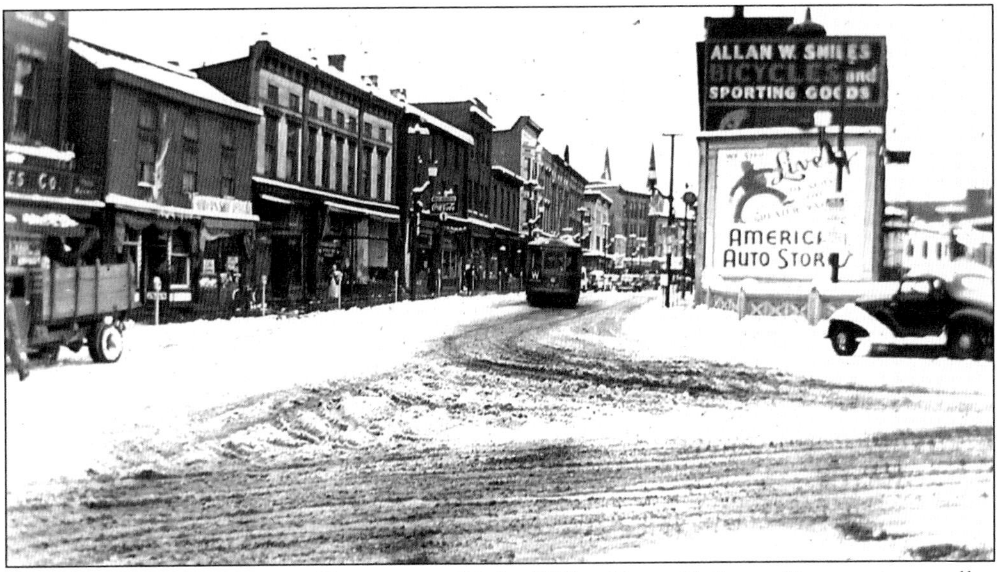

NORTH MAIN STREET IN PITTSTON, 1938. Wilkes-Barre Railway Corporation trolley No. 712 is at Fort Jenkins Bridge on the West Pittston line on Thursday, April 7, 1938. Fort Jenkins Bridge connecting Pittston and West Pittston was dedicated on February 2, 1926. The bridge was named for Fort Jenkins, which was built along the Susquehanna River during the American Revolution.

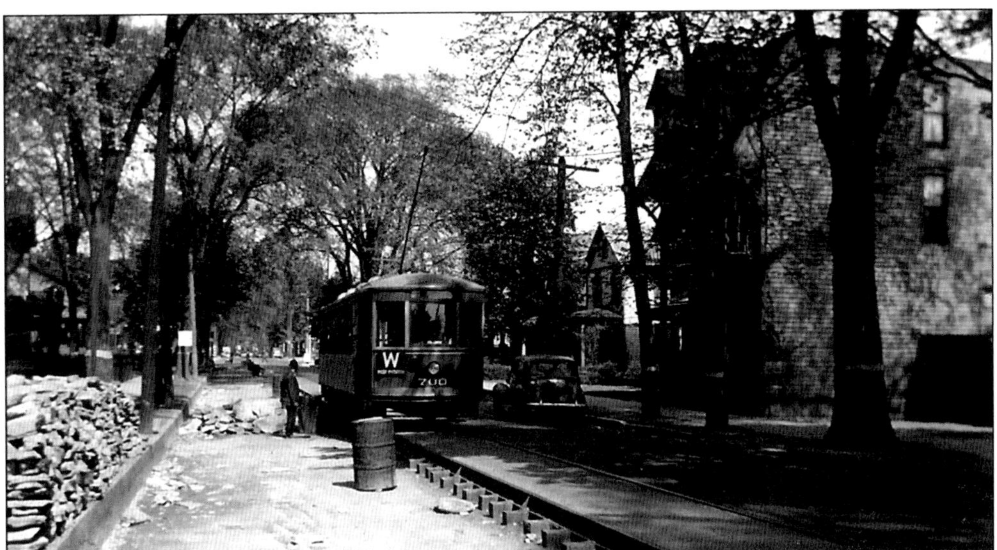

WYOMING AVENUE NEAR LINDEN STREET IN WEST PITTSTON, 1938. Wilkes-Barre Railway Corporation trolley No. 700 works on the West Pittston line on Monday, May 2, 1938. All trolleys on the West Pittston line were changed to single-motorman operation on October 1, 1926. The trolley was sold to the San Diego Electric Railway in 1942.

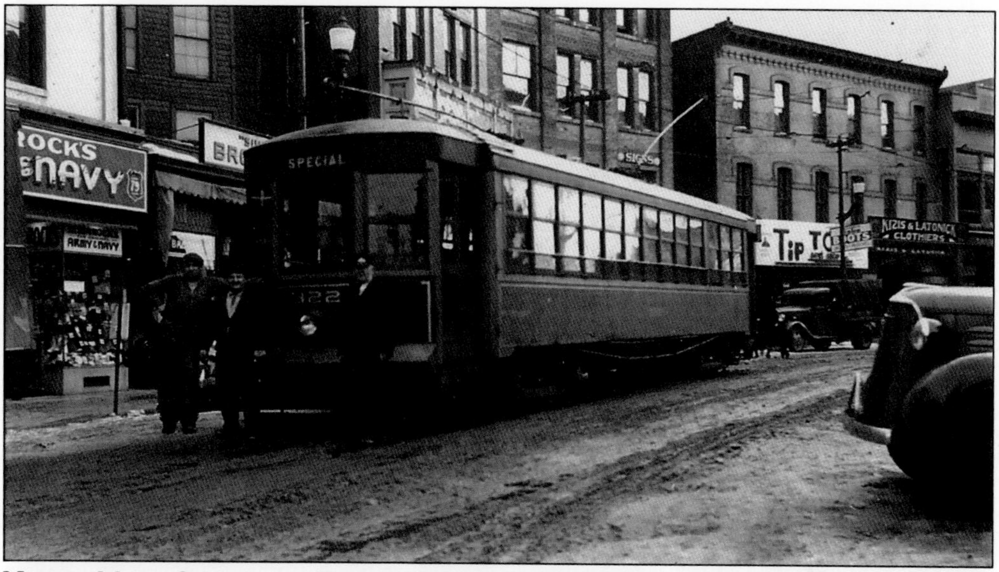

North Main Street at Butler Street in Pittston, 1938. Wilkes-Barre Railway Corporation trolley No. 322 travels on the West Pittston line on Tuesday, November 29, 1938. The trolley was breaking through the snow-blocked line caused by the Thanksgiving Day storm on November 24. In front of the trolley are Edward McCormack, James La Moss, and Matthew Bilbow.

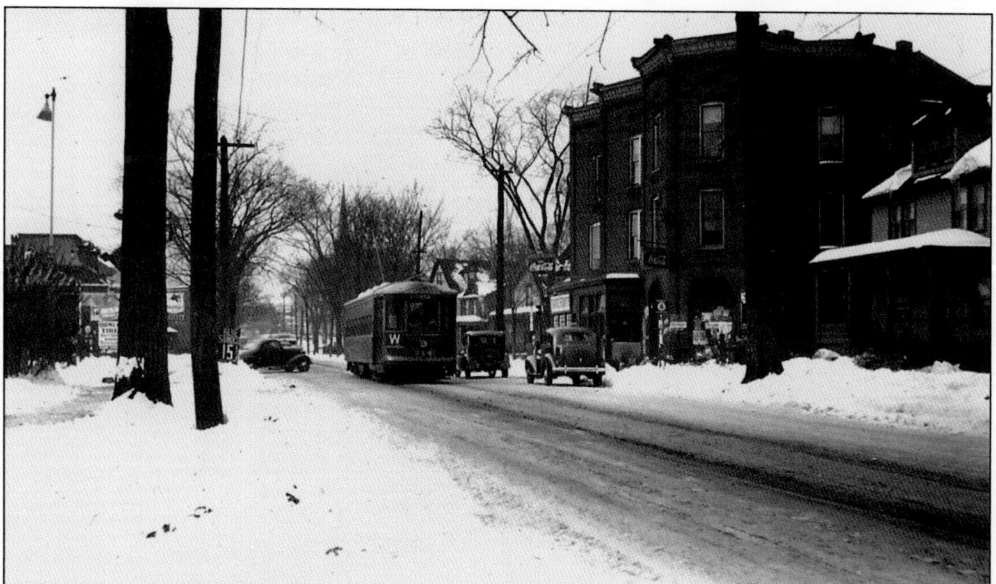

Wyoming Avenue at Luzerne Avenue in West Pittston, 1938. Wilkes-Barre Railway Corporation trolley No. 714 is on the West Pittston line on Monday, November 28, 1938. The 45-foot trolley ran on the West Pittston line until it was discontinued on Christmas Day 1939. In 1942, the trolley was sold to the San Diego Electric Railway in California.

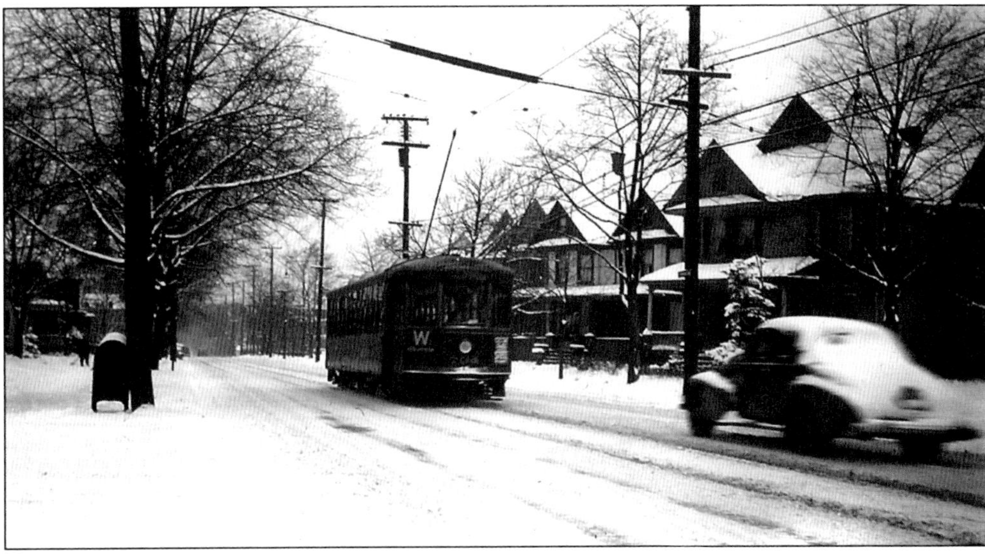

WYOMING AVENUE IN WEST PITTSTON, 1939. Wilkes-Barre Railway Corporation trolley No. 704 is pictured at Philadelphia Avenue on the West Pittston line on Saturday, January 24, 1939. After the West Pittston line was abandoned in 1939, trolley No. 704 was used in the upper Wyoming Valley until it was sold to the San Diego Electric Railway in 1942.

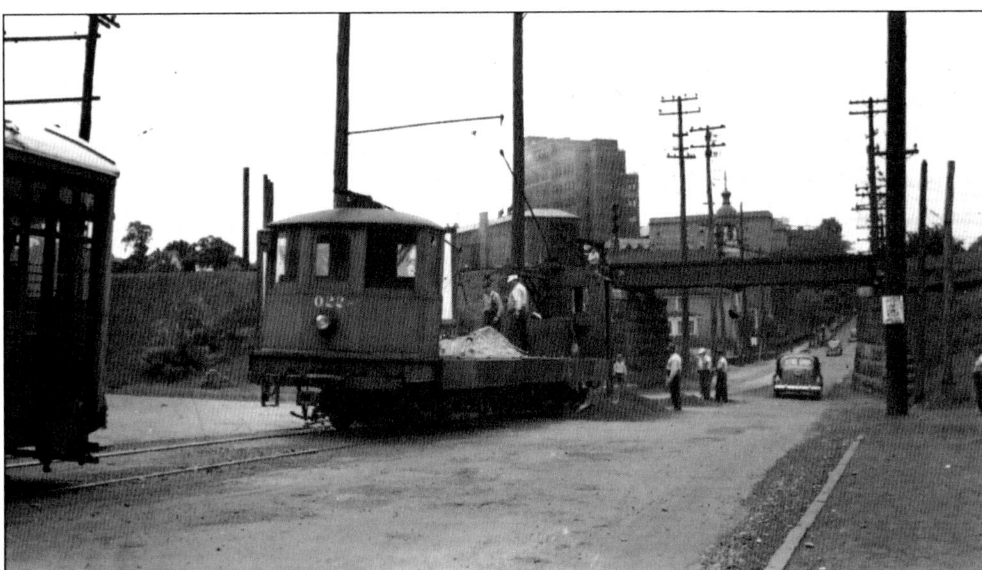

RIVER STREET AT WILKES-BARRE CITY LINE IN PLAINS, 1939. Wilkes-Barre Railway Corporation work trolley No. 022 is shown on the Hudson line on Friday, June 2, 1939. The trolley was equipped with steel cranes used for lifting heavy loads, including rails. In the background is the Lehigh Valley Railroad overpass. The photograph was taken near the Prospect Colliery owned by the Lehigh Valley Coal Company.

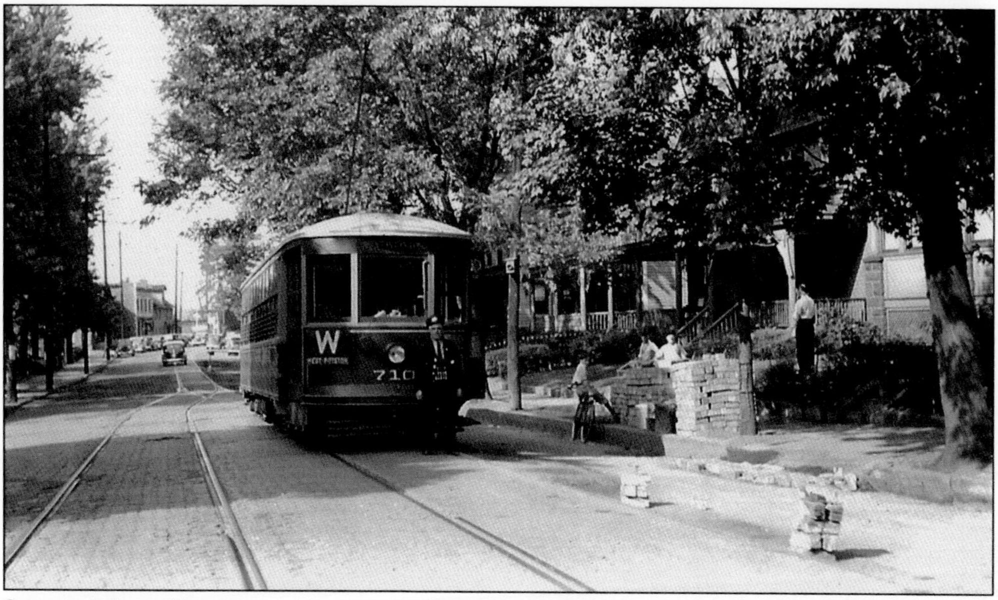

SOUTH MAIN STREET AT SWALLOW STREET IN PITTSTON, 1939. Wilkes-Barre Railway Corporation trolley No. 710 is pictured at the end of the West Pittston line on Friday, June 16, 1939. In front of the trolley was motorman Johnson Van Buren Coolbaugh. After the Fort Jenkins Bridge was dedicated, the West Pittston line was extended through Pittston to Swallow Street on May 12, 1926.

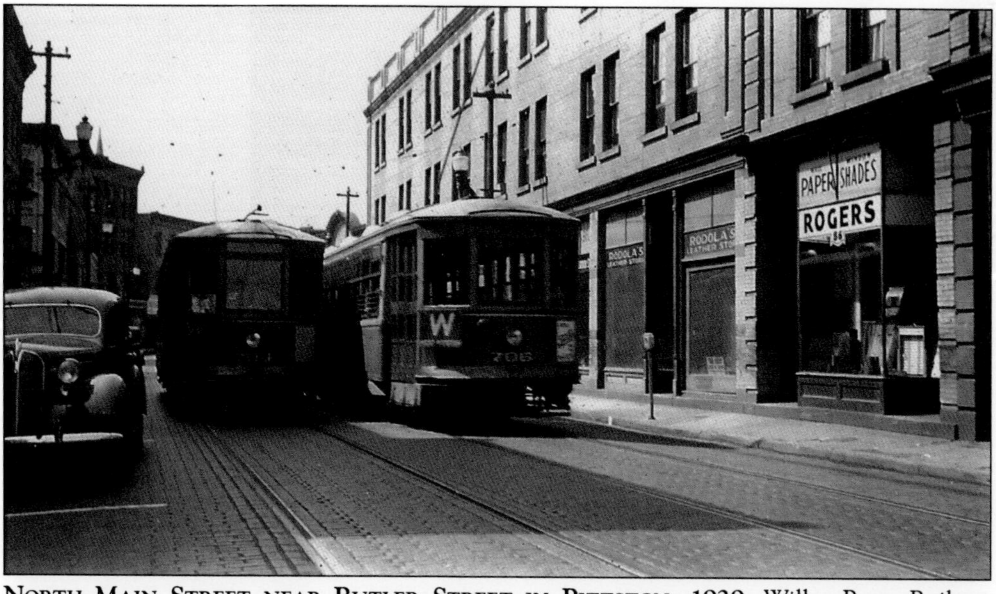

NORTH MAIN STREET NEAR BUTLER STREET IN PITTSTON, 1939. Wilkes-Barre Railway Corporation trolleys No. 704 and No. 706 are on the West Pittston line on Tuesday, July 4, 1939. Both trolleys were ordered from the J. G. Brill Company on March 22, 1923, and were equipped with Westinghouse motors. Both trolleys were sold to the San Diego Electric Railway in California.

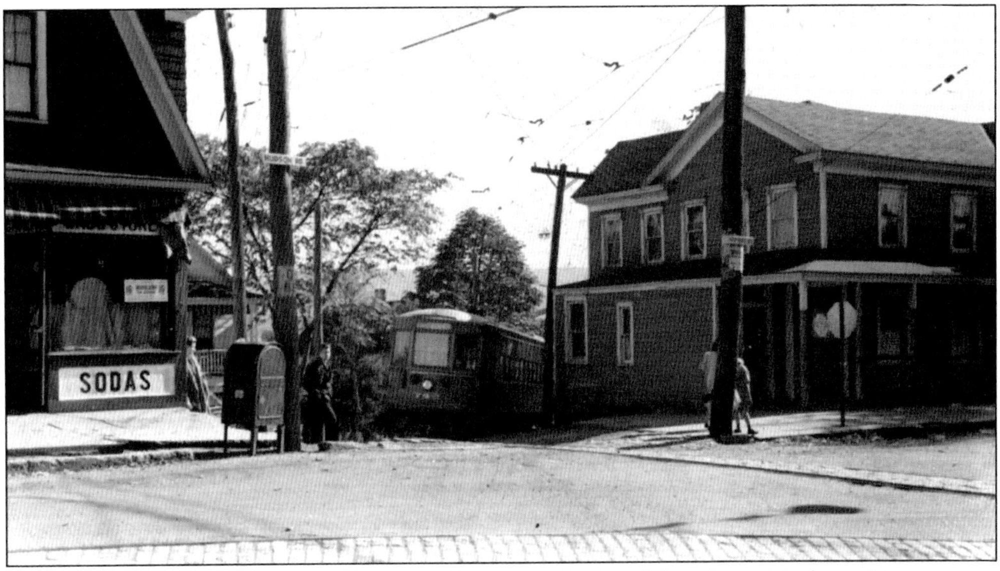

CAREY STREET AND HUDSON ROAD IN PLAINS, 1939. Wilkes-Barre Railway Corporation trolley No. 742 is pictured on Sunday, October 15, 1939, at the end of the Plains line. The 45-foot trolley was ordered with Westinghouse motors on May 3, 1926. The last trolley ran on the Plains line on November 15, 1939. Trolley No. 742 was sold to the Virginia Electric and Power Company in July 1940.

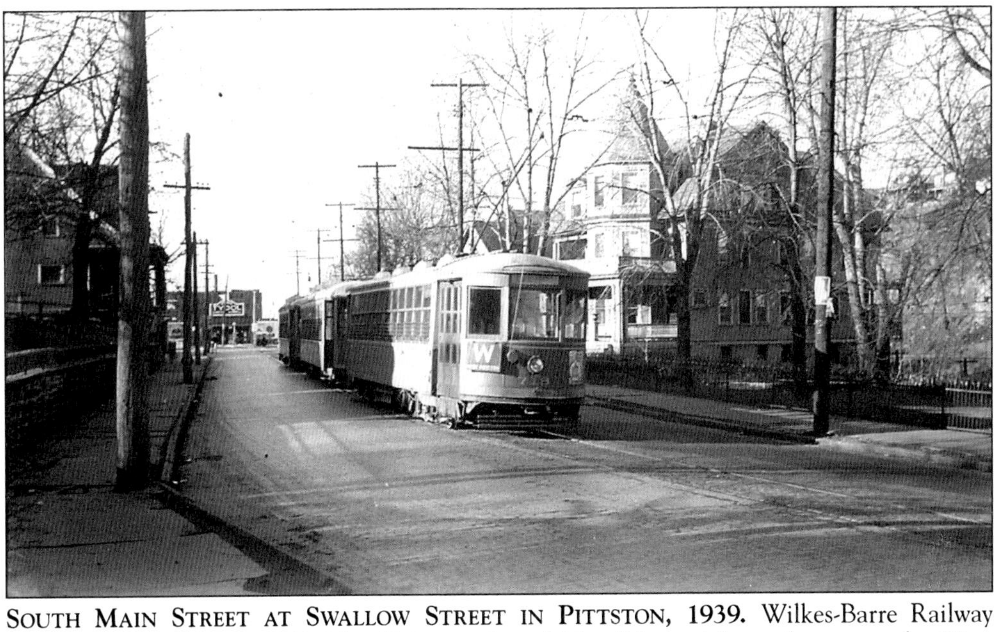

SOUTH MAIN STREET AT SWALLOW STREET IN PITTSTON, 1939. Wilkes-Barre Railway Corporation trolleys No. 718, No. 620 special, and No. 618 special are shown on the West Pittston line on Saturday, November 11, 1939. Behind trolley No. 718 were trolleys No. 620 and No. 618, two Armistice Day special trolleys chartered by the West Pittston American Legion that were going to a veterans' parade in Wilkes-Barre.

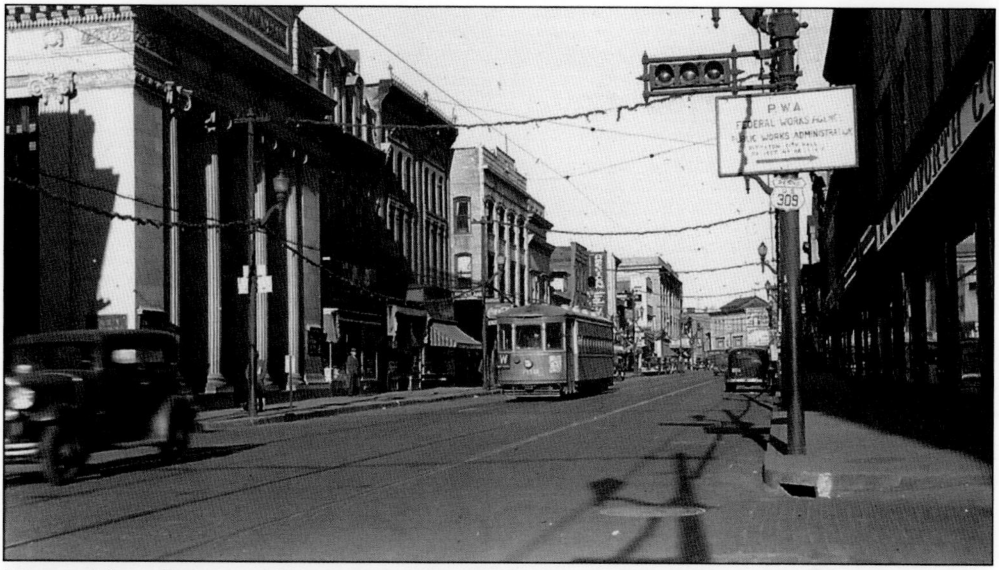

NORTH MAIN STREET IN PITTSTON, 1939. Wilkes-Barre Railway Corporation trolley No. 702 is heading southbound at Water Street and Broad Street on Sunday, December 24, 1939, the day before the West Pittston line was abandoned. Anthracite coal mining remained active in the Wyoming Valley until shortly after the Knox Mine disaster in Port Griffith, Jenkins Township, on January 22, 1959.

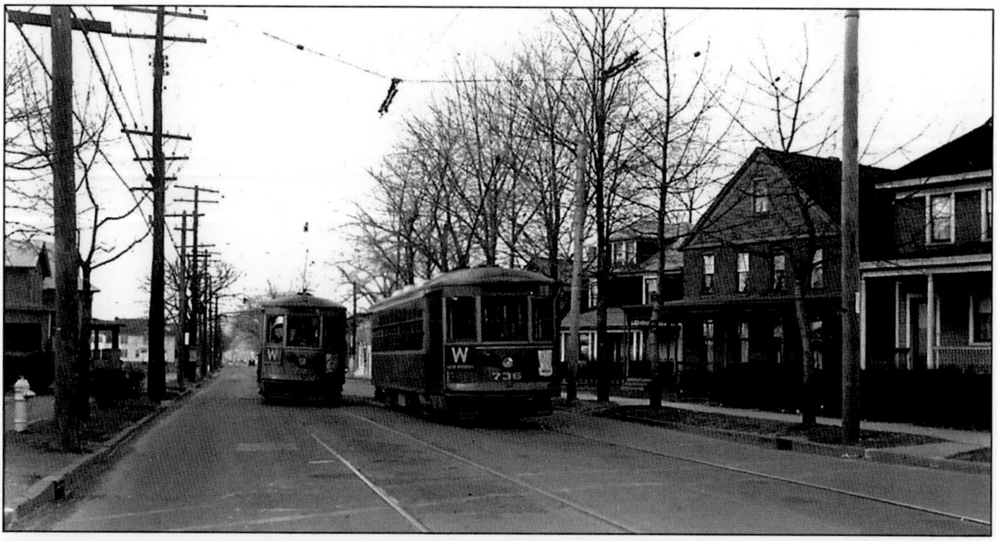

WYOMING AVENUE AT BALTIMORE STREET IN WEST PITTSTON, 1939. Wilkes-Barre Railway Corporation trolleys No. 734 and No. 736 travel on the West Pittston line on Christmas Eve 1939. Both trolleys were ordered from the J. G. Brill Company on May 3, 1926. The interior of the 730-series trolleys were well appointed with electric dome lights and leather seats.

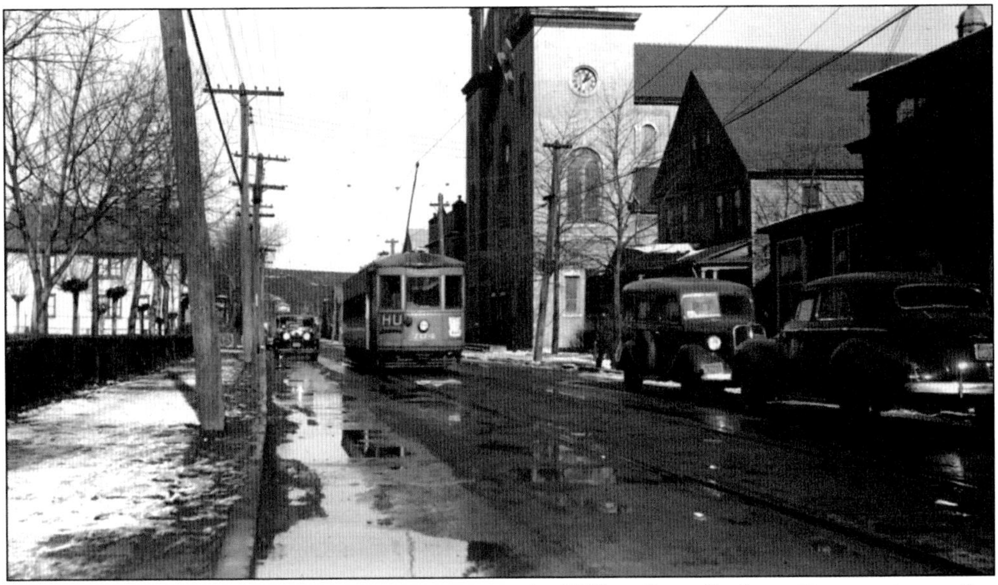

HUDSON ROAD AT CAREY STREET IN PLAINS, 1940. Wilkes-Barre Railway Corporation trolley No. 704 works on the Hudson line on Saturday, February 3, 1940. The Hudson line opened on August 9, 1909, and it went to Miner Street at School Street. The final day of trolley service on the Hudson line was Monday, September 15, 1941.

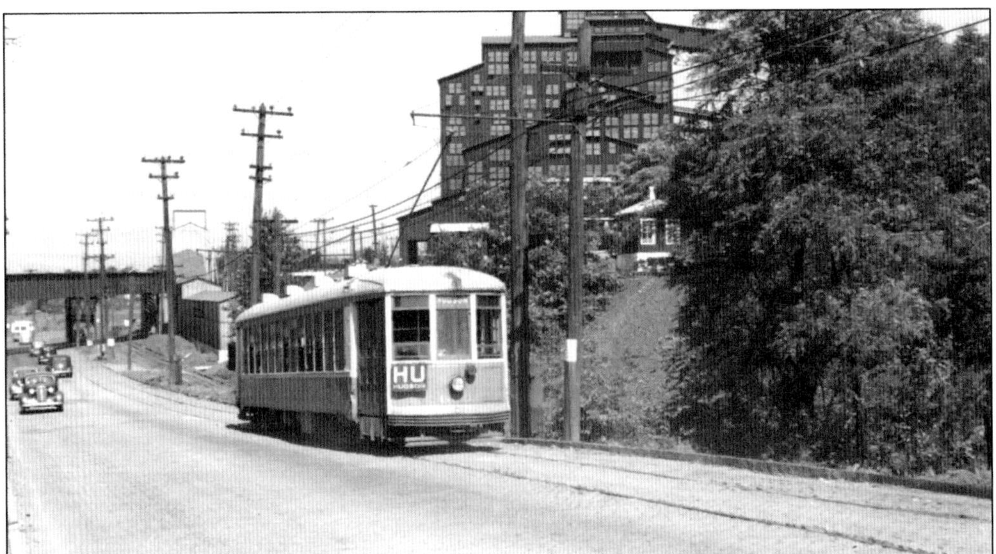

RIVER STREET IN PLAINS, 1941. Wilkes-Barre Railway Corporation trolley No. 600 is pictured on the Hudson line on Saturday, August 30, 1941. In the background is the Lehigh Valley Railroad overpass and the Prospect Colliery owned by the Lehigh Valley Coal Company. In 1893, an accident during an inspection tour of a mine owned by the Lehigh Valley Coal Company caused the deaths of Joseph Burrell, miner Jacob Gates, Col. Addison G. Mason, Robert S. Mercur, and William Wilson.

Four

West Side

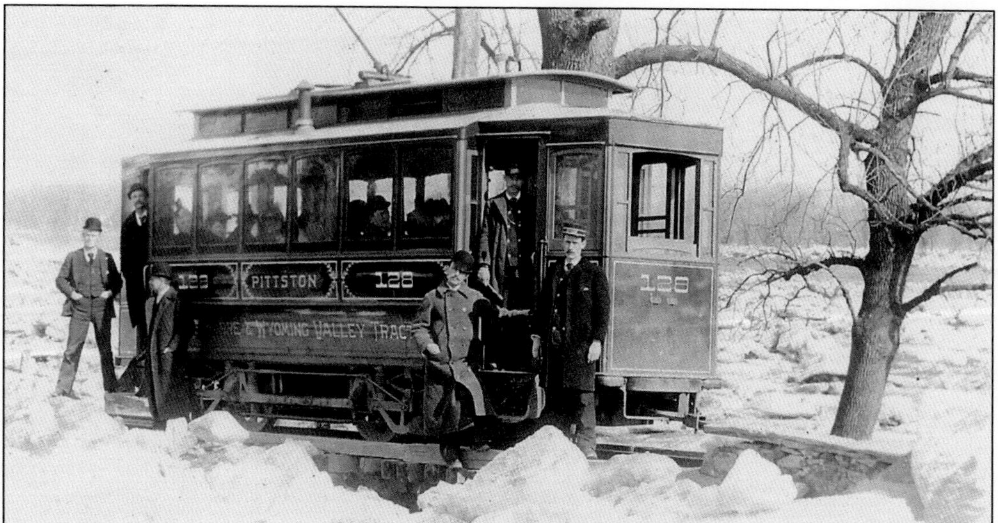

Wyoming Avenue at the Stone Bridge in Forty Fort, 1904. Wilkes-Barre and Wyoming Valley Traction Company trolley No. 128 was built by the St. Louis Streetcar Company in 1893. Due to the growing number of people living on Wyoming Avenue in Forty Fort, a new trolley line was established to the Stone Bridge in 1911. Trolley No. 220 was destroyed by a Delaware, Lackawanna and Western Railroad coal train on Wyoming Avenue near Union Street in Kingston on October 30, 1908.

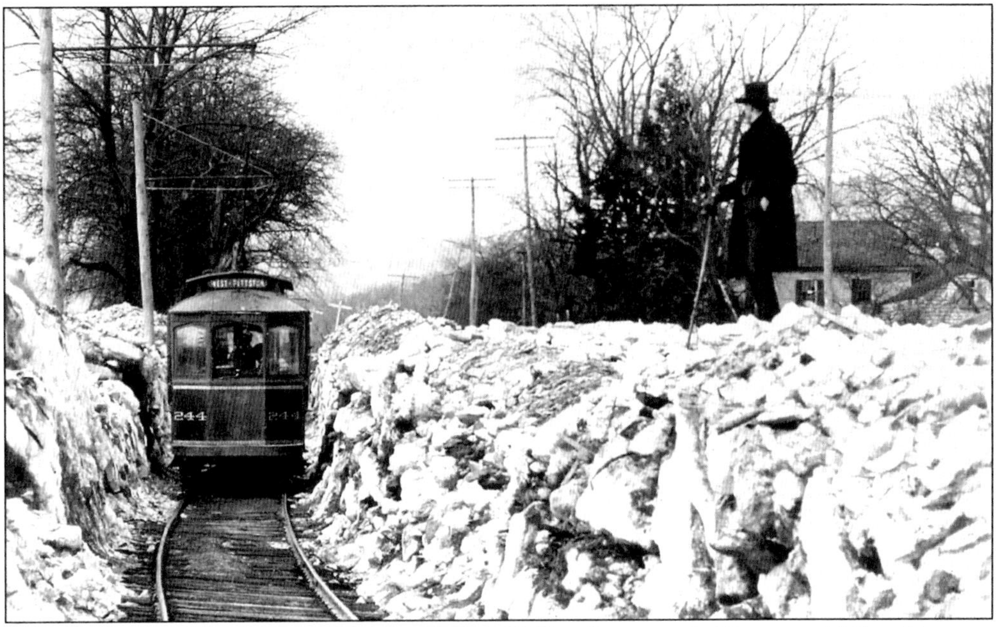

Wyoming Avenue in Forty Fort, 1904. Wilkes-Barre and Wyoming Valley Traction Company trolley No. 244 is travelling along the snowbanked West Pittston line near the present site of the Wyoming Valley Airport in March 1904. The trolley was ordered on October 3, 1895, and it was scrapped in 1928. Forty Fort, Fort Jenkins, and Fort Wintermute were three forts along the Susquehanna River that were destroyed during the Battle of Wyoming in 1778. (Misericordia University Archives.)

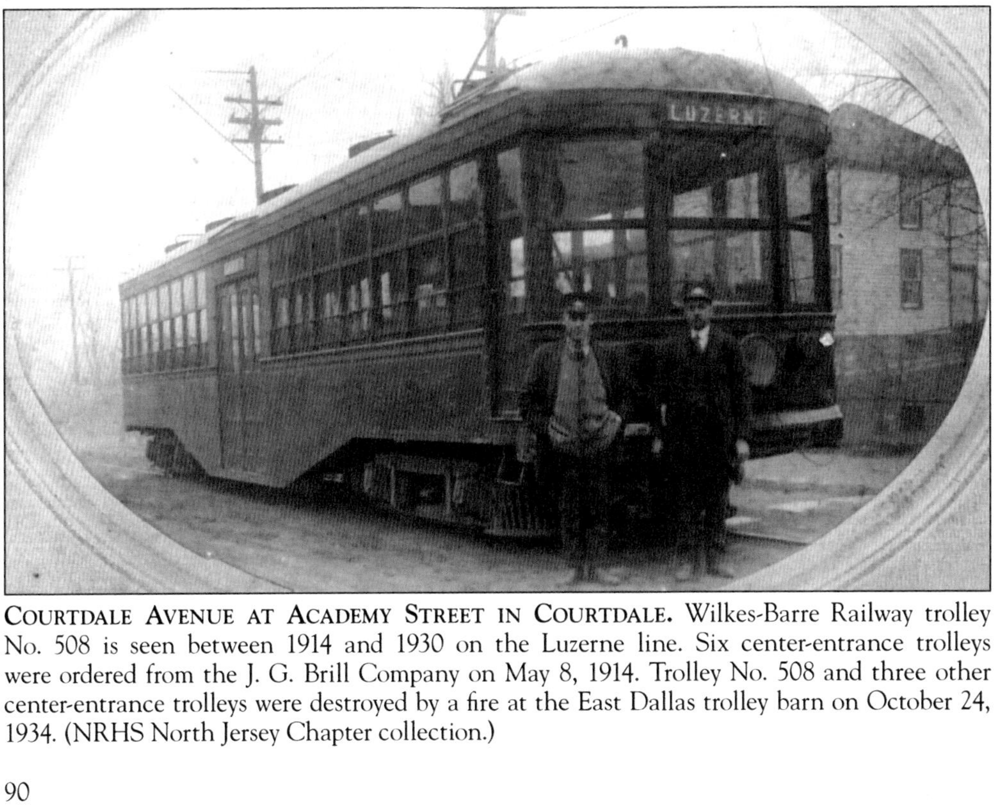

Courtdale Avenue at Academy Street in Courtdale. Wilkes-Barre Railway trolley No. 508 is seen between 1914 and 1930 on the Luzerne line. Six center-entrance trolleys were ordered from the J. G. Brill Company on May 8, 1914. Trolley No. 508 and three other center-entrance trolleys were destroyed by a fire at the East Dallas trolley barn on October 24, 1934. (NRHS North Jersey Chapter collection.)

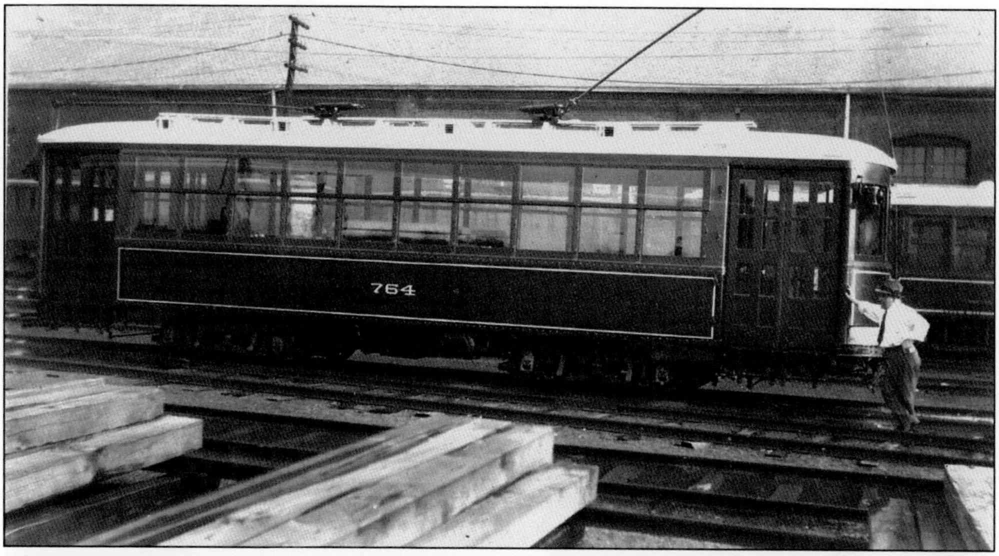

WESTMOOR YARD ON MARKET STREET IN KINGSTON, C. 1933. Wilkes-Barre Railway Corporation trolley No. 764 is pictured with Percy Miles leaning against the front of the trolley. The former Eastern Pennsylvania Railway trolley No. 313 was delivered to the Wilkes-Barre Railway in 1933. Trolley No. 764 was scrapped in August 1948.

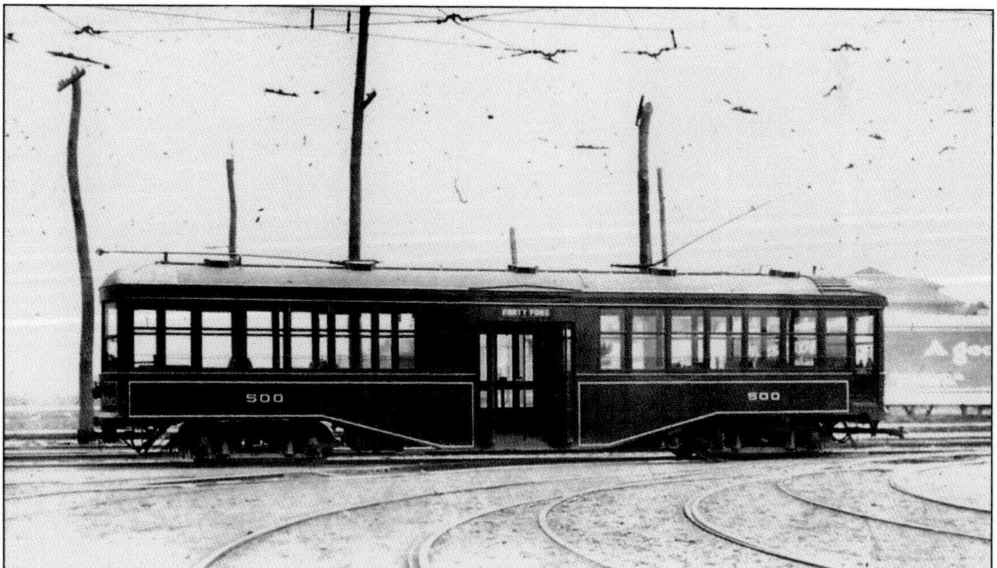

WESTMOOR YARD ON MARKET STREET IN KINGSTON. Wilkes-Barre Railway trolley No. 500 was built in 1914 for the Wilkes-Barre and Hanover Street Railway. The center-entrance trolleys were not a popular design and could not be converted to single-motorman operation and were retired early. Trolley No. 500 was destroyed by a fire at the East Dallas trolley barn in 1934. (NRHS North Jersey Chapter collection.)

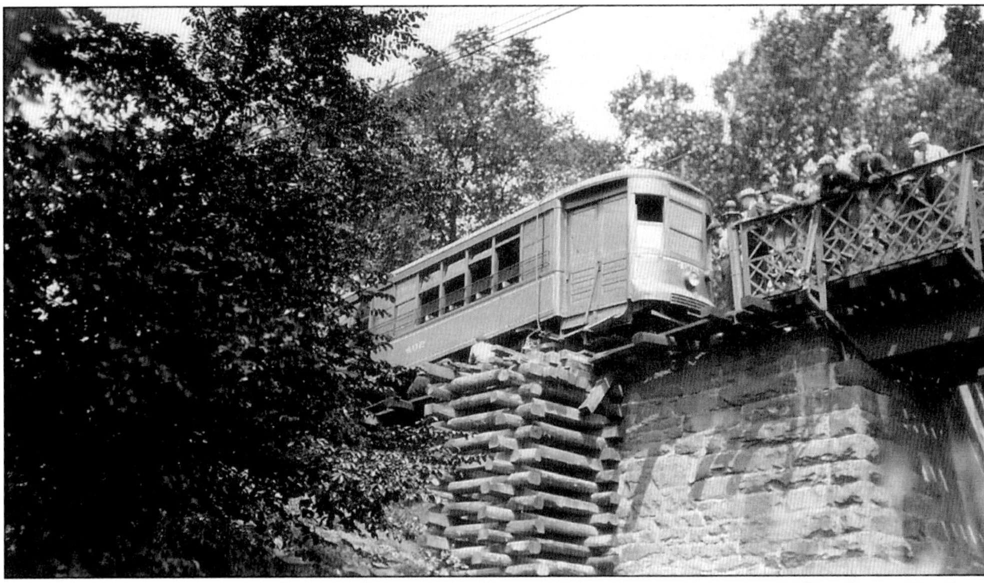

DERAILMENT NEAR THE MARKET STREET BRIDGE IN KINGSTON, 1923. Wilkes-Barre Railway trolley No. 402 derailed on the westerly approach to the Market Street Bridge in Kingston in August 1923. The trolley was ordered from the J. G. Brill Company for the Wilkes-Barre Railway on February 20, 1913, and it was delivered in August 1913. (NRHS North Jersey Chapter collection.)

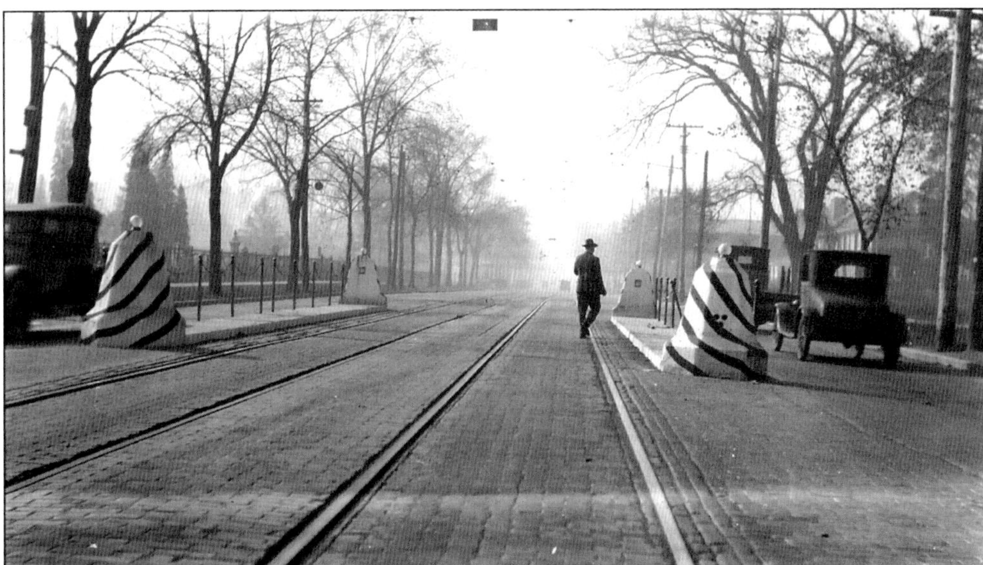

LOADING PLATFORM ON WYOMING AVENUE IN FORTY FORT, 1927. Seen here is the Wilkes-Barre Railway loading platform between Yates Street and Shoemaker Street on May 24, 1927. In 1924, Forty Fort line trolleys were converted to single-motorman operation. The trolley line was extended to Eighth Street in Wyoming on July 16, 1927. In 1930, the loading platform on Wyoming Avenue was removed. Forty Fort was named for the fort built by Connecticut colonists who first settled in the Wyoming Valley.

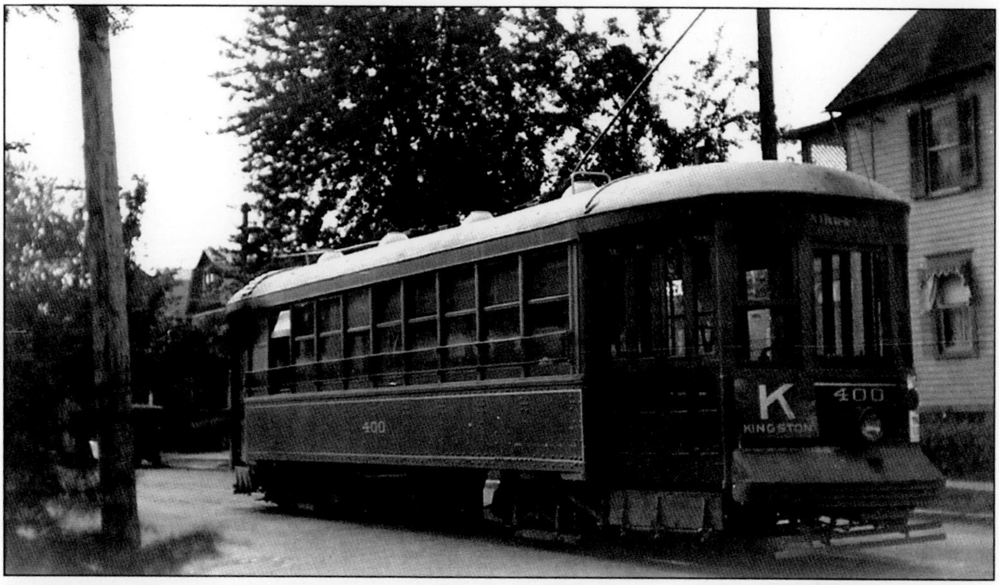

Schuyler Avenue at Division Street in Kingston, 1934. Wilkes-Barre Railway Corporation trolley No. 400 is at the end of the Kingston line. The 22-ton orange and yellow trolley was ordered from the J. G. Brill Company, and it was delivered in August 1913. Trolley No. 400 was retired in 1935 and stored in Kingston.

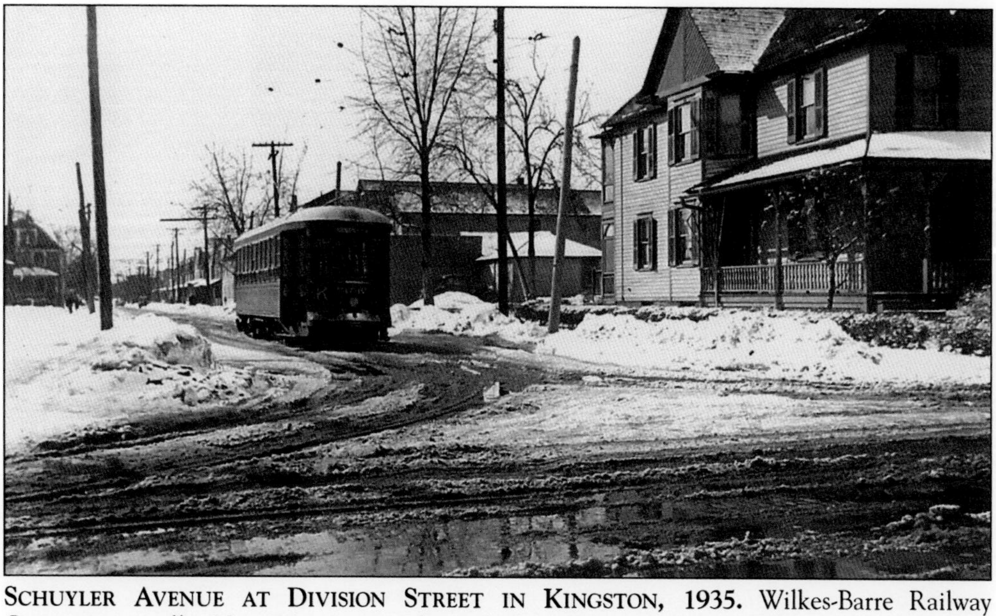

Schuyler Avenue at Division Street in Kingston, 1935. Wilkes-Barre Railway Corporation trolley No. 406 is seen at the end of the Kingston line on February 18, 1935. The trolley was delivered in 1913 to update the Kingston line. Trolley No. 406 was in service until the final day of the Kingston line on Saturday, June 19, 1937.

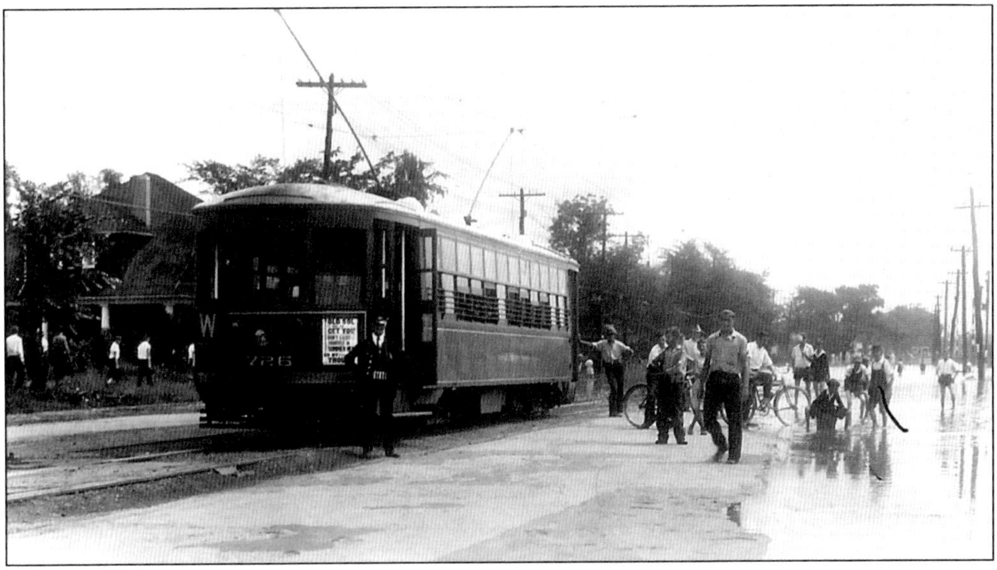

WYOMING AVENUE AT PEARL STREET IN FORTY FORT, 1935. Wilkes-Barre Railway Corporation trolley No. 726 is shown in July 1935. The 45-foot trolley was ordered from the J. G. Brill Company on May 3, 1926. It was in service until the final day of the Forty Fort line on Wednesday, January 24, 1940. The trolley was sold to the San Diego Electric Railway in 1942, and it was scrapped in 1947.

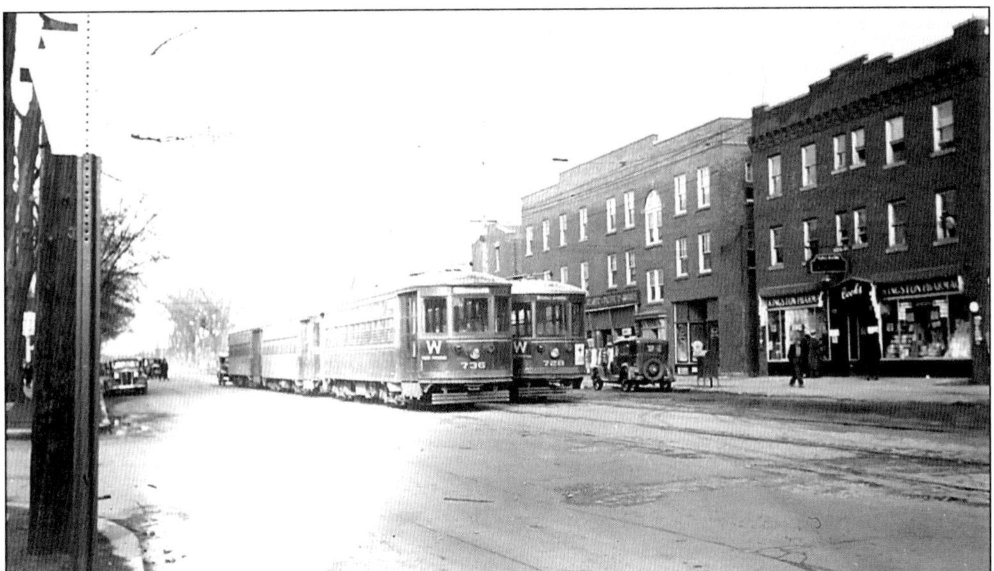

WYOMING AVENUE DURING THE 1936 FLOOD IN KINGSTON. Wilkes-Barre Railway Corporation trolleys including No. 736 and No. 728 are on the West Pittston line parked along Wyoming Avenue in Kingston on March 20, 1936. The 1936 flood crested above 33 feet on March 21. The flood cut trolley service to Ashley, Sugar Notch, West Pittston, and Wilkes-Barre.

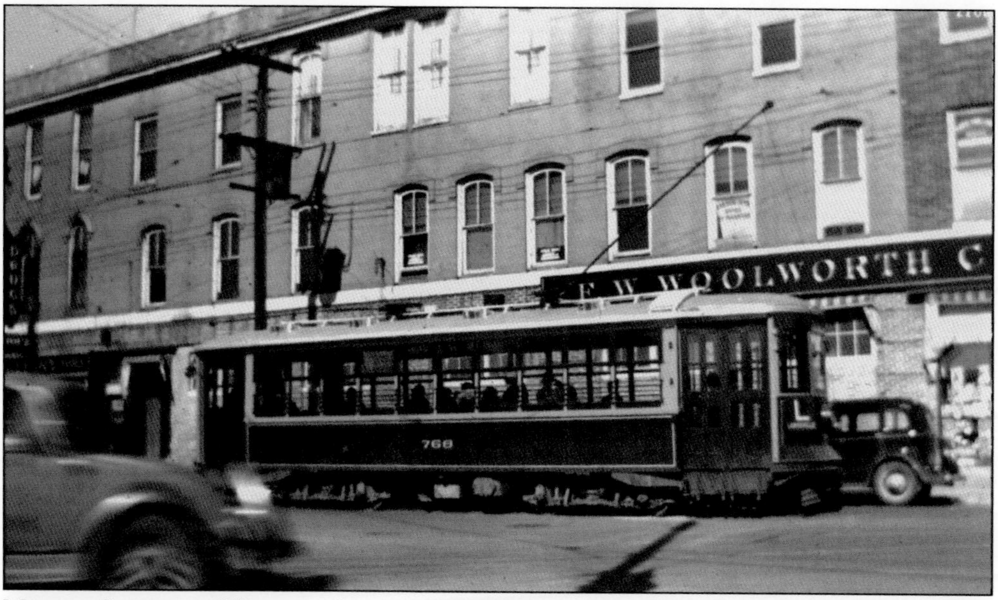

MARKET STREET AT WYOMING AVENUE IN KINGSTON, 1937. Wilkes-Barre Railway Corporation trolley No. 768 is seen on the Larksville line on Sunday, March 7, 1937. The trolley was ordered from the J. G. Brill Company for the Eastern Pennsylvania Railway in Pottsville, and it was purchased by the Wilkes-Barre Railway in 1933. Trolley No. 768 was scrapped at the Wood Street trolley yard by Shapiro scrap dealers of Wilkes-Barre in March 1950.

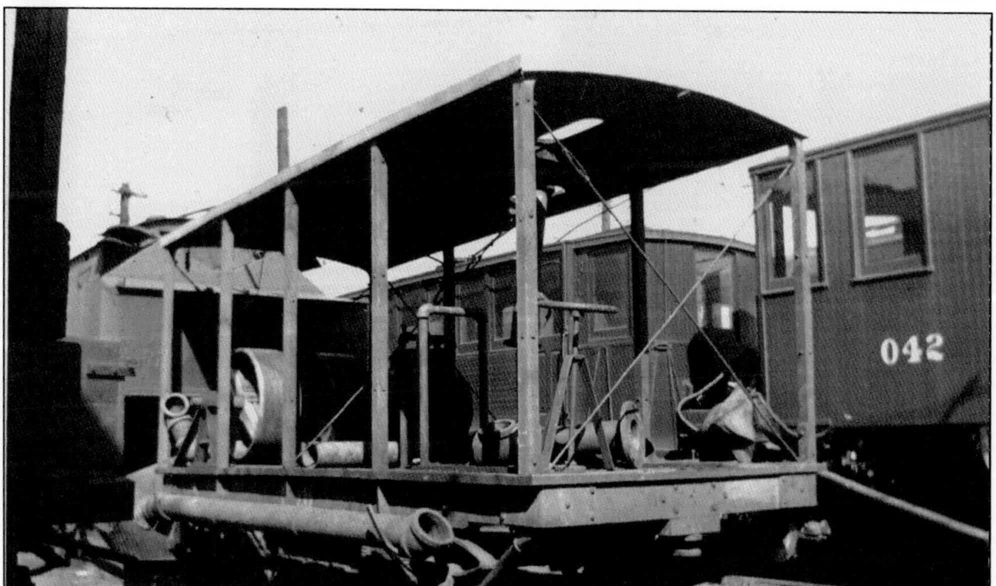

PUMP CAR IN STORAGE AT THE MARKET STREET YARD IN KINGSTON, 1937. Wilkes-Barre Railway Corporation trolley No. 056 is pictured on Saturday, April 24, 1937. The trolley's superstructure was scrapped in December 1937, and the undercarriage was scrapped in June 1940. During the flood in April 1940, the Westmoor trolley barn and the Market Street trolley yard were completely flooded.

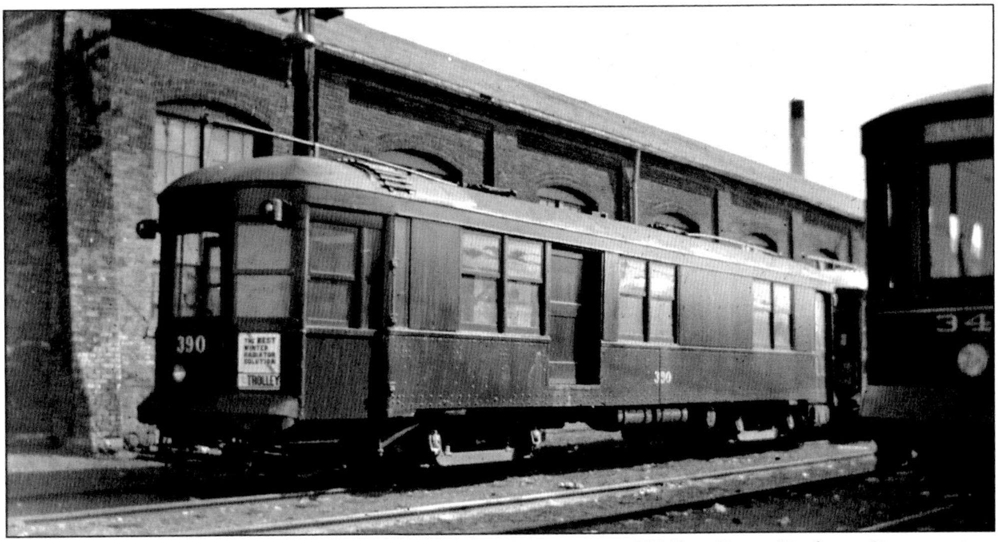

EMERGENCY TROLLEY AT THE MARKET STREET YARD, 1937. Wilkes-Barre Railway Corporation work trolley No. 390, shown on Saturday, April 24, 1937, was rebuilt from a passenger trolley in September 1936. The final day of trolley service on the Kingston line was Saturday, June 19, 1937. Work trolley No. 390 was taken to the Louis Cohen and Son scrap yard, and it was scrapped in 1950.

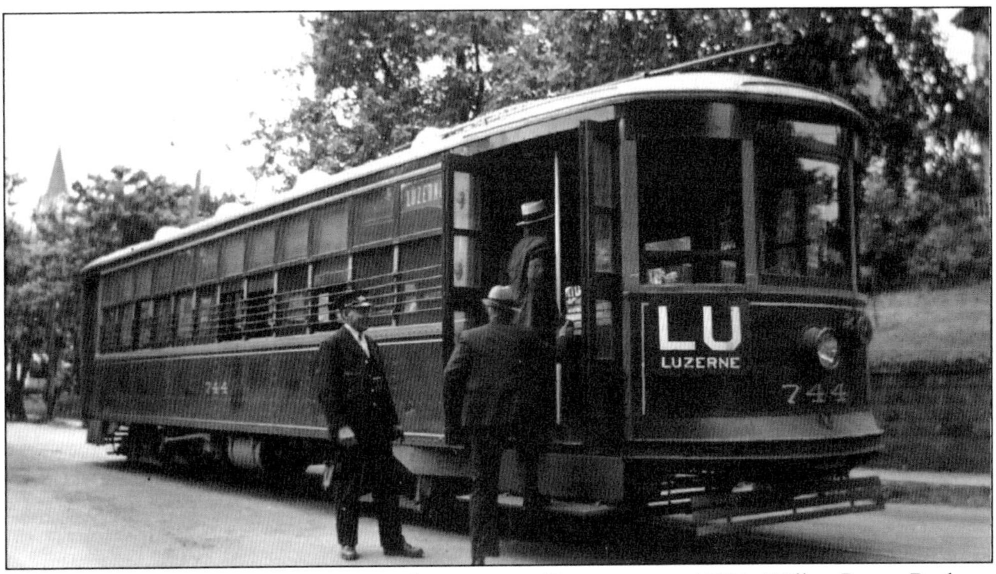

COURTDALE AVENUE AT ACADEMY STREET IN COURTDALE, 1937. Wilkes-Barre Railway Corporation trolley No. 744 travels on the Luzerne line on Sunday, June 13, 1937. Standing at the trolley door is motorman George Youngblood. It was ordered from the J. G. Brill Company in 1926. In 1940, the trolley was sold to the Virginia Electric and Power Company in Norfolk.

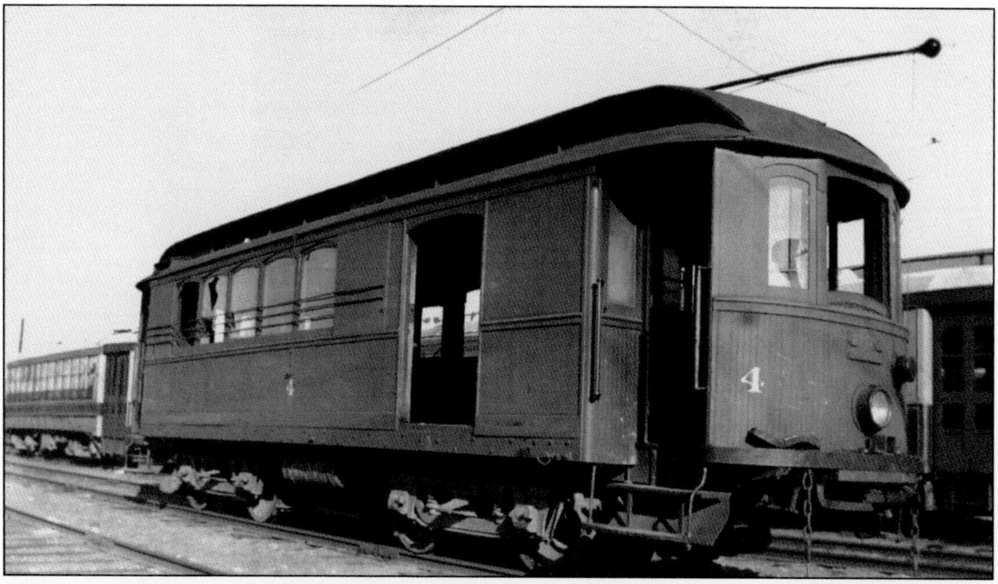

Westmoor Yard on Market Street in Kingston, 1937. Wilkes-Barre Railway Corporation work trolley No. 4, pictured on Sunday, September 12, 1937, was ordered from Jackson and Sharp as a passenger trolley on October 8, 1896, for the Wilkes-Barre, Dallas and Harvey's Lake Railway. The work trolley was powered by four General Electric motors, and it was used on the Harvey's Lake line until 1931. It was scrapped in 1941. (William Johns collection.)

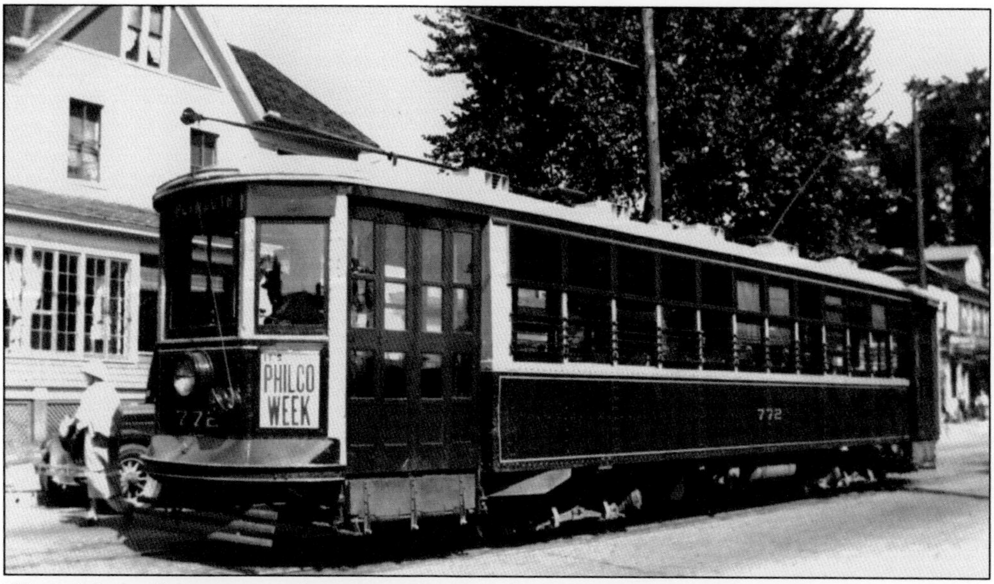

West Main Street at Academy Street In Plymouth, 1937. Wilkes-Barre Railway Corporation trolley No. 772, seen on Thursday, September 23, 1937, was ordered from the J. G. Brill Company for the Eastern Pennsylvania Railway. In 1933, the trolley was purchased by the Wilkes-Barre Railway. Trolley No. 772 was scrapped in November 1949.

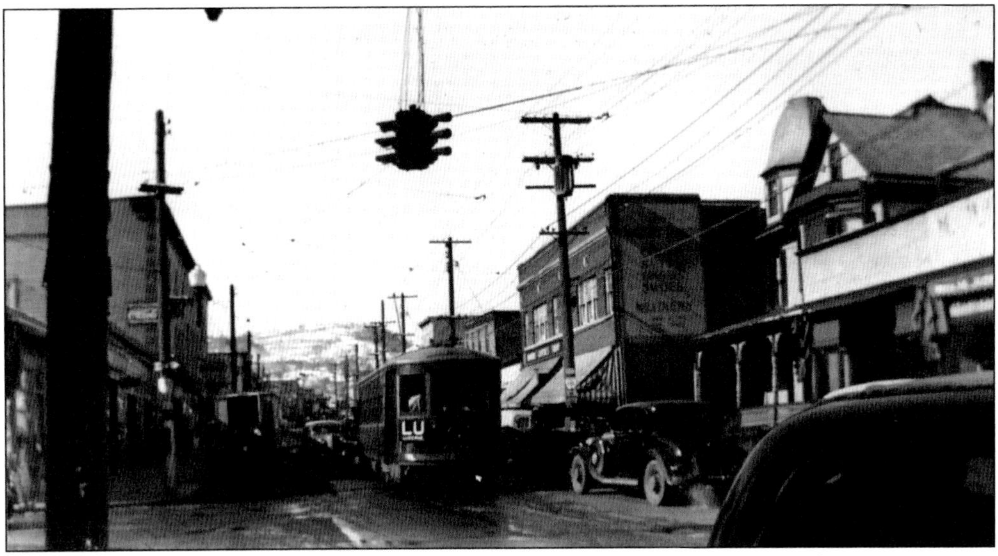

MAIN AVENUE AT BUCKINGHAM AVENUE IN LUZERNE, 1938. Wilkes-Barre Railway Corporation trolley No. 726 is pictured on the Luzerne line on Tuesday, February 1, 1938. The 45-foot trolley was ordered from the J. G. Brill Company on May 3, 1926. The interiors of most trolleys in the Wyoming Valley were equipped with rattan seats, but trolley No. 726 was upholstered in leather. In 1942, the trolley was sold, and it was sent to San Diego, California.

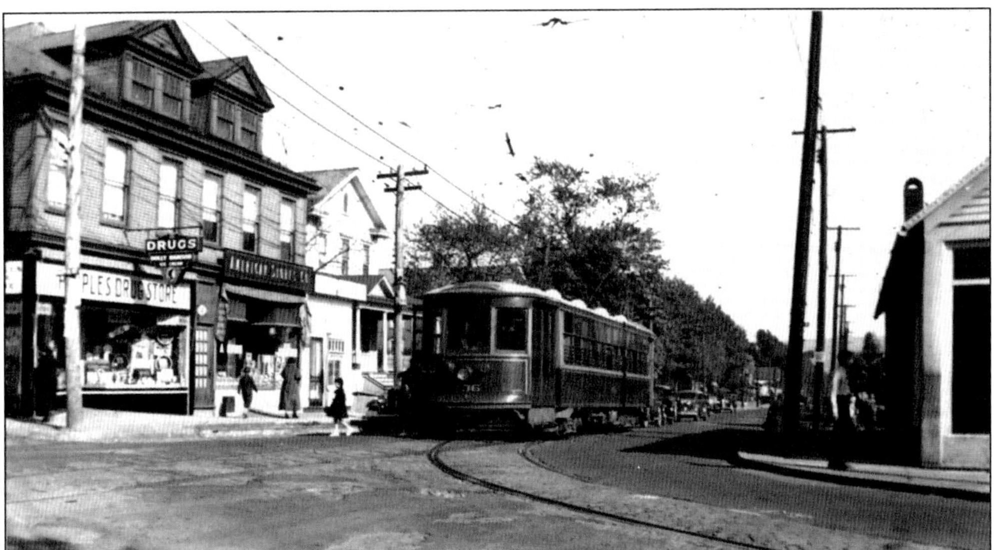

BENNETT STREET IN LUZERNE, 1938. Wilkes-Barre Railway Corporation trolley No. 736 was captured at Chapel Street and Main Avenue on the Luzerne line on Sunday, May 1, 1938. The trolley was sold to the San Diego Electric Railway in 1942, and it was scrapped in 1947. The first passenger trolley on the Luzerne line went to Main Street and Bennett Street on July 26, 1890.

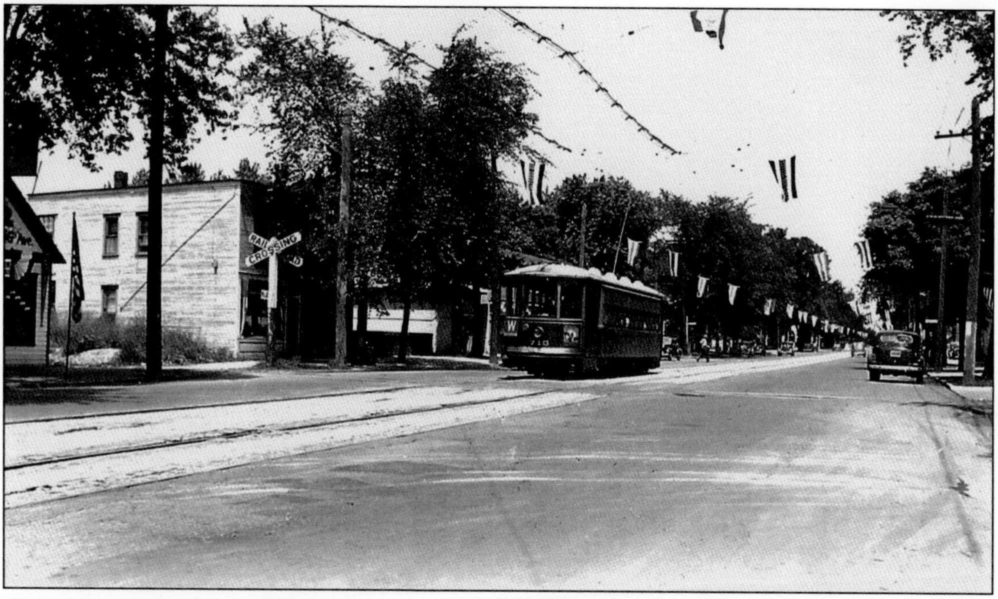

WYOMING AVENUE AT RAILROAD CROSSING IN KINGSTON, 1938. Wilkes-Barre Railway Corporation trolley No. 710 is seen at the Delaware, Lackawanna and Western Railroad crossing in Kingston between Vaughn Street and John Street on the West Pittston line on Tuesday, June 14, 1938. The 45-foot trolley was powered by four Westinghouse motors, and it was sold to the San Diego Electric Railway in 1942.

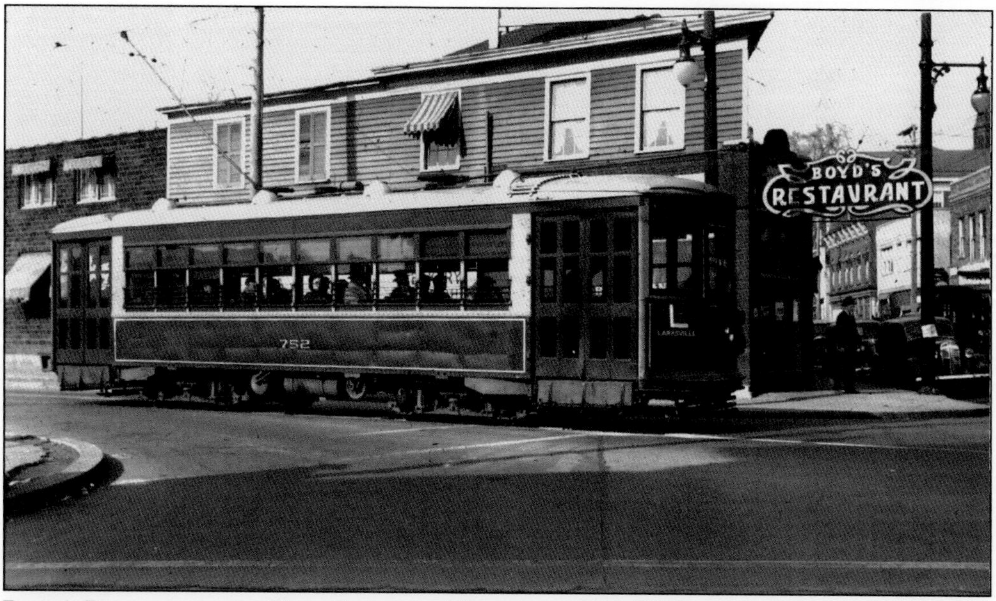

BOYD'S RESTAURANT ON MAIN STREET IN KINGSTON, 1938. Wilkes-Barre Railway Corporation trolley No. 752 is on the Larksville line on Wednesday, November 2, 1938. The trolley was ordered from the J. G. Brill Company in 1925 for the Coast Cities Railway. The former Coast Cities Railway trolley No. 401 was purchased by the Wilkes-Barre Railway in 1932. Trolley No. 752 was scrapped in 1948.

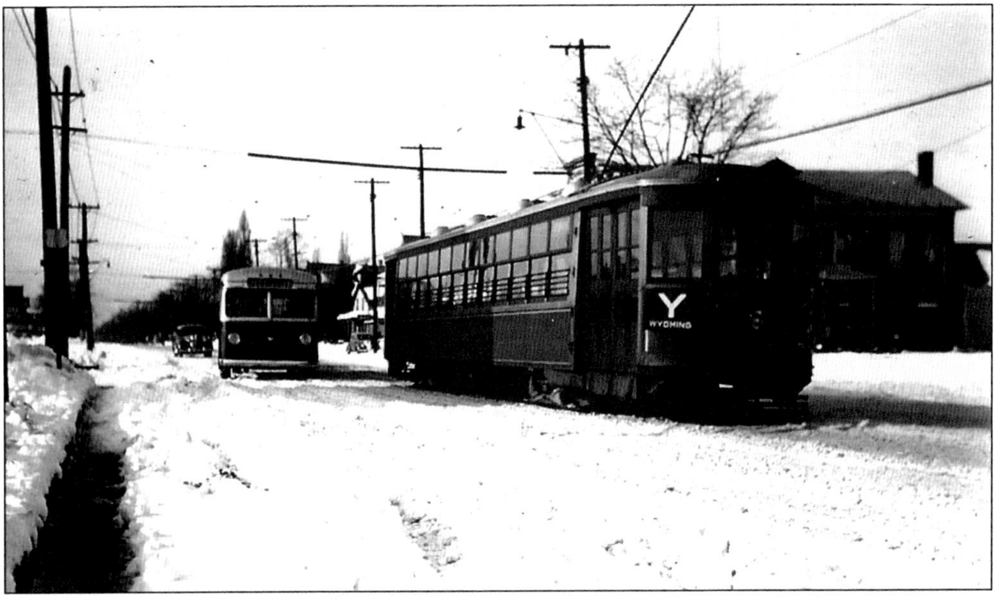

WYOMING AVENUE AT SECOND STREET IN WYOMING, 1938. Wilkes-Barre Railway Corporation trolley No. 704 on the Wyoming line and a bus on the Pittston line are pictured on Sunday, November 21, 1938. The Wyoming line was blocked beyond this point by a Thanksgiving Day snowstorm on November 24. Service on the Wyoming and West Pittston trolley lines was discontinued early because of the decline in passenger business along Wyoming Avenue.

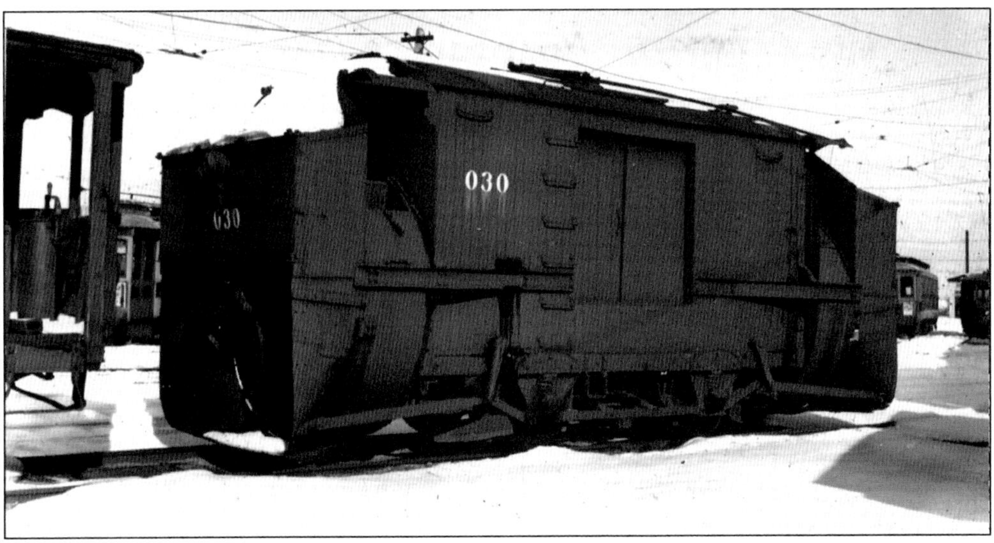

WESTMOOR YARD ON MARKET STREET IN KINGSTON, 1938. Wilkes-Barre Railway Corporation rotary snowplow No. 030 is seen on November 29, 1938. The trolley was built for the Wilkes-Barre, Dallas and Harvey's Lake Railway in November 1899 by the Peckham Motor Truck and Wheel Company in Kingston, New York. In 1941, the trolley was sold to the Copper Cliffs Suburban Electric Railway in Sulbury, Ontario.

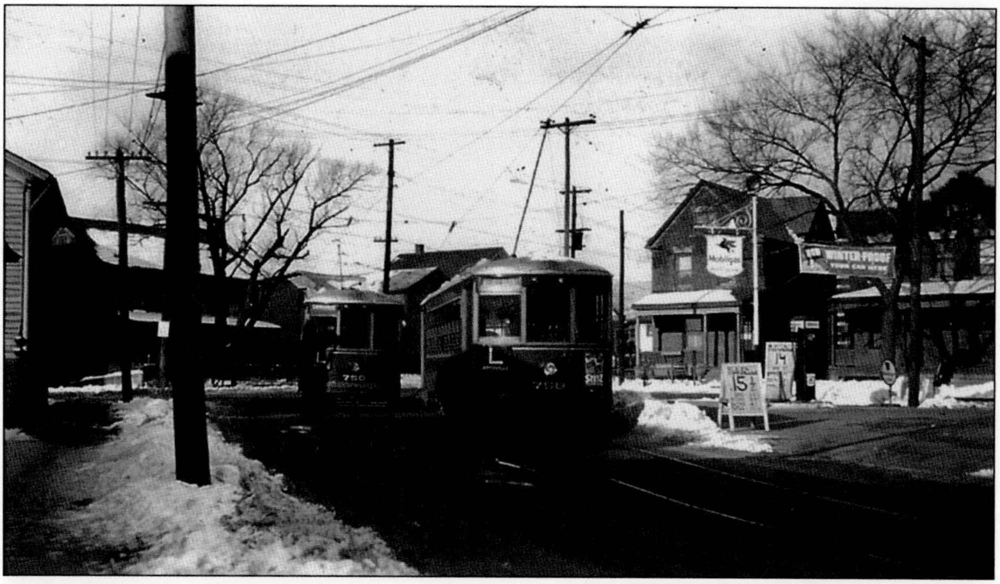

Main Street at Maple Avenue in Kingston, 1938. Wilkes-Barre Railway Corporation trolleys No. 750 and No. 758 travel on the Larksville line on Tuesday, November 29, 1938. The switch was removed in 1944. The 40-foot trolleys were ordered from the J. G. Brill Company on October 28, 1924, for the Coast Cities Railway of Asbury Park, New Jersey. Both trolleys were sold to the Wilkes-Barre Railway in 1932 and were in service until 1947.

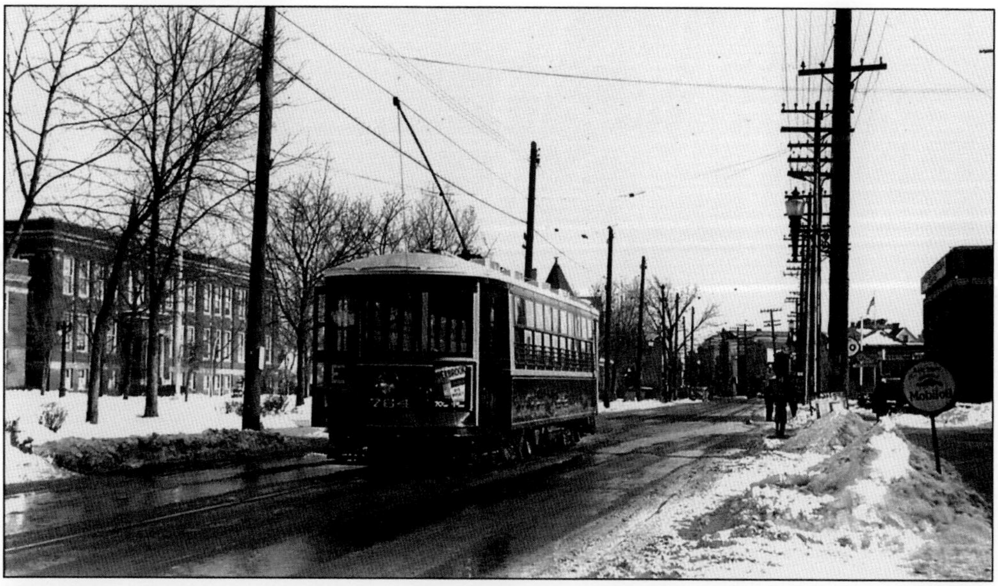

West Main Street in Plymouth, 1938. Wilkes-Barre Railway Corporation trolley No. 764 is seen between Wadham Street and Academy Street at the Parrish Switch in Plymouth at the end of the Edwardsville line on Tuesday, November 29, 1938. The high school can be seen on the left. The final day of service on the Plymouth line was Sunday, August 31, 1947. The trolley was scrapped in August 1948.

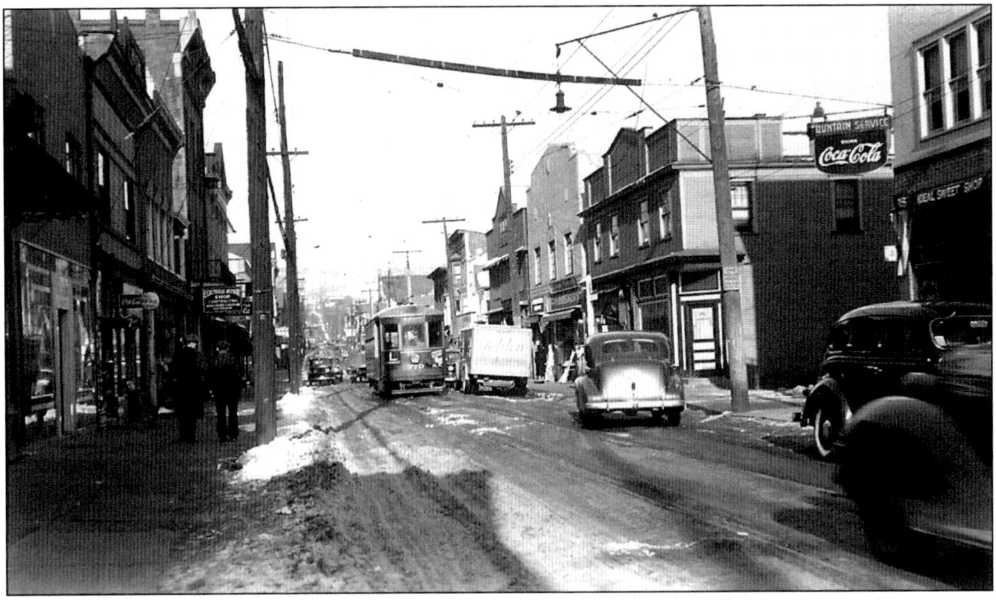

MAIN STREET AT CENTER STREET IN EDWARDSVILLE, 1938. Wilkes-Barre Railway Corporation trolley No. 770 is on the Larksville line on Tuesday, November 29, 1938. The trolley was ordered from the J. G. Brill Company on April 2, 1924, for the Eastern Pennsylvania Railway in Pottsville. The trolley was purchased by the Wilkes-Barre Railway in 1933.

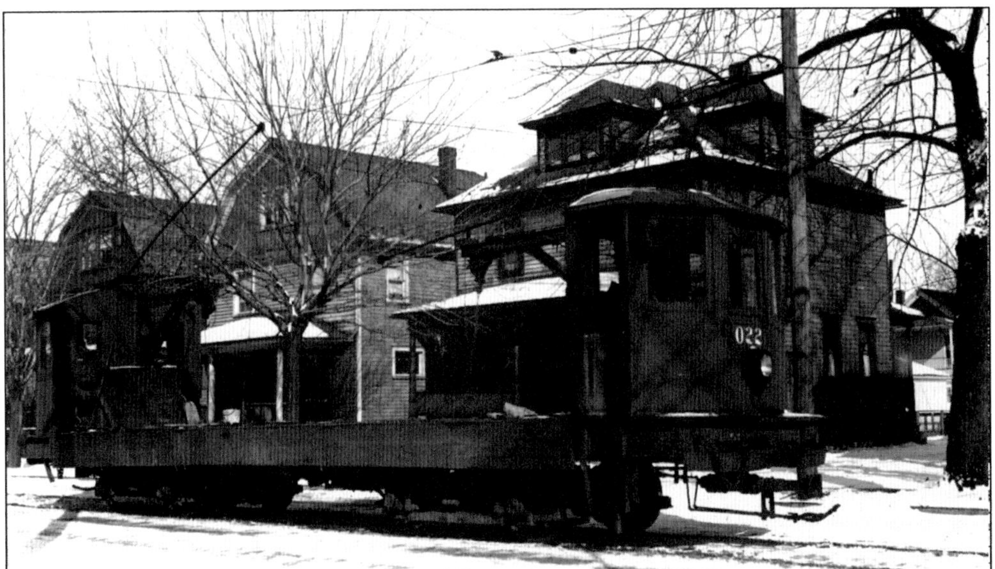

DIVISION STREET NEAR CHESTNUT AVENUE IN KINGSTON, 1939. Wilkes-Barre Railway Corporation work trolley No. 022 is seen on Wednesday, February 1, 1939. The steel crane trolley was ordered from the J. G. Brill Company. It was scrapped at the Louis Cohen and Son scrap yard in March 1952. The final day of trolley service on the Kingston line was Saturday, June 19, 1937.

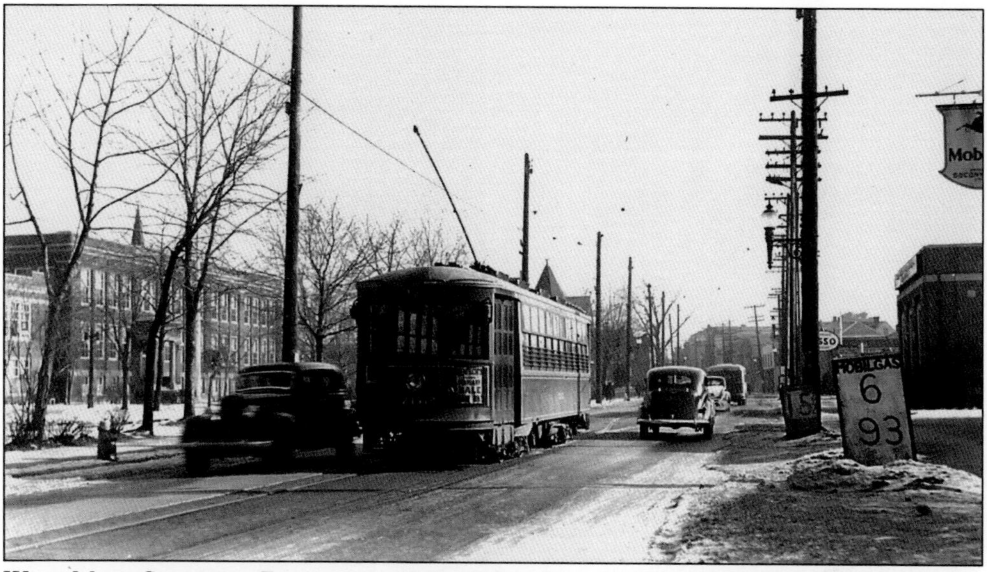

West Main Street in Plymouth, 1939. Wilkes-Barre Railway Corporation trolley No. 762 is seen between Wadham Street and Academy Street at the Parrish switch on Sunday, February 5, 1939. The high school is on the left, and the Larksville line trolleys operated to this point on Sunday afternoons only. The final day of service on the Larksville line was Tuesday, August 10, 1948. Trolley No. 762 was scrapped in 1950.

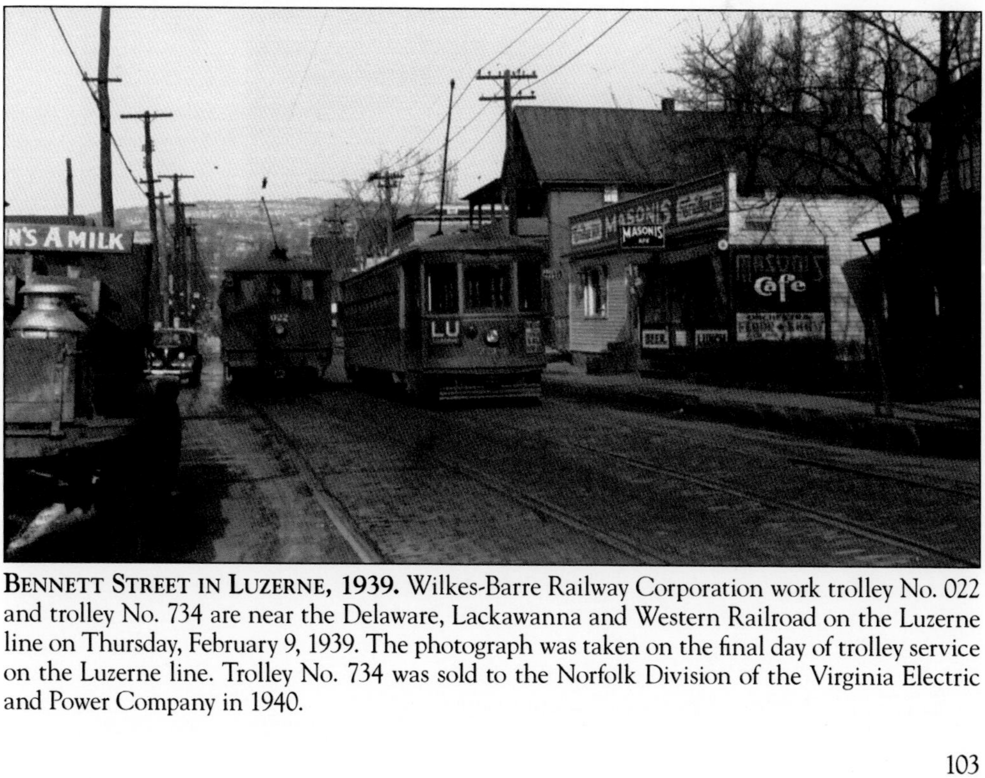

Bennett Street in Luzerne, 1939. Wilkes-Barre Railway Corporation work trolley No. 022 and trolley No. 734 are near the Delaware, Lackawanna and Western Railroad on the Luzerne line on Thursday, February 9, 1939. The photograph was taken on the final day of trolley service on the Luzerne line. Trolley No. 734 was sold to the Norfolk Division of the Virginia Electric and Power Company in 1940.

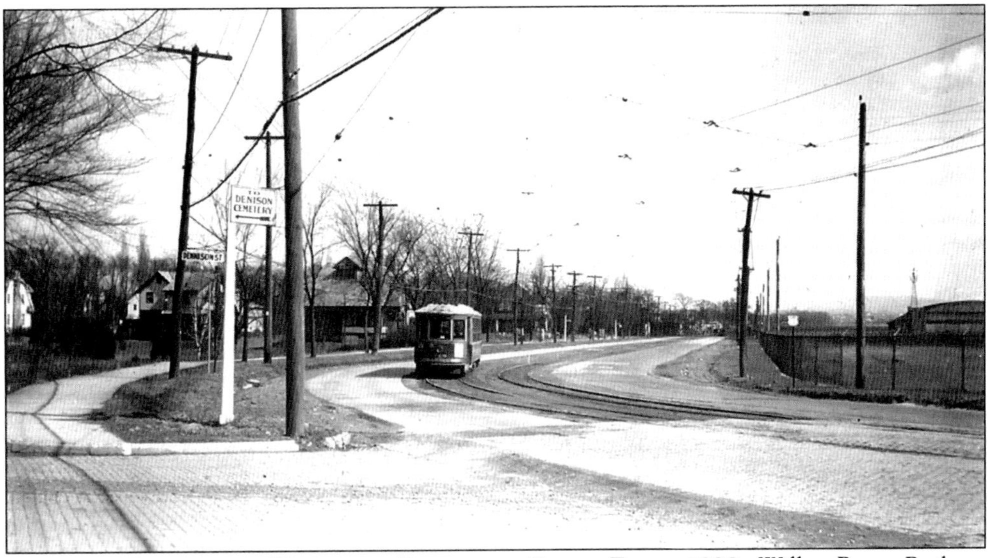

WYOMING AVENUE AT DENNISON STREET IN FORTY FORT, 1939. Wilkes-Barre Railway Corporation trolley No. 718 is on the West Pittston line on Friday, March 10, 1939. The photograph was taken with the Wyoming Valley Airport on the right and the Dennison house and family cemetery on the left. The final day of trolley service on the West Pittston line was Christmas Day 1939. In 1942, the 45-foot trolley was sent to San Diego, California.

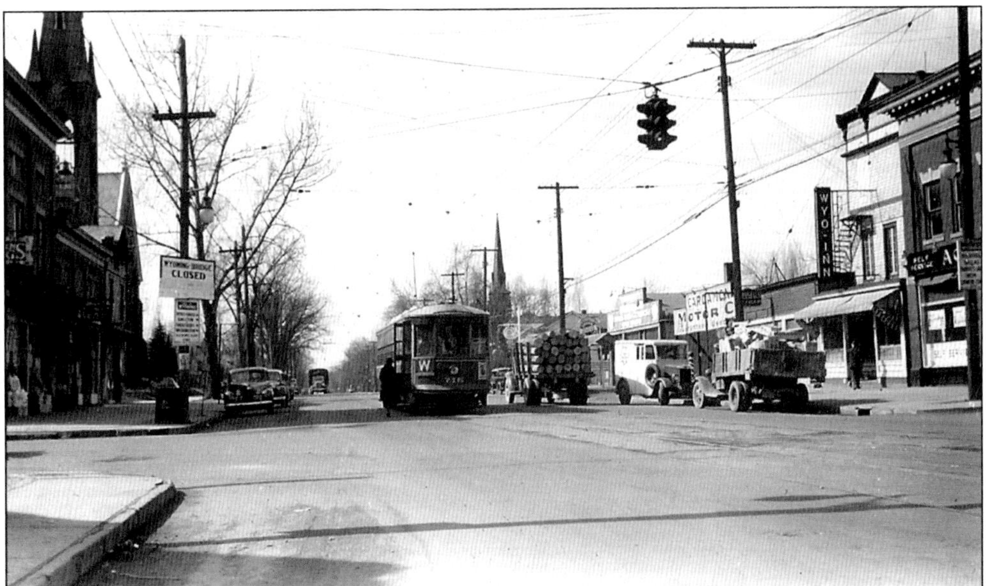

WYOMING AVENUE AT EIGHTH STREET IN WYOMING, 1939. Wilkes-Barre Railway Corporation trolley No. 716 travels on the West Pittston line on Friday, March 10, 1939. The trolley was ordered on March 22, 1923, and it was sold to the San Diego Electric Railway in 1942. Approximately 300 Americans were killed and more than 1,000 homes were burned by British loyalists and Iroquois raiders during the Battle of Wyoming on July 3, 1778.

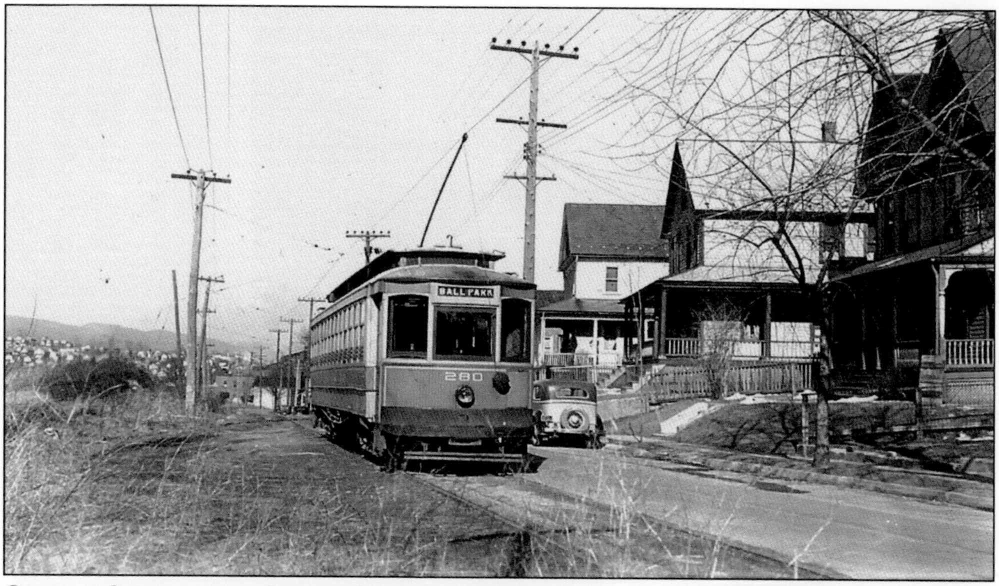

Church Street near Cherry Street in Edwardsville, 1939. The Wilkes-Barre Railway Corporation trolley No. 280 special chartered by the NRHS is seen on the Edwardsville line on Sunday, March 19, 1939. The 19-ton trolley was ordered from the J. G. Brill Company on December 12, 1903. Trolley No. 280 was delivered with General Electric motors, but it was reequipped with Westinghouse motors before it was retired in 1939.

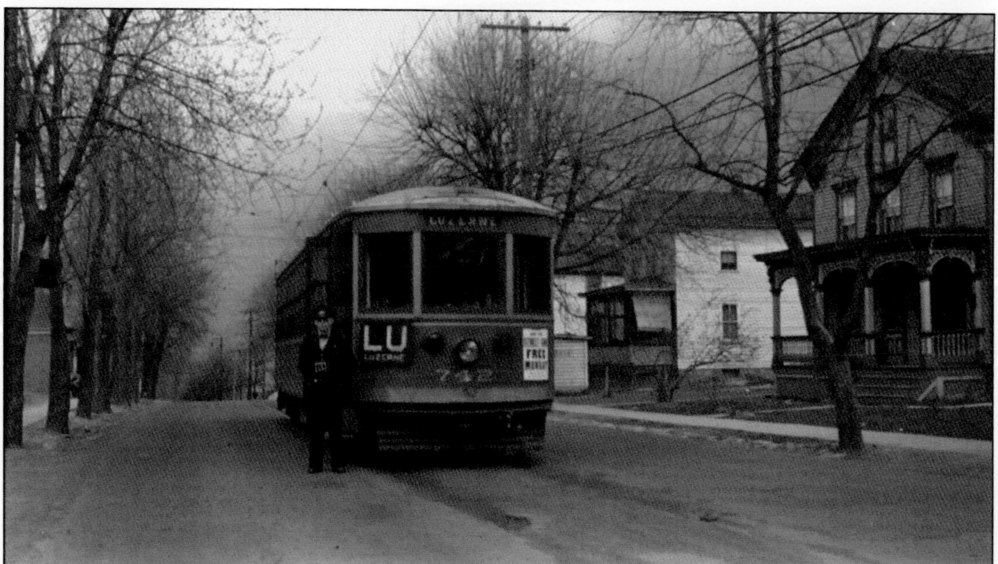

Courtdale Avenue at Academy Street in Courtdale, 1939. Wilkes-Barre Railway Corporation trolley No. 742 is at the end of the Luzerne line on Sunday, April 30, 1939. The photograph was taken on the final day of trolley service on the Luzerne line. In front of the trolley is motorman Charles Gelsleichter. The 45-foot trolley was sold to the Virginia Electric and Power Company.

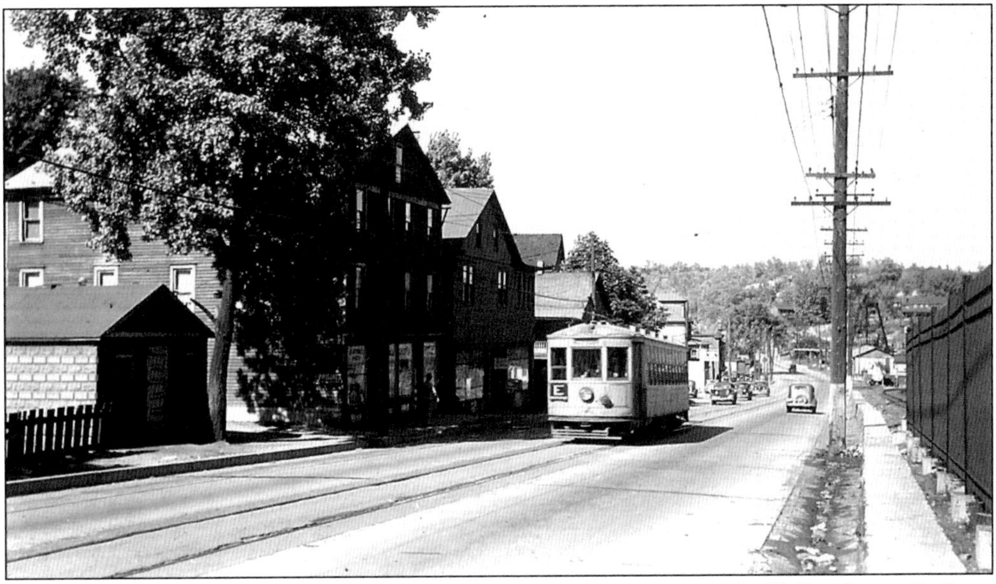

EAST MAIN STREET AT CHESTNUT STREET IN LARKSVILLE, 1939. Wilkes-Barre Railway Corporation trolley No. 782 works on the Edwardsville line on Thursday, May 18, 1939. Trolley business was in direct competition with automobiles, but after mining operations declined, the Edwardsville trolley line was reduced in service and only went as far as the Parrish switch. The final day of trolley service on the Edwardsville line was August 28, 1948.

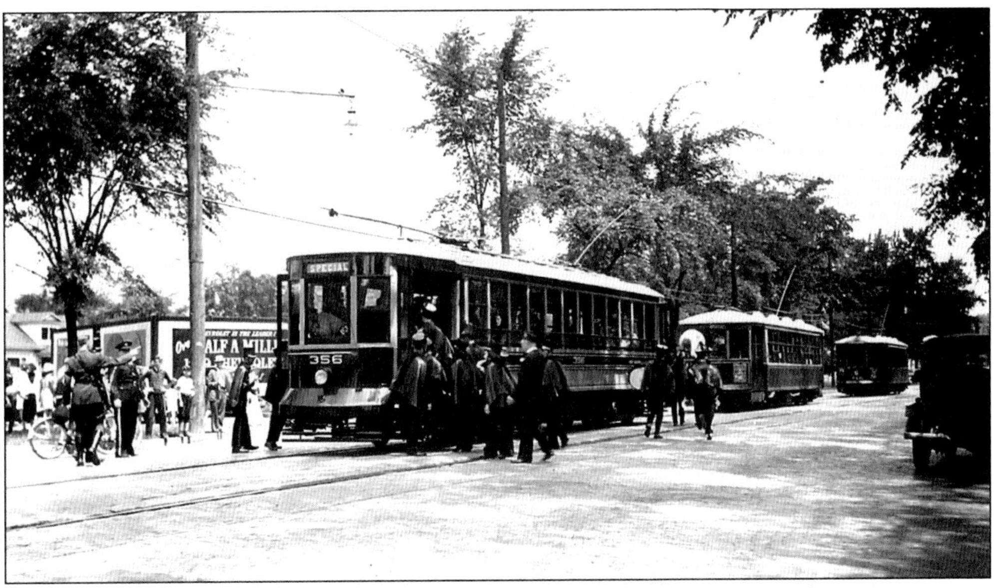

TROLLEYS ON WYOMING AVENUE IN FORTY FORT, 1939. Wilkes-Barre Railway Corporation trolleys No. 356 special, No. 710, and No. 716 are seen at Shoemaker Street on the Forty Fort line on Tuesday, May 30, 1939. Trolley No. 356 special was chartered by the Edwardsville High School. The final day of trolley service on the Forty Fort line was Wednesday, January 24, 1940, and the trolleys were replaced by trackless trolleys the following day.

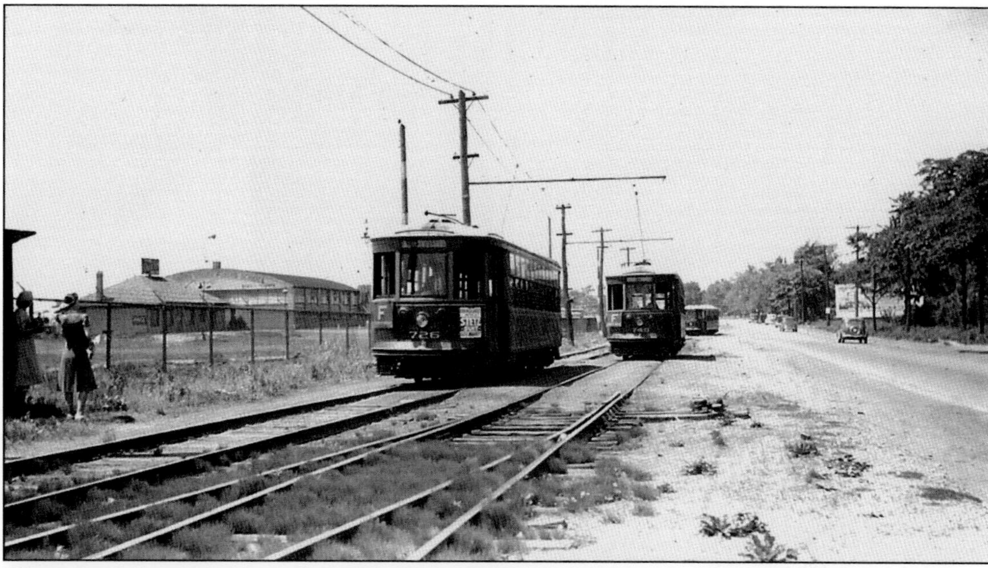

Wyoming Avenue at the Wyoming Valley Airport, 1939. Wilkes-Barre Railway Corporation trolleys No. 726, No. 740, and No. 702 are pictured on the Forty Fort line on Tuesday, May 30, 1939. In the background is the Wyoming Valley Flying School that was operated by Russell Smith. He owned an airplane hangar on Harvey's Lake and offered flight instruction and charter flights. The Smith Flying Service on Harvey's Lake later became the Harvey's Lake Yacht Club.

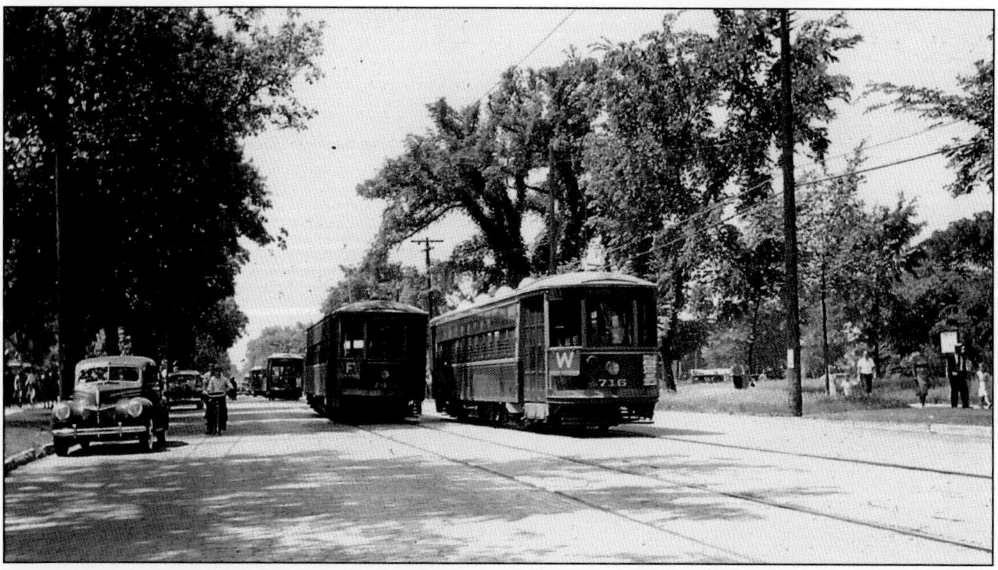

Trolleys at the Memorial Day Parade in Forty Fort, 1939. Wilkes-Barre Railway Corporation trolleys No. 702, No. 716, No. 726, No. 740, and No. 744 are seen on Wyoming Avenue at Shoemaker Street on Tuesday, May 30, 1939. The trolleys were on the Forty Fort and West Pittston lines. The crowd from the parade is on the left. The West Pittston line was abandoned on Christmas Day 1939, and the Forty Fort line was discontinued less than a month later in 1940.

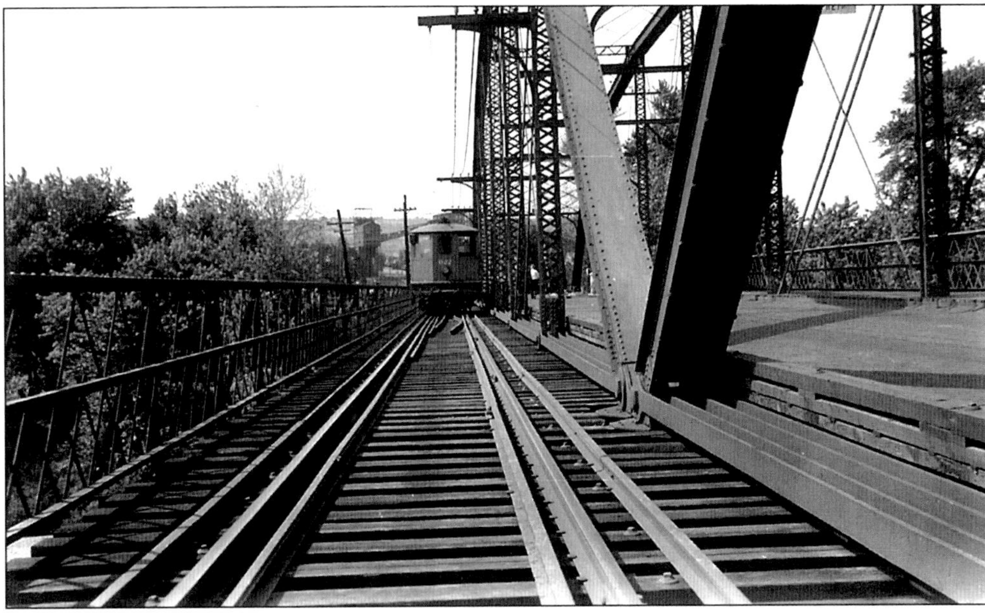

CAREY AVENUE BRIDGE LOOKING SOUTH TOWARD PLYMOUTH, 1939. Wilkes-Barre Railway Corporation work trolley No. 022 travels on the Plymouth line on Friday, June 16, 1939. The Carey Avenue Bridge was replaced, and the new two-lane concrete bridge was dedicated to the 1st Battalion of the 109th Field Artillery of the Pennsylvania National Guard.

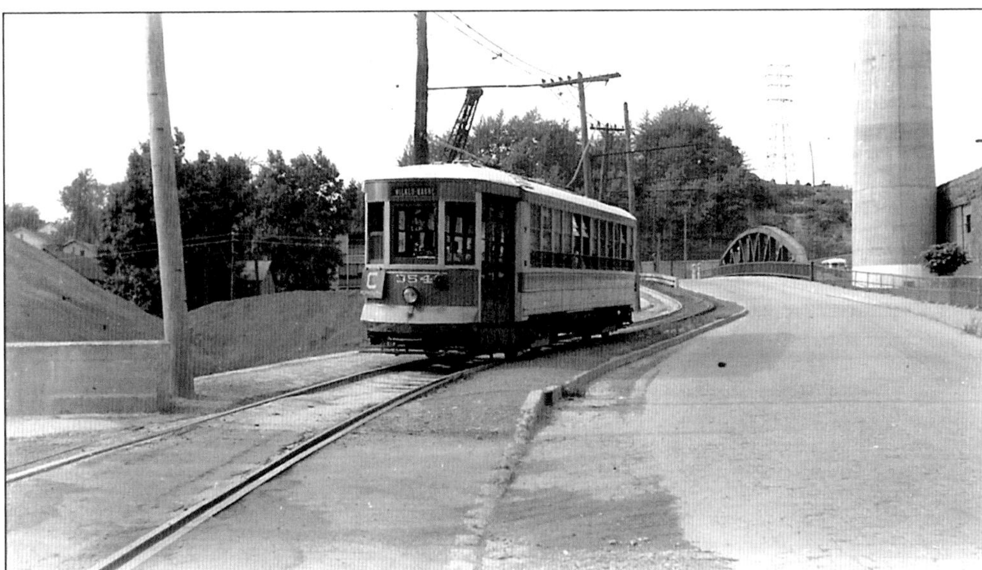

BRIDGE STREET AT BEADE STREET IN PLYMOUTH, 1939. Wilkes-Barre Railway Corporation trolley No. 354 works on the Plymouth line on Saturday, August 26, 1939. In 1911, the trolley was delivered to the Wilkes-Barre Railway. In April 1942, it was sold to the Sudbury–Copper Cliff Suburban Electric Railway in Ontario, Canada, where it became trolley No. 38.

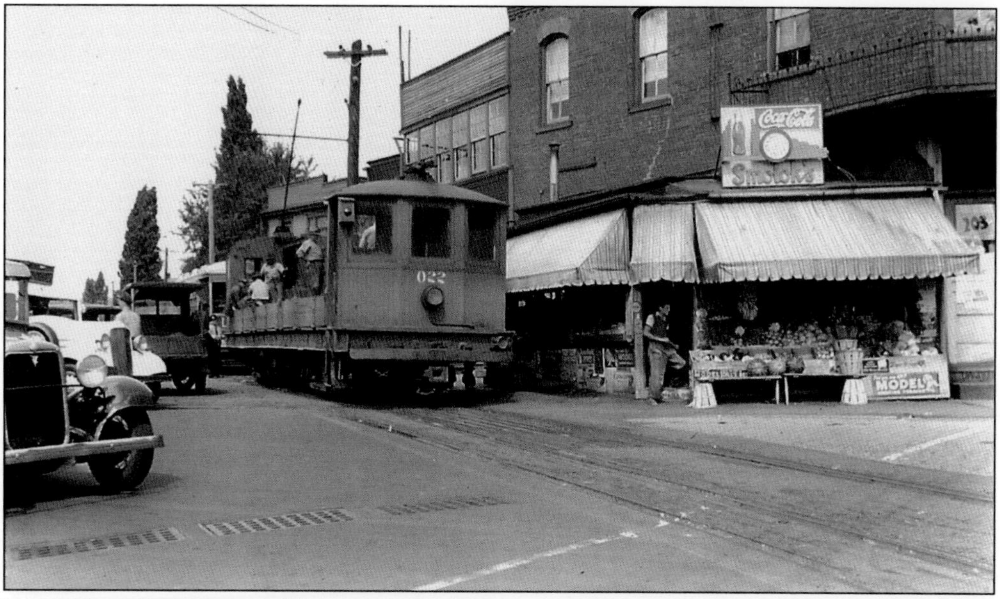

East Main Street and West Cherry Street in Plymouth, 1939. Wilkes-Barre Railway Corporation work trolley No. 022 is pictured on the Larksville line on Tuesday, September 5, 1939. The photograph was taken next to Smolok's grocery store in Plymouth. The 43-foot steel crane trolley was equipped with General Electric motors. The trolleys on the Larksville line were converted to single-motorman operation on July 25, 1928.

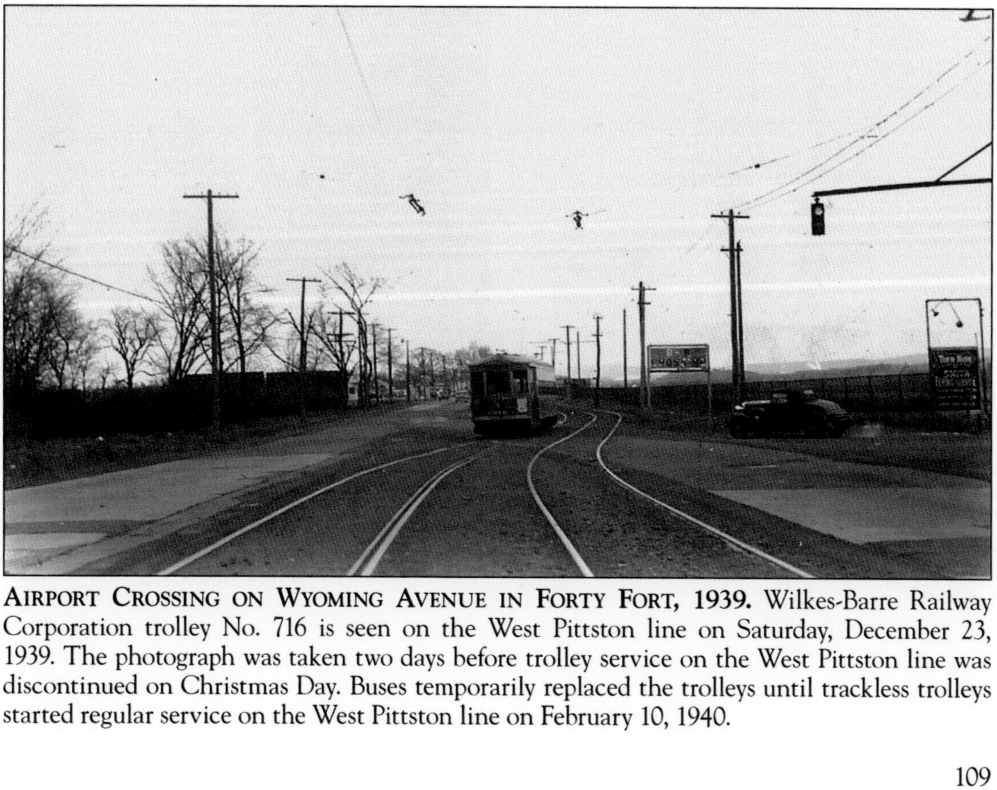

Airport Crossing on Wyoming Avenue in Forty Fort, 1939. Wilkes-Barre Railway Corporation trolley No. 716 is seen on the West Pittston line on Saturday, December 23, 1939. The photograph was taken two days before trolley service on the West Pittston line was discontinued on Christmas Day. Buses temporarily replaced the trolleys until trackless trolleys started regular service on the West Pittston line on February 10, 1940.

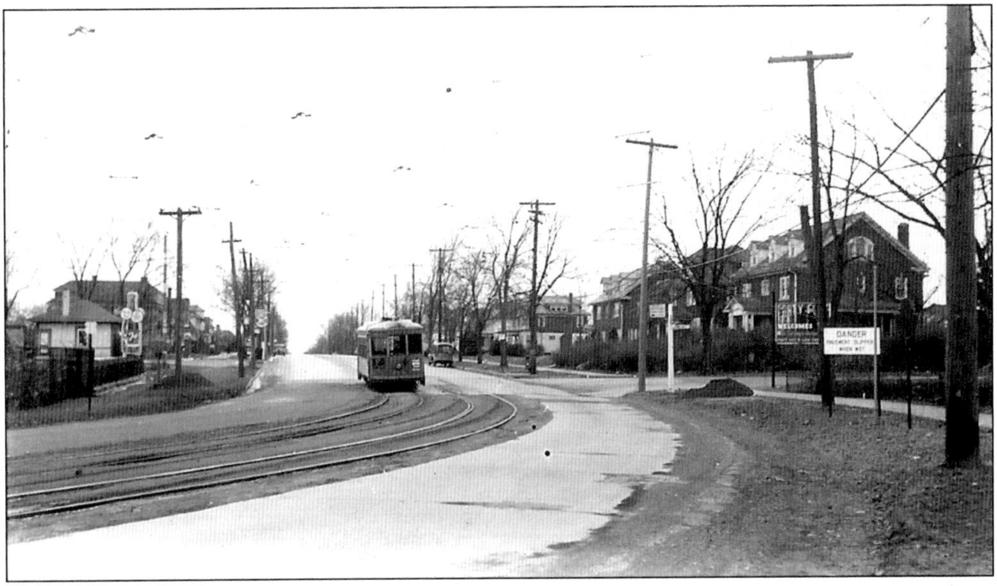

Wyoming Avenue at Dennison Street in Forty Fort, 1939. Wilkes-Barre Railway Corporation trolley No. 754 is on the Forty Fort line on Saturday, December 23, 1939. The Dennison house is on the right across from the Wyoming Valley Airport. The final day of service on the Forty Fort line on Wyoming Avenue was Wednesday, January 24, 1940, and trackless trolleys replaced trolley service the following day.

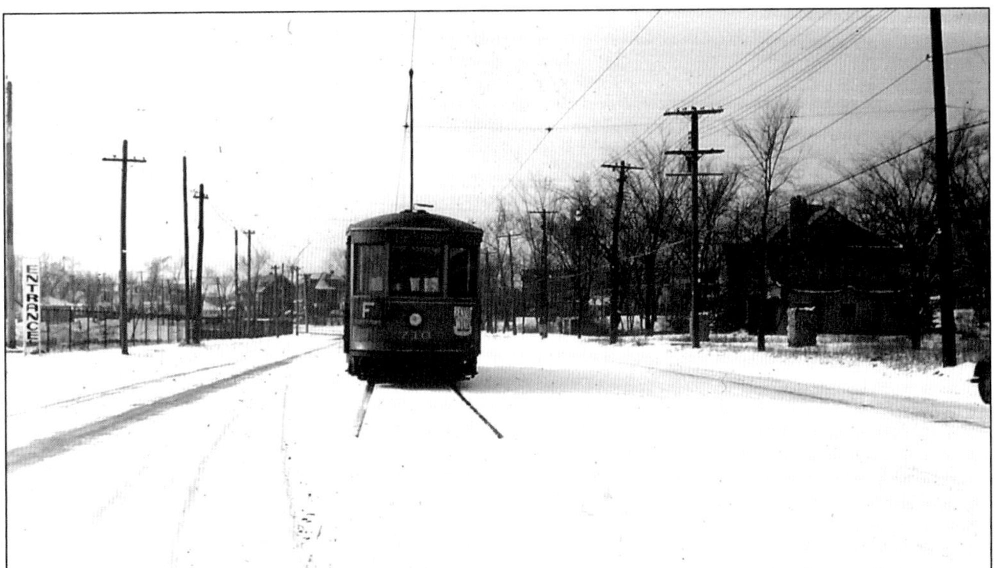

Wyoming Avenue at Terrace Street in Forty Fort, 1939. Wilkes-Barre Railway Corporation trolley No. 710 is pictured on Saturday, December 30, 1939. This was the end of the Forty Fort line following the abandonment of the West Pittston line on Christmas Day. Track was laid for the trolley line over Fort Jenkins Bridge from October to December 1925.

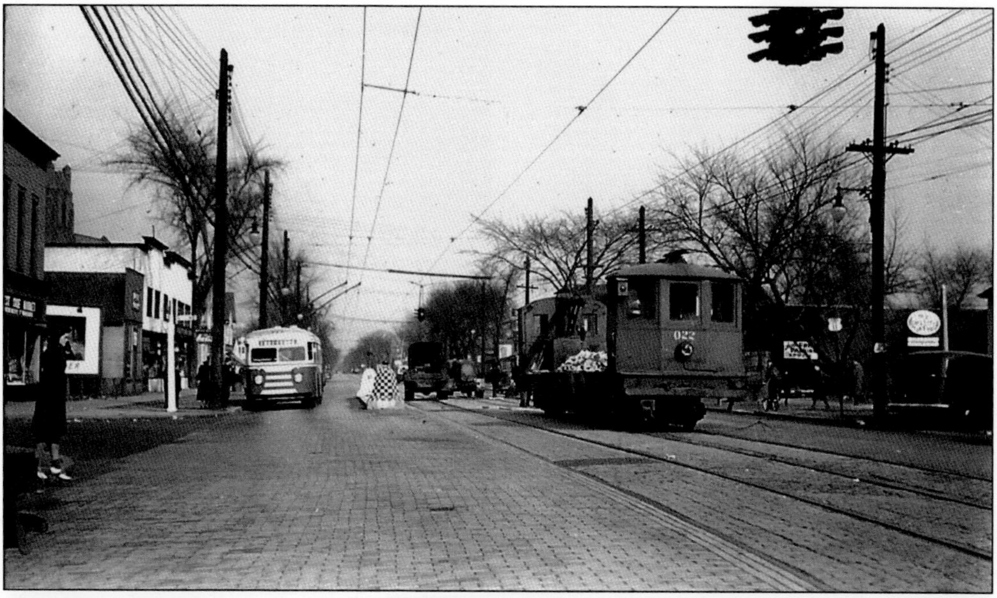

Wyoming Avenue at Slocum Street in Forty Fort, 1940. Wilkes-Barre Railway Corporation work trolley No. 022 is seen on the Forty Fort line on Tuesday, January 30, 1940. Workmen are removing safety zones and loading platforms from the recently abandoned Forty Fort line. The final day of regular trolley service on the Forty Fort line was Wednesday, January 24, 1940.

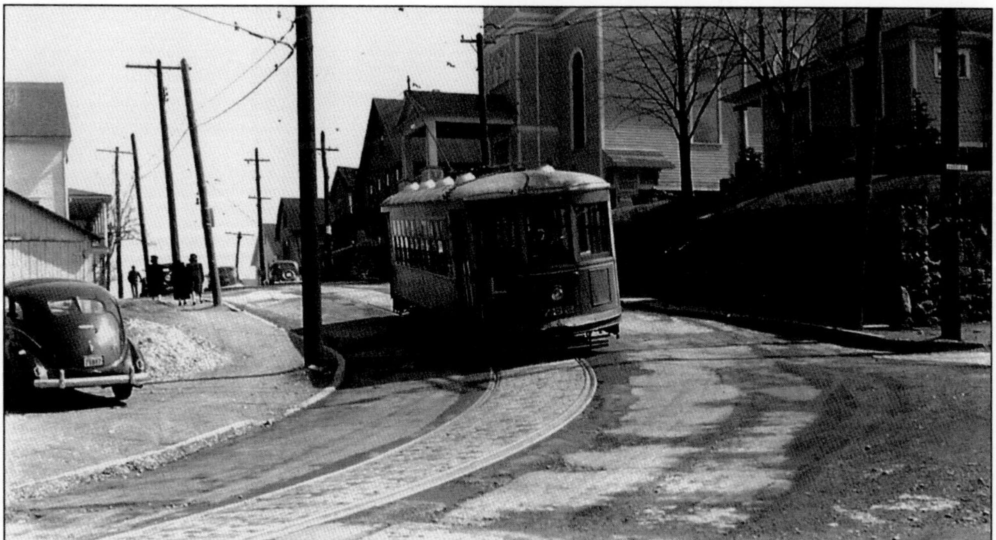

Orchard Street in Larksville, 1940. Wilkes-Barre Railway Corporation trolley No. 752 is heading outbound on the Larksville line near Jackson Avenue at Wilson Street in Larksville just outside Edwardsville on Sunday, March 31, 1940. St. Anthony's Church is in the background across from Arch Street close to the Larksville and Edwardsville border. The Edwardsville borough was incorporated on June 16, 1884.

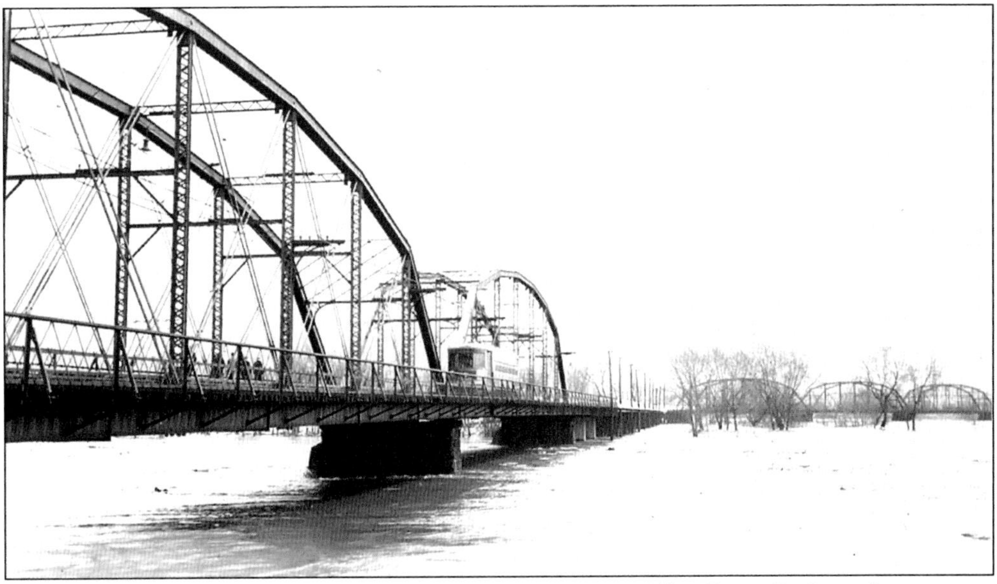

PLYMOUTH END OF THE CAREY AVENUE BRIDGE, 1940. Wilkes-Barre Railway Corporation trolley No. 790 is seen on Sunday, March 31, 1940. Plymouth was incorporated in 1866. The Plymouth trolley line was originally connected to Wilkes-Barre in 1892 through Edwardsville and Kingston across the Market Street bridge before the construction of the Carey Avenue bridge.

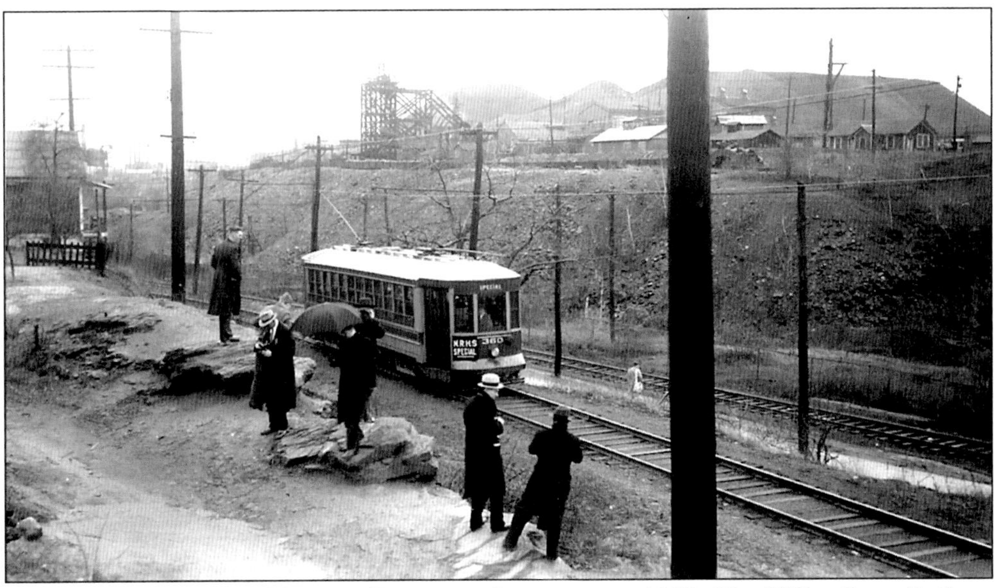

EAST MAIN STREET AT NESBITT STREET IN LARKSVILLE, 1940. The Wilkes-Barre Railway Corporation trolley No. 360 special was chartered by the NRHS near the Broadway station on the Edwardsville line on Sunday, April 21, 1940. The photograph was taken with the Loree Breaker in the background. In 1921, Larksville mining operations produced 1,590,000 tons of anthracite coal. The trolley was sold to the Sudbury–Copper Cliff Suburban Electric Railway in Ontario.

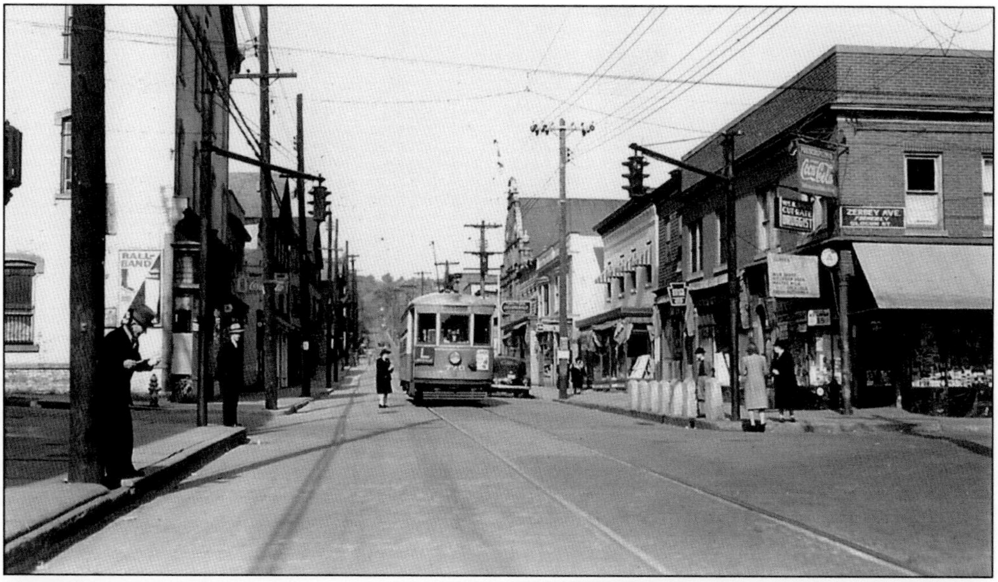

MAIN STREET AT ZERBY AVENUE IN EDWARDSVILLE, 1940. Wilkes-Barre Railway Corporation trolley No. 770 travels on the Larksville line on Sunday, October 20, 1940. The former Eastern Pennsylvania Railway trolley collided with a coal truck on the Larksville line on December 28, 1946. The trolley was not repaired, and it was scrapped in 1948. Zerby Avenue in Edwardsville was formerly Slocum Street.

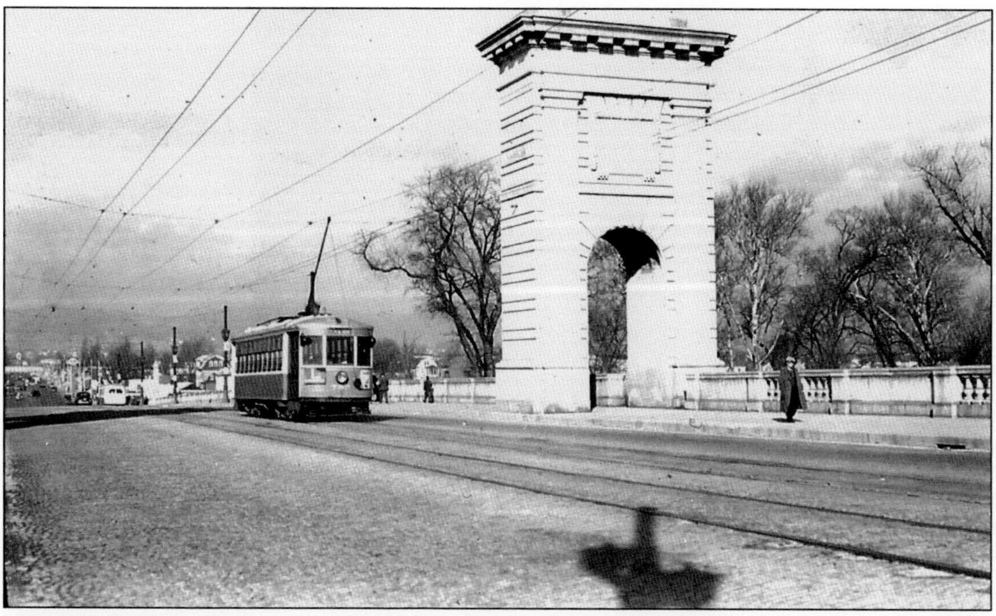

MARKET STREET BRIDGE IN KINGSTON, 1940. Wilkes-Barre Railway Corporation trolley No. 762 is seen on the Larksville line on Friday, November 22, 1940. The trolley was ordered from the J. G. Brill Company on April 2, 1924, for the Eastern Pennsylvania Railway. In 1933, it was delivered to the Wilkes-Barre Railway. The trolley was scrapped in 1950.

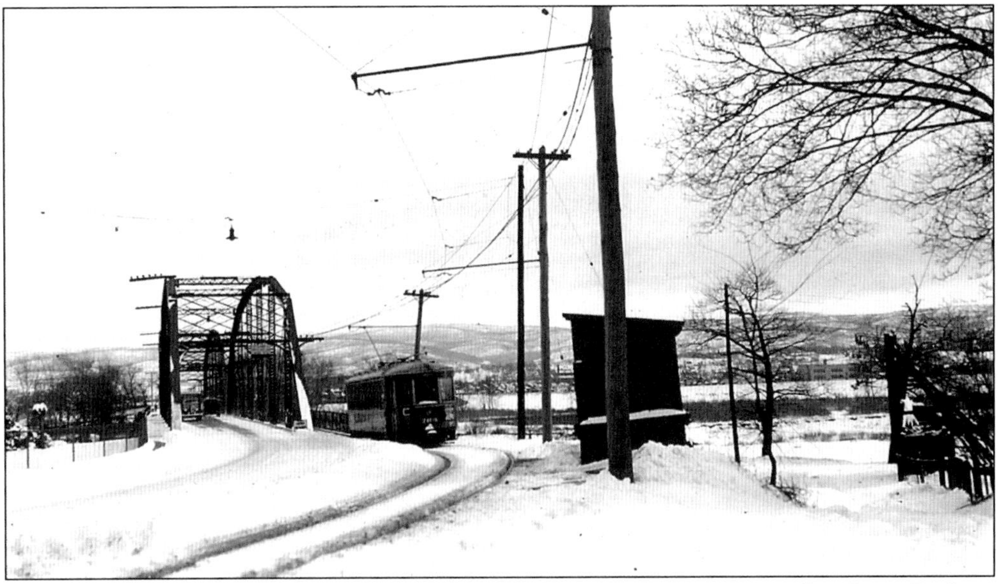

BRIDGE STREET AT THE CAREY AVENUE BRIDGE IN PLYMOUTH, 1941. Wilkes-Barre Railway Corporation trolley No. 784 is pictured on the Plymouth line on Saturday, March 1, 1941. In 1930, Route 11 was rerouted from Plymouth Road, Carey Avenue, River Street, and River Road in Wilkes-Barre to its current route on Wyoming Avenue through Forty Fort, Kingston, Edwardsville, and Plymouth.

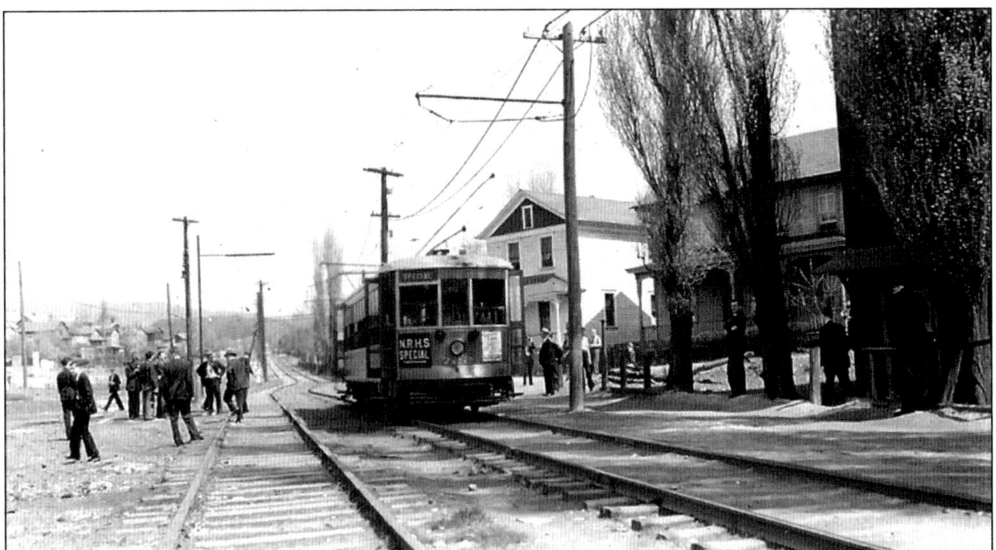

ELM STREET NEAR EDWARDS STREET IN PLYMOUTH, 1941. The Wilkes-Barre Railway Corporation trolley No. 722 special was chartered by the NRHS on the Larksville line on Sunday, April 20, 1941. The trolley was ordered from the Wason Company in 1923 for the Sistersville and New Martinsville Traction Company in West Virginia. The trolley was delivered to the Wilkes-Barre Railway on December 29, 1925, and it was in service until 1948.

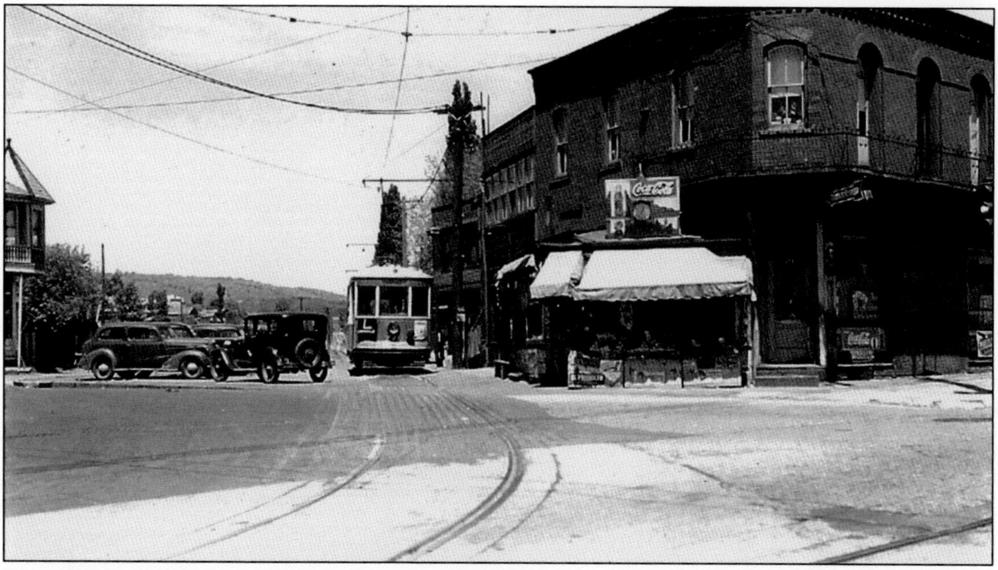

East Main Street and West Cherry Street in Plymouth, 1941. Wilkes-Barre Railway Corporation trolley No. 770 is on the Larksville line on Sunday, May 18, 1941. After the abandonment of the trolley line on Tuesday, August 10, 1948, it became Washington Avenue. Until 1926, sections of Wyoming Avenue between Plymouth and Kingston remained unpaved.

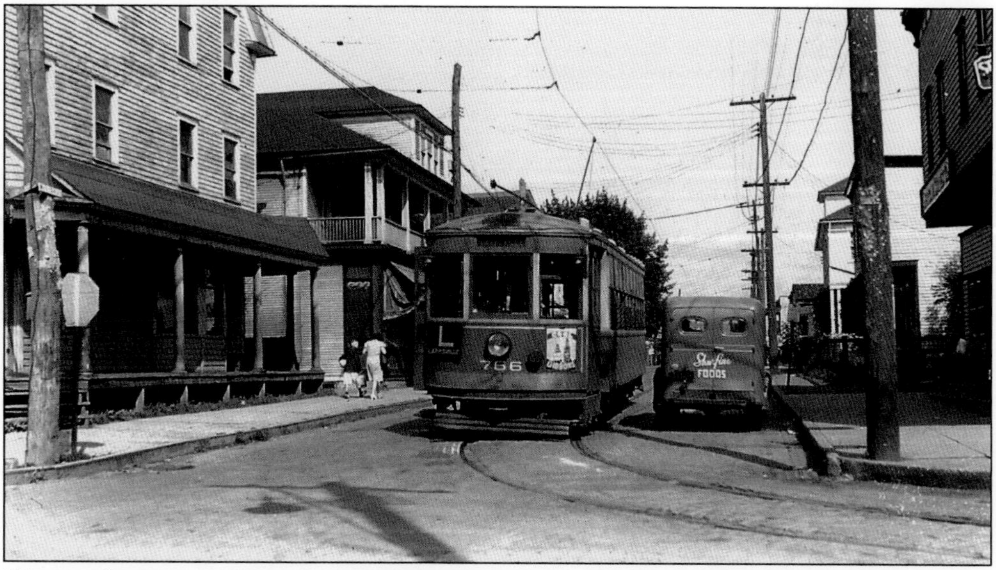

Wilson Street at West Luzerne Avenue in Larksville, 1941. Wilkes-Barre Railway Corporation trolley No. 766 is seen on the Larksville line on Saturday, July 5, 1941. The trolley was ordered in 1924 for the Eastern Pennsylvania Railway in Pottsville. In 1933, it was delivered to the Wilkes-Barre Railway. Trolley No. 766 was scrapped in March 1950.

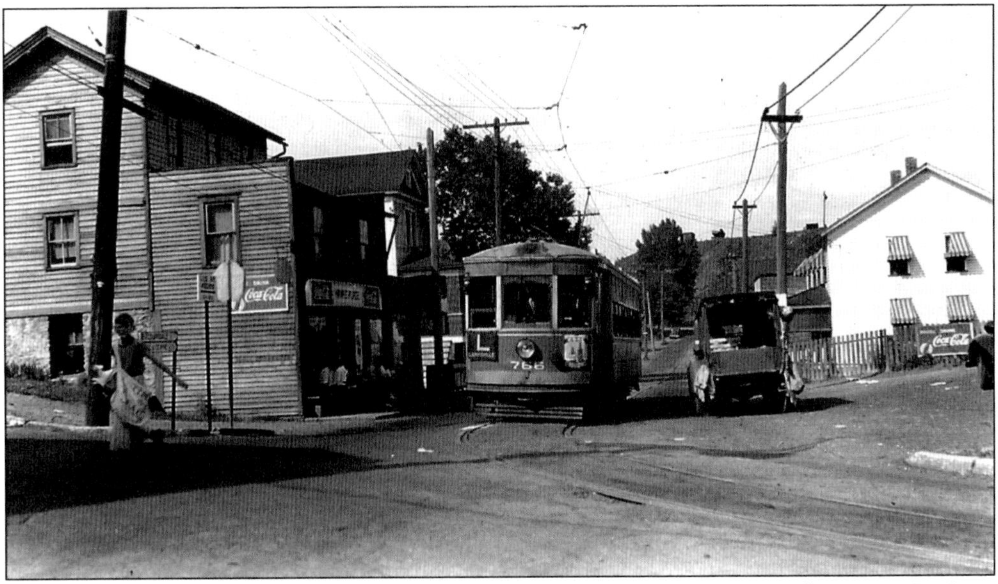

West State Street at Washington Avenue in Larksville, 1941. Wilkes-Barre Railway Corporation trolley No. 766 travels on the Larksville line on Saturday, July 5, 1941. The trolley remained on the Larksville line until it was discontinued in 1948. The trolley was equipped with air-operated doors on the right side and manual doors on the left side that were operated by the motorman.

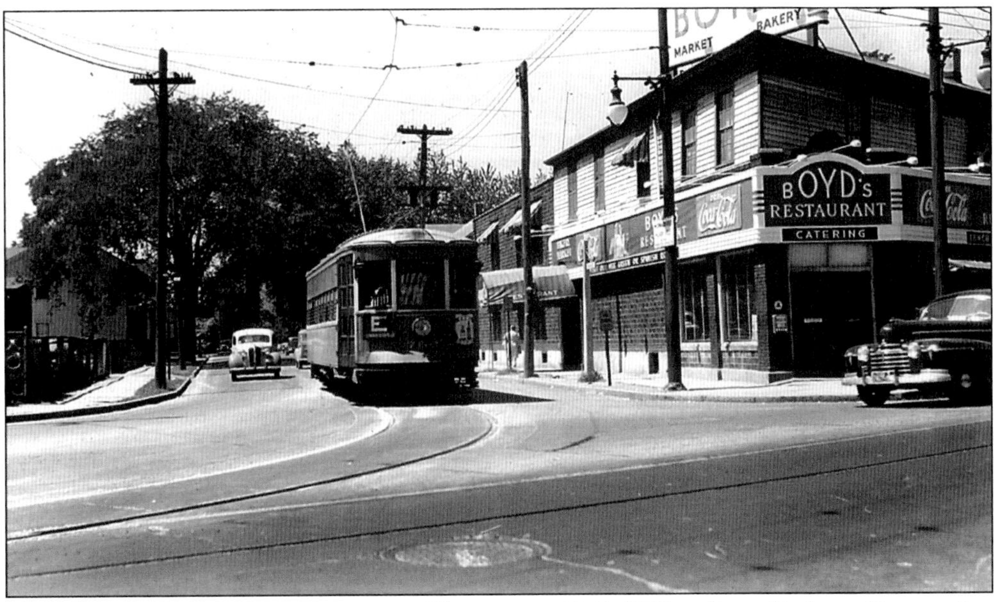

Main Street at Market Street in Kingston, 1941. Wilkes-Barre Railway Corporation trolley No. 762 is pictured at Boyd's Restaurant on the Edwardsville line on Friday, August 8, 1941. There were 598 people living in Kingston Borough when it was incorporated on November 23, 1857. In 1940, the population of Kingston was 20,679. The trolley was equipped with General Electric motors.

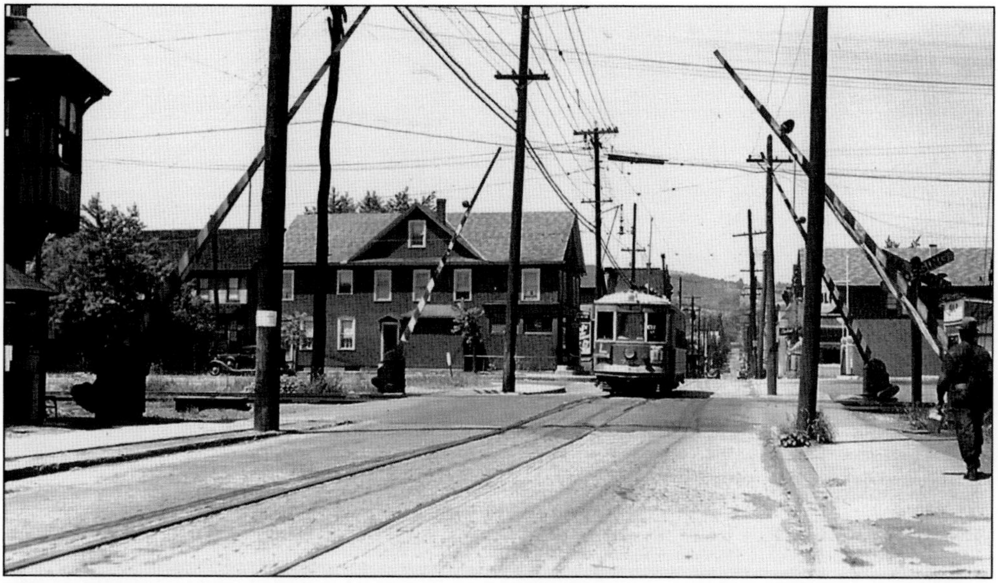

MAIN STREET AT RAILROAD CROSSING IN EDWARDSVILLE, 1941. Wilkes-Barre Railway Corporation trolley No. 764 is at the Delaware, Lackawanna and Western Railroad crossing on the Larksville line on Friday, August 8, 1941. The population of Edwardsville reached its height in 1910 when 8,407 people lived in the borough in proximity to the mines.

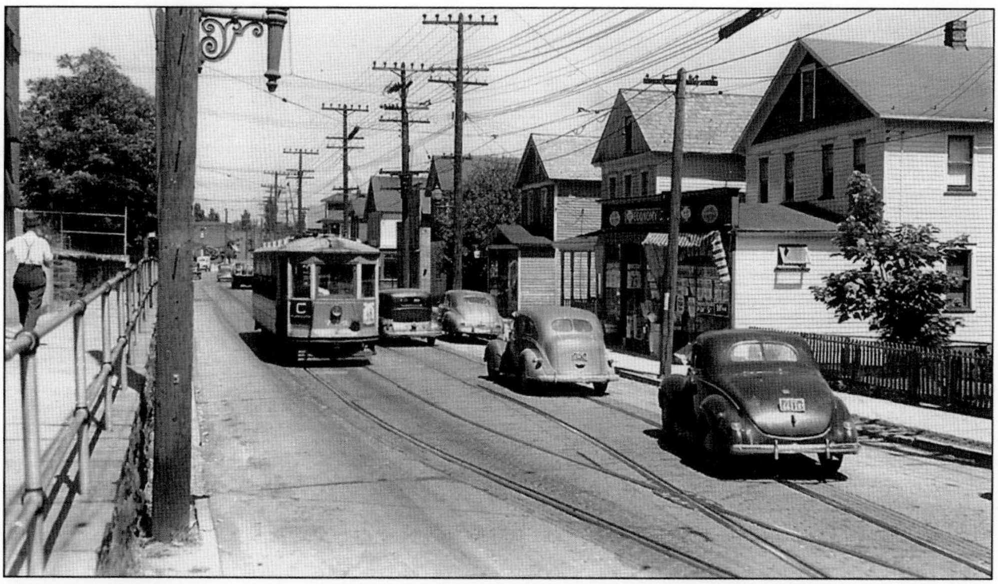

WEST MAIN STREET NEAR FLAT ROAD IN PLYMOUTH, 1941. Wilkes-Barre Railway Corporation trolley No. 774 is seen on the Plymouth line on Friday, August 8, 1941. The former Pottsville trolley was delivered to the Wilkes-Barre Railway in 1933, and it was in service until the Plymouth trolley line was abandoned in 1947. The trolley was scrapped in 1950.

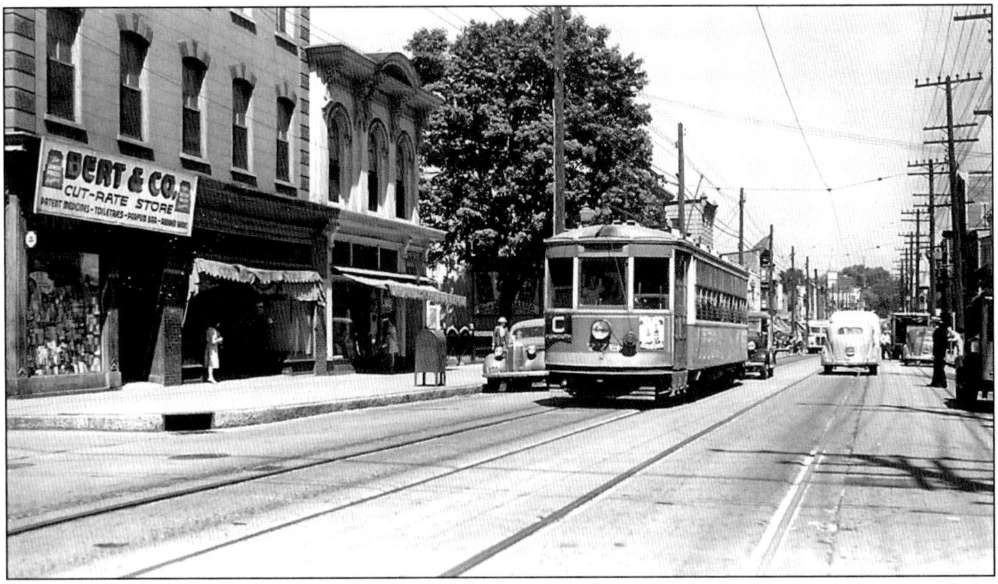

WEST MAIN STREET AT CENTER AVENUE IN PLYMOUTH, 1941. Wilkes-Barre Railway Corporation trolley No. 778 works on the Plymouth line on Friday, August 8, 1941. The trolley was ordered on April 2, 1924, and it was sent to the Eastern Pennsylvania Railway in Pottsville. It was delivered to the Wilkes-Barre Railway in 1933. The trolley was sold to the Virginia Electric and Power Company in 1942.

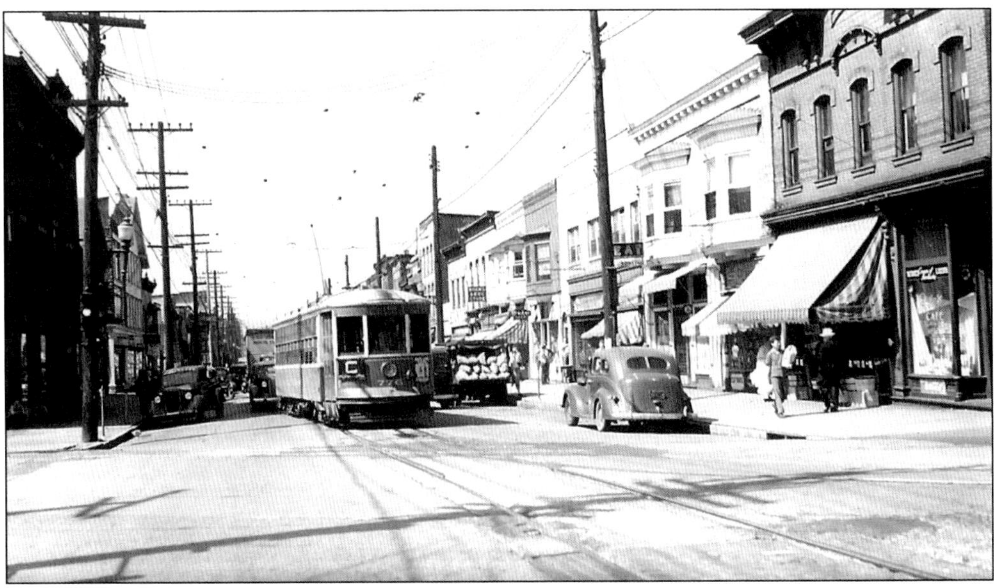

EAST MAIN STREET AT WEST CHERRY STREET IN PLYMOUTH, 1941. Wilkes-Barre Railway Corporation trolley No. 776 is on the Plymouth line on Saturday, August 30, 1941. Plymouth was the site of the Avondale Mine disaster on September 6, 1869, when 110 mine workers lost their lives at the Avondale Colliery owned by the Delaware, Lackawanna and Western Railroad Company.

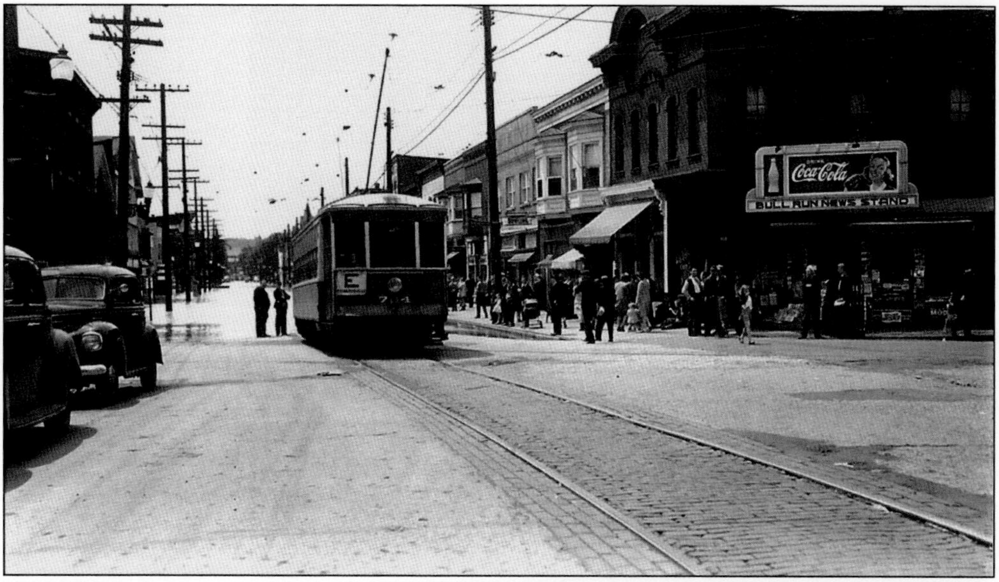

East Main Street at West Cherry Street in Plymouth, 1946. Wilkes-Barre Railway Corporation trolley No. 784 is on the Edwardsville line on Wednesday, May 29, 1946. Main Street was flooded by Brown's Creek. The population in Plymouth reached its zenith in 1910 when 16,996 people lived in the borough. An explosion at the Nottingham Mine in Plymouth killed 15 mine workers on January 15, 1947.

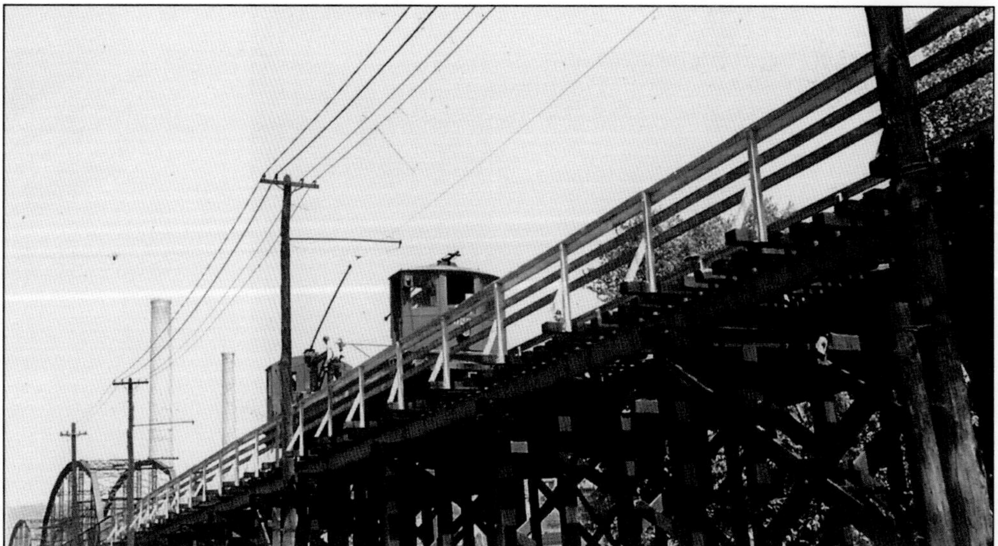

Carey Avenue Bridge, 1946. Wilkes-Barre Railway Corporation work trolley No. 022 travels on the Plymouth line between Hanover and Plymouth on Friday, May 31, 1946. The work trolley was inspecting the bridge after flooding on May 29. During flooding in 1936 and 1940, trolleys were parked on Wyoming Avenue in Kingston, but flooding in 1946 caused minimal damage. The last day of service on the Plymouth line was Sunday, August 31, 1947.

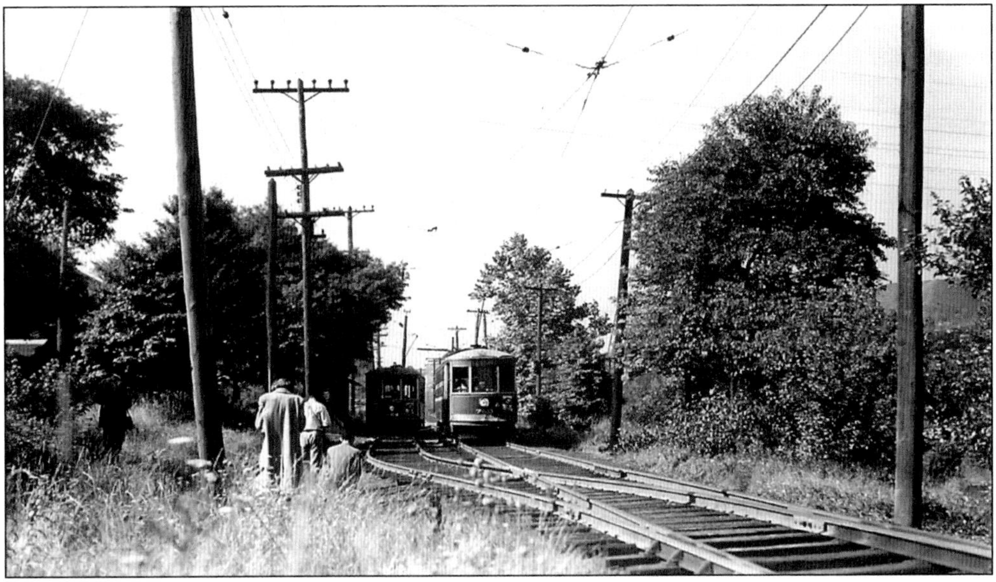

EAST MAIN STREET AT NESBITT STREET IN LARKSVILLE, 1946. Wilkes-Barre Railway Corporation trolleys No. 754 and No. 780 special chartered by the Electric Railway Association are seen at the Broadway station along the Edwardsville line on Sunday, August 25, 1946. The last trolley ran on the Edwardsville line on Saturday, August 28, 1948, and the trolleys were replaced by buses until trackless trolley service began in 1949.

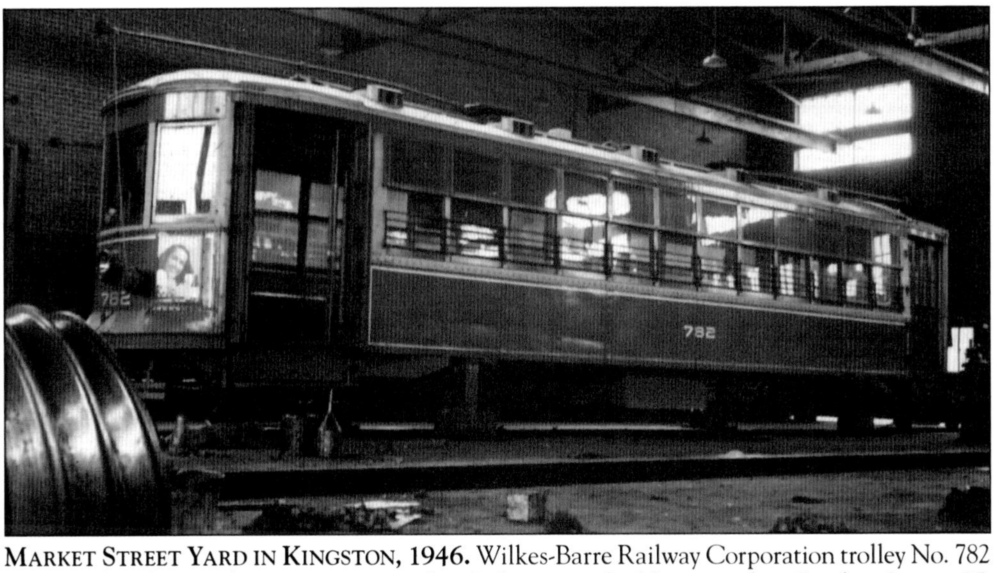

MARKET STREET YARD IN KINGSTON, 1946. Wilkes-Barre Railway Corporation trolley No. 782 is pictured with its undercarriage removed and after it was freshly painted on Sunday, August 25, 1946. The Hoyt Library on Wyoming Avenue in Kingston opened its doors on January 2, 1928. It was the former residence of Samuel Hoyt, and the house was bequeathed by his son Frank Weston Hoyt.

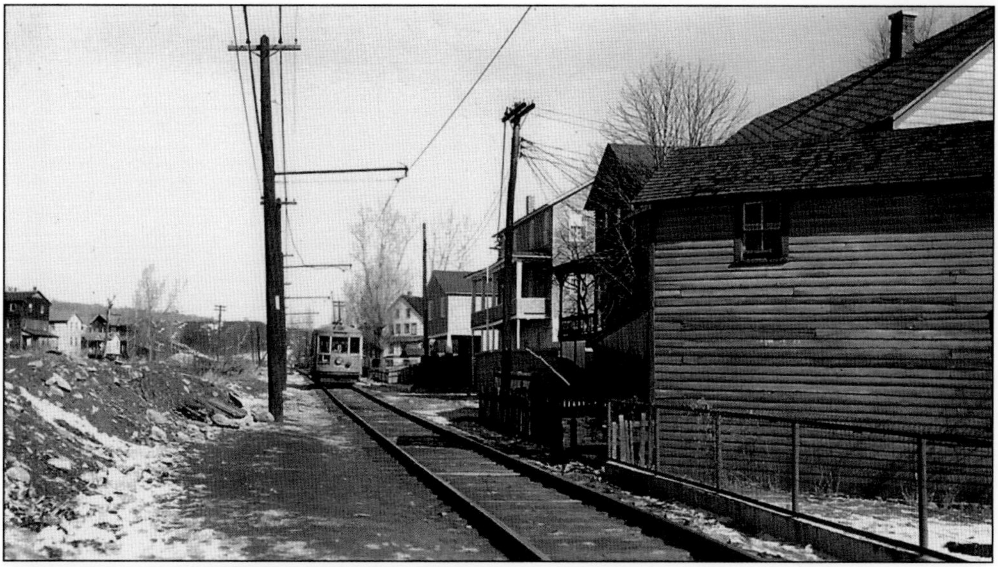

ALONG BROWN'S CREEK NEAR ELM STREET IN PLYMOUTH, 1947. Wilkes-Barre Railway Corporation trolley No. 764 travels on the Larksville line on Wednesday, February 12, 1947. The trolley was ordered in 1924 for the Eastern Pennsylvania Railway. It was bought by the Wilkes-Barre Railway in 1933. The former Larksville trolley line was resurfaced, and it became Washington Avenue.

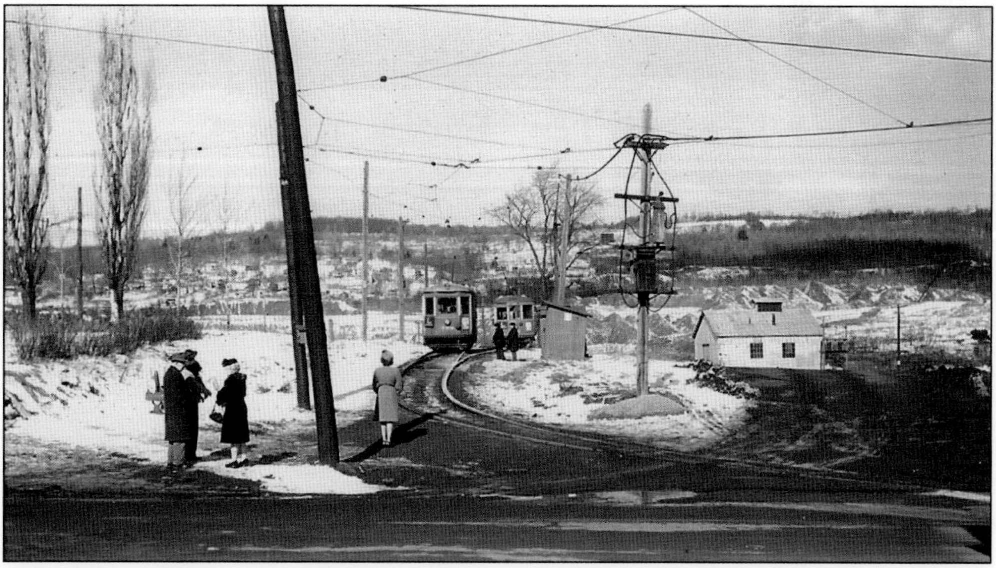

EAST STATE STREET AND NESBITT STREET IN LARKSVILLE, 1947. Wilkes-Barre Railway Corporation trolleys No. 774 and No. 756 are at Snyder's switch on the Larksville line on Wednesday, February 12, 1947. Trolley No. 756 was 40 feet long, and it was in service on the Larksville and Plymouth trolley lines before it was scrapped in March 1950.

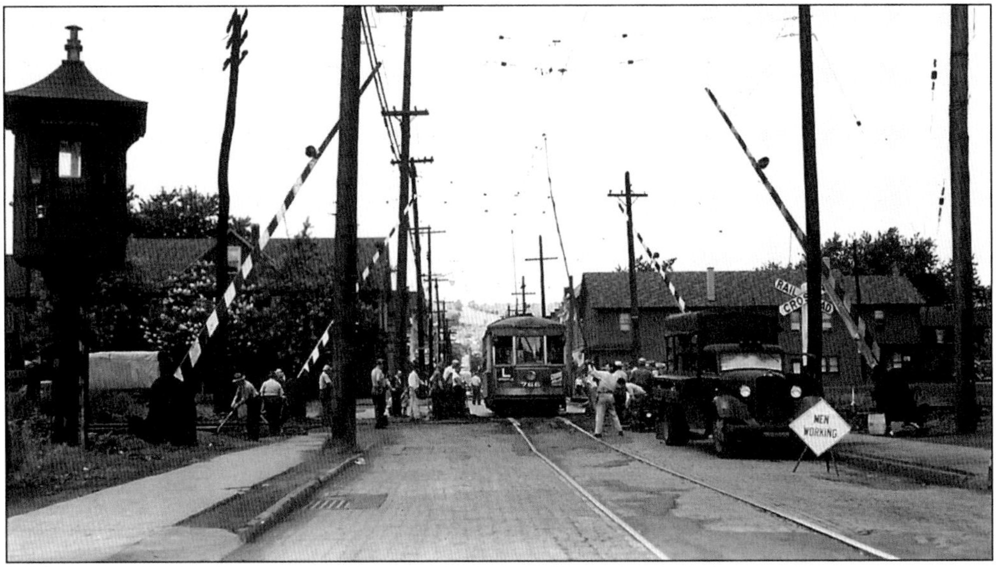

MAIN STREET AT RAILROAD CROSSING IN KINGSTON, 1947. Wilkes-Barre Transit Corporation trolley No. 766 works on the Larksville line on Thursday, July 3, 1947. Workers at the railroad crossing were realigning the tracks after the tracks were washed out. The trolley was ordered from the J. G. Brill Company for the Eastern Pennsylvania Railway, and it was delivered to the Wilkes-Barre Railway in 1933.

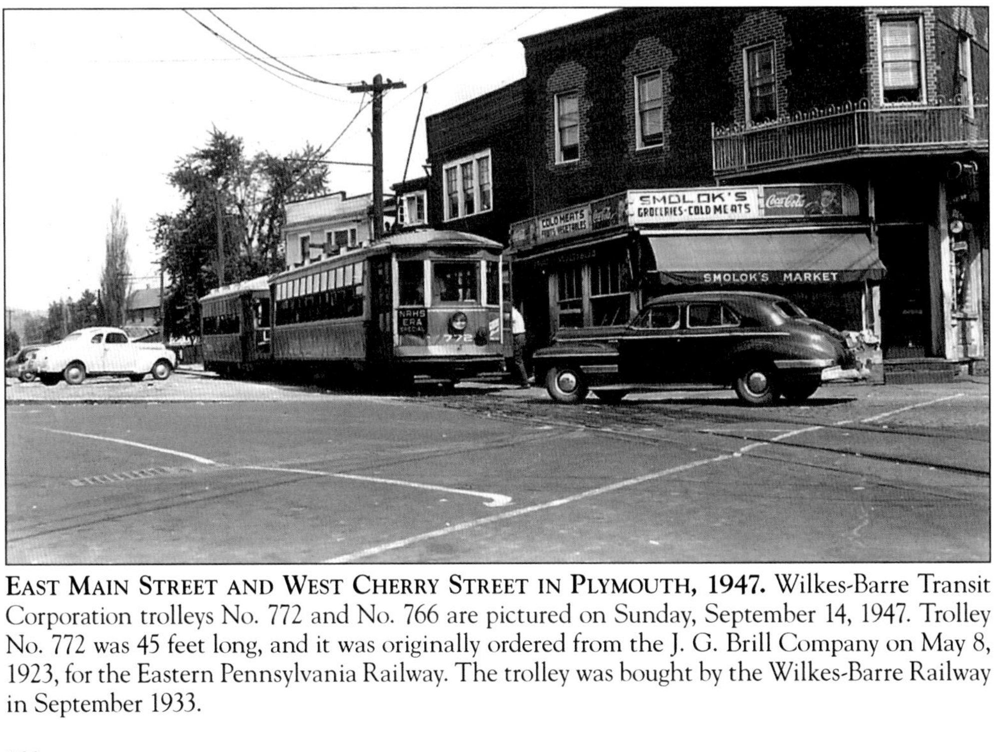

EAST MAIN STREET AND WEST CHERRY STREET IN PLYMOUTH, 1947. Wilkes-Barre Transit Corporation trolleys No. 772 and No. 766 are pictured on Sunday, September 14, 1947. Trolley No. 772 was 45 feet long, and it was originally ordered from the J. G. Brill Company on May 8, 1923, for the Eastern Pennsylvania Railway. The trolley was bought by the Wilkes-Barre Railway in September 1933.

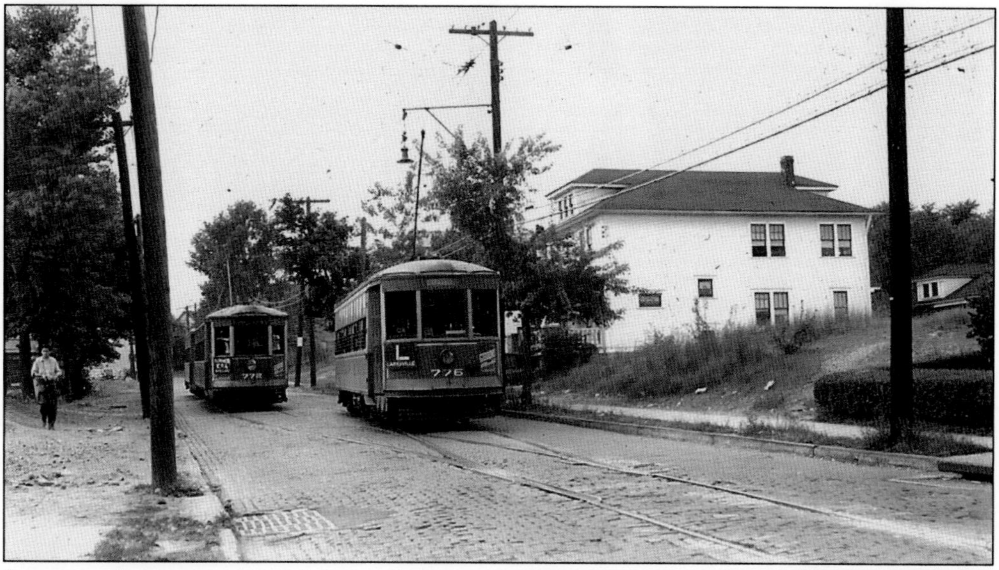

JACKSON AVENUE NEAR MARTIN STREET IN EDWARDSVILLE, 1947. Wilkes-Barre Transit Corporation trolleys No. 772, No. 774, and No. 776 are on the Larksville line on Sunday, September 14, 1947. The trolleys were ordered from the J. G. Brill Company for the Eastern Pennsylvania Railway and were delivered to the Wilkes-Barre Railway in 1933. Trolleys No. 776, No. 778, No. 780, and No. 784 were reequipped with Westinghouse motors and were sold to the Virginia Electric and Power Company in 1942.

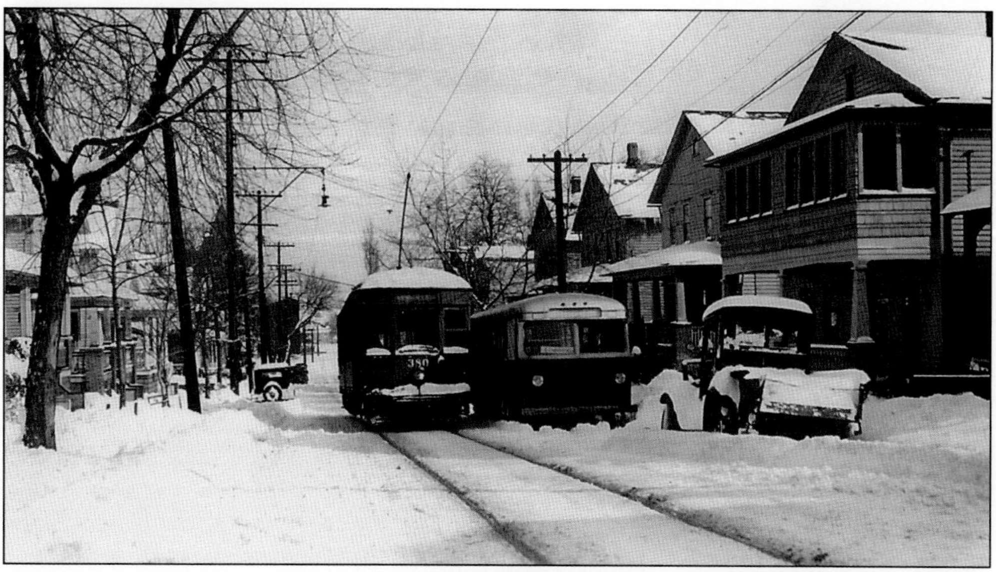

CHURCH STREET NEAR SWALLOW STREET IN EDWARDSVILLE, 1948. Wilkes-Barre Transit Corporation trolley No. 380 and bus No. 106 are on the Edwardsville line on Sunday, January 25, 1948. Buses were used to supplement service when trolley service was limited by snow or ice. The last day of trolley service on the Edwardsville line was Saturday, August 28, 1948.

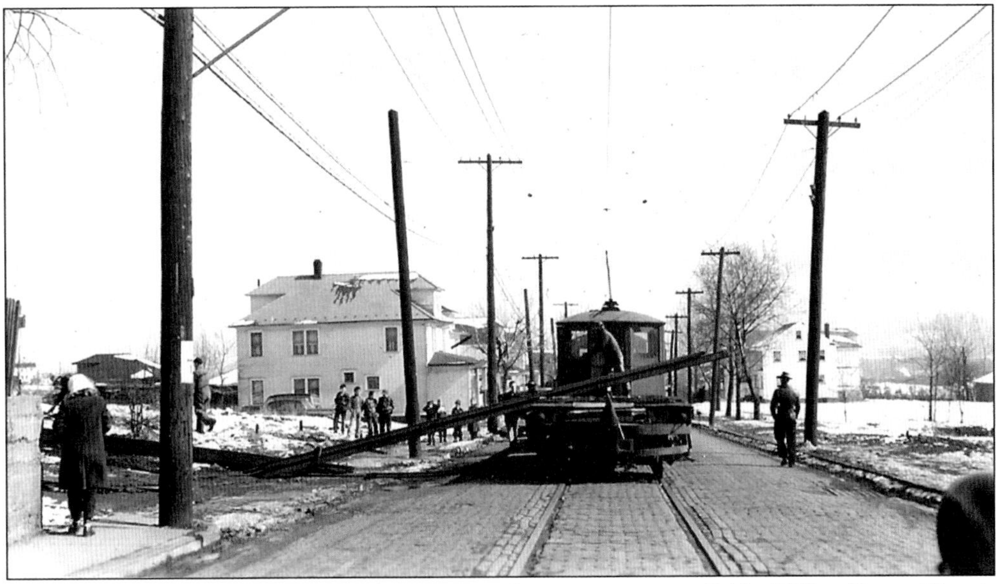

JACKSON AVENUE AT MARTIN STREET IN EDWARDSVILLE, 1948. Wilkes-Barre Transit Corporation work trolley No. 022 and flatbed No. 08 remove abandoned tracks along the Larksville line on Tuesday, February 24, 1948. The trolleys on the Larksville line were converted to single-motorman operation on July 25, 1928. The final day of service on the Larksville line was Tuesday, August 10, 1948.

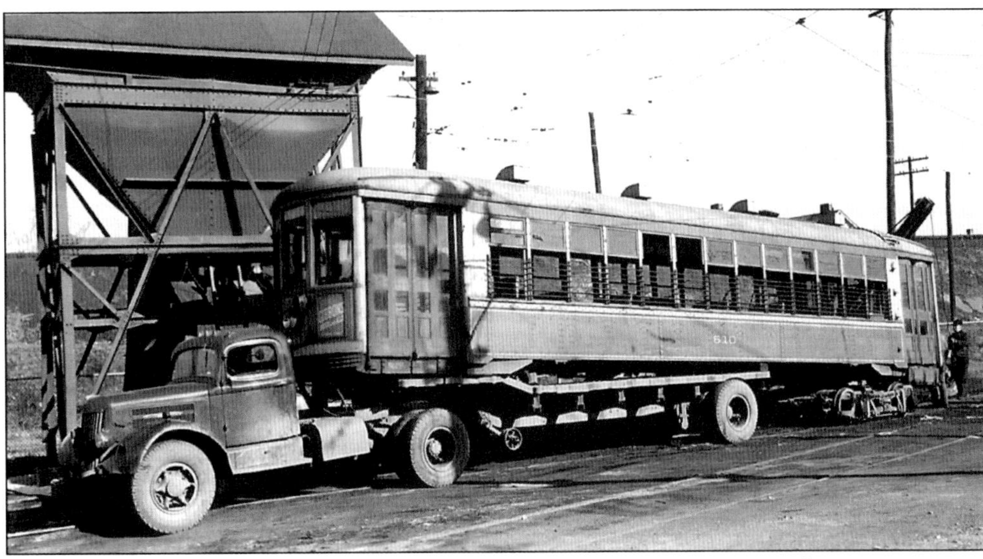

TROLLEY BEING TOWED TO THE MARKET STREET YARD, 1948. Wilkes-Barre Transit Corporation trolley No. 610 was loaded on a tractor trailer after the undercarriage was removed, and taken to the Market Street trolley yard in Kingston on Thursday, March 25, 1948. In 1948, after trolley No. 610 was taken out of service, it was sent to the Louis Cohen and Son scrap yard on Fellows Street in Breslon in Hanover Township.

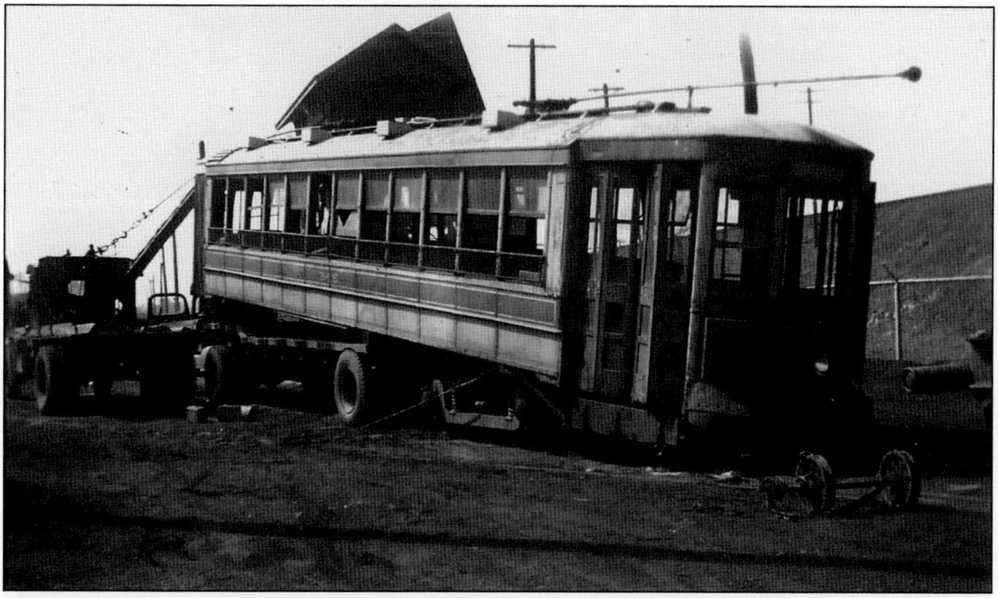

TRACTOR TRAILER TOWING TROLLEY TO KINGSTON, 1948. Wilkes-Barre Transit Corporation trolley No. 346 is being towed to the Market Street Yard on Tuesday, March 30, 1948. In the 1920s and 1930s, while transit companies struggled, trolleys in the Wyoming Valley continued to supply the majority of local transportation. Between 1937 and 1940, trolley lines that were abandoned along Wyoming Avenue included service to Forty Fort, Kingston, Luzerne, Pittston, and West Pittston.

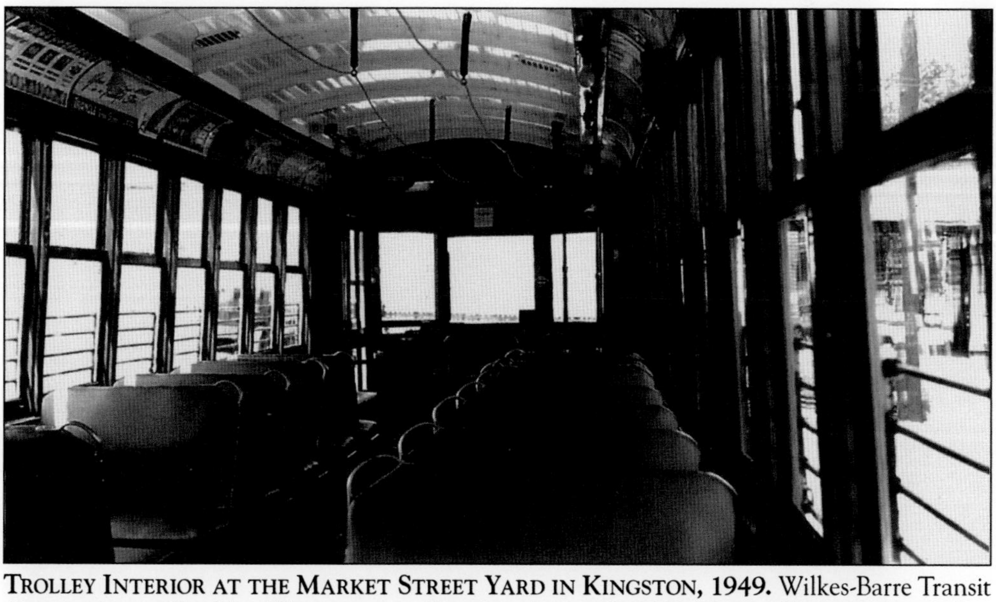

TROLLEY INTERIOR AT THE MARKET STREET YARD IN KINGSTON, 1949. Wilkes-Barre Transit Corporation trolley No. 790 is seen on Tuesday, August 9, 1949. The trolley was scrapped in 1950. The first train in the Wyoming Valley was the Lackawanna-Bloomsburg Railroad. The railroad ran between Kingston and Scranton and went as far as Kingston on June 24, 1856.

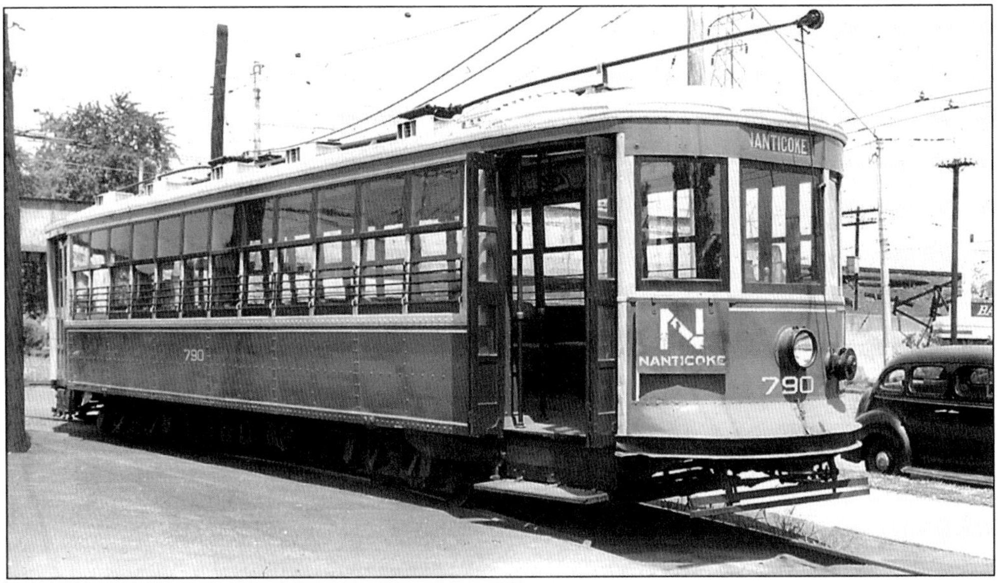

Market Street in Kingston, 1949. Wilkes-Barre Transit Corporation trolley No. 790 is pictured on Tuesday, August 9, 1949. It was ordered from the J. G. Brill Company in 1924 for the Eastern Pennsylvania Railway. In 1933, the trolley was purchased by the Wilkes-Barre Railway. The trolley had an aluminum roof and rattan seats. The coachwork was painted vermilion and yellow with maroon doors, and the undercarriage was painted black. The trolley was scrapped in 1950.

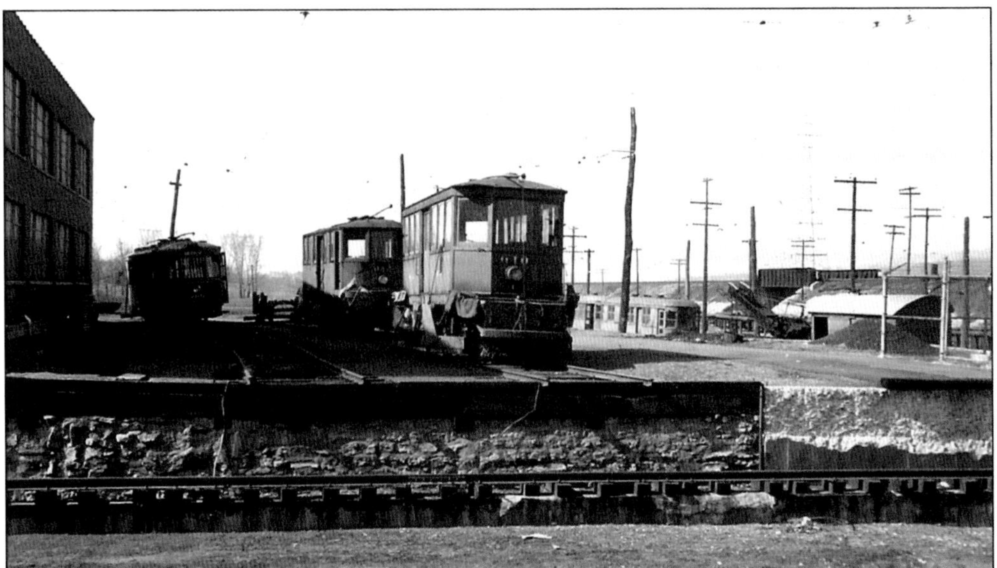

Trolleys Stored at the Market Street Yard, 1950. Wilkes-Barre Transit Corporation trolley No. 768, and sweeper trolleys No. 040 and No. 042 are seen in Kingston on Wednesday, March 15, 1950. Both sweeper trolleys were ordered from the J. G. Brill Company, trolley No. 040 in 1899 and trolley No. 042 10 years later. Trolley No. 768 and the sweeper trolleys were scrapped in 1950. Trolley service in the Wyoming Valley ended after nearly 63 years on Saturday, October 14, 1950.

BIBLIOGRAPHY

Bodnar, John. *Anthracite People: Families, Unions, and Work, 1900-1940.* Harrisburg, Pennsylvania: Pennsylvania Historical and Museum Commission, 1983.

Cox, Harold E. *Wyoming Valley Trolleys: Street Railways of Wilkes-Barre, Nanticoke and Pittston, Pennsylvania.* Forty Fort, Pennsylvania: Harold E. Cox, 1988.

Greenberg, William T., Frederick A. Kramer and Theodore F. Gleichmann Jr. *The Handsomest Trains in the World: Passenger Service on the Lehigh Valley Railroad.* New York: Quadrant Press, Inc., 1978.

Hanley, Edward F. *The Wyoming Valley: an American portrait.* Sun Valley, California: American Historical Press, 2003.

Harvey, Oscar Jewell. *A History of Wilkes-Barre, Luzerne County, Pennsylvania, from Its Beginnings to the Present Time.* 6 vols. Wilkes-Barre: 1909–1930.

Lottick, Sally Teller. *Bridging Change: a Wyoming Valley Sketchbook.* Wilkes-Barre: Wyoming Historical and Geological Society, 1992.

Petrillo, F. Charles. *Harvey's Lake.* Wilkes-Barre: the Bookmakers, 1991.

Powell, Howard Benjamin. *Philadelphia's First Fuel Crisis: Jacob Cist and the Developing Market for Pennsylvania Anthracite.* University Park, Pennsylvania: Pennsylvania State University Press, 1978.

Roberts, Ellis W. *The Breaker Whistle Blows: Mining Disasters and Labor Leaders in the Anthracite Region.* Scranton, Pennsylvania: Anthracite Press, 1984.

Rohrbeck, Benson W. *Wilkes-Barre Railways Co.* Pennsylvania Traction Series. West Chester, Pennsylvania: B. Rohrbeck Traction Publications, 1975.

Schooley, Frank Budd. *The Word.* Dallas, Pennsylvania: Payne Printery, 1971.

Wick, Harrison. *Pennsylvania's Back Mountain.* Charleston, South Carolina: Arcadia Publishing, 2009.

Williamson, James R. *The Susquehanna Frontier: Northeastern Pennsylvania during the Revolutionary Years.* Wilkes-Barre: Wilkes University Press, 1997.

Wolensky, Robert P. *The Knox Mine Disaster, January 22, 1959: The Final Years of the Northern Anthracite Industry and the Effort to Rebuild a Regional Economy.* Harrisburg, Pennsylvania: Pennsylvania Historical and Museum Commission, 1999.

Zbiek, Paul J. *Luzerne County: History of the People and Culture.* Wyoming Historical and Geological Society. Lancaster, Pennsylvania: Strategic Publications, 1994.

Consistent with our mission to preserve history on a local level, this book was printed in South Carolina on American-made paper and manufactured entirely in the United States. Products carrying the accredited Forest Stewardship Council (FSC) label are printed on 100 percent FSC-certified paper.

MADE IN THE USA